Almost Home

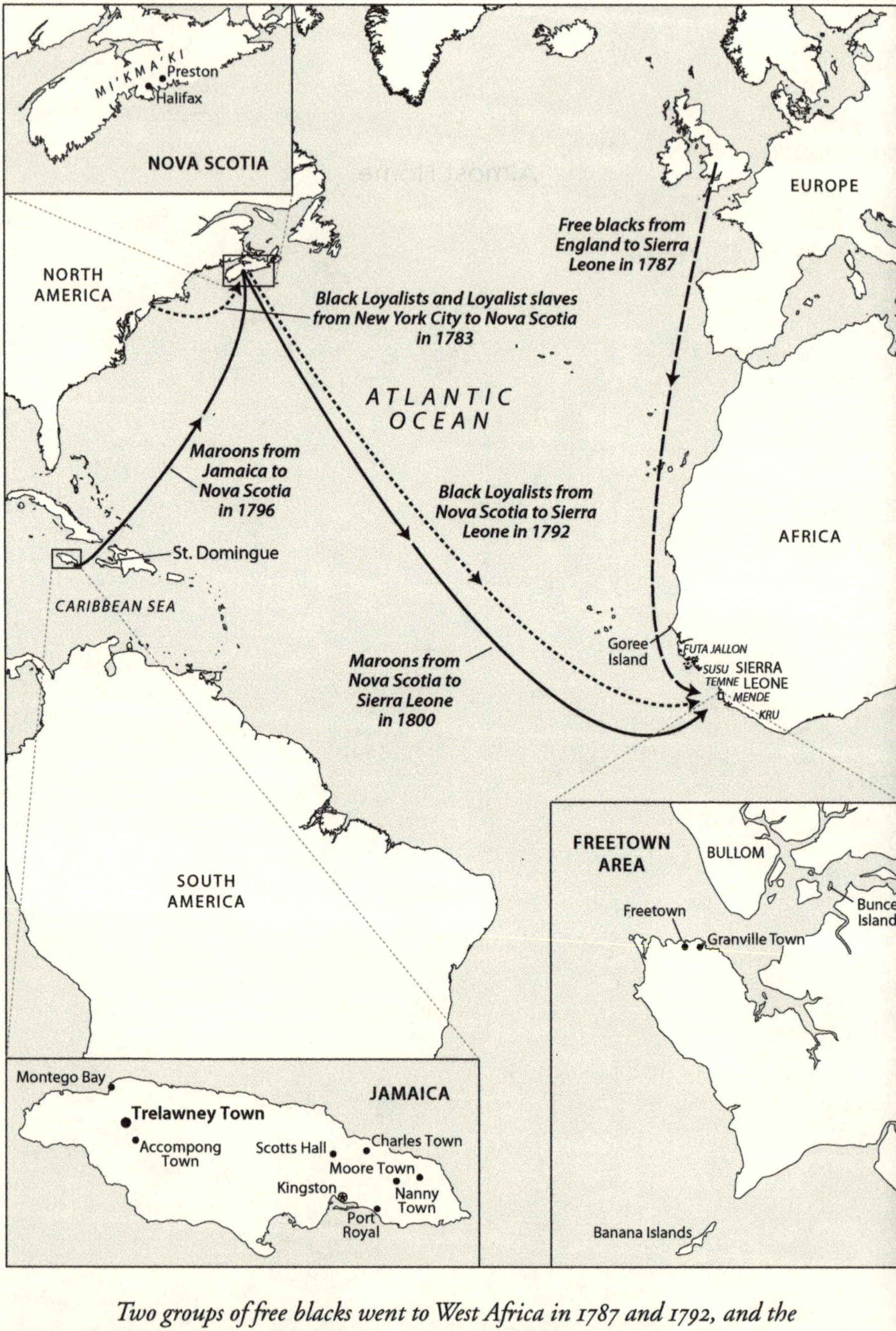

Two groups of free blacks went to West Africa in 1787 and 1792, and the Maroons followed in 1800. (Cartography by Bill Nelson.)

ALMOST HOME

MAROONS BETWEEN SLAVERY AND FREEDOM IN JAMAICA, NOVA SCOTIA, AND SIERRA LEONE

RUMA CHOPRA

Yale
UNIVERSITY PRESS
New Haven and London

Yale University Press books may be purchased in quantity for educational, business, or promotional use. For information, please e-mail sales .press@yale.edu (U.S. office) or sales@yaleup.co.uk (U.K. office).

An earlier version of Chapter 4 was previously published as "Maroons and Mi'kmaq in Nova Scotia, 1796–1800" in the pages of *Acadiensis: Journal of the History of the Atlantic Region* 46, no. 1 (Winter/Spring 2017): 5–23, and is reproduced by permission.

Set in Adobe Garamond type by IDS Infotech, Ltd.
Printed in the United States of America.

Library of Congress Control Number: 2017953471
ISBN 978-0-300-22046-9 (hardcover: alk. paper)

A catalogue record for this book is available from the British Library.

This paper meets the requirements of ANSI/NISO Z39.48-1992 (Permanence of Paper).

10 9 8 7 6 5 4 3 2 1

For Zohab

Contents

Almost Home

INTRODUCTION

The Maroons agonized daily over the only decision that mattered: whether to hide in the cockpit country or to surrender. The situation was dire. British soldiers surrounded the area, and trained mastiffs, rented from Cuba, tracked their scent. Trusted slaves joined the Jamaican militia in the mission to discover and destroy Maroon haunts and retreats, to remove so troublesome an internal enemy. Rumors spread that a hungry bloodhound had mistakenly mangled a soldier's wife. Slowly, the Maroons gave up. The men came at night with women, children, the sick, and convalescents. By spring 1796, after eight months of struggle, most of the village of Trelawney Town, a community of about 550 runaway slaves and their descendants, had surrendered.

The insurrection in the mountainous interior by a community of free blacks had caught the colony by surprise. The Jamaican elite had not previously worried much about a few hundred Maroons in the distant northwest village of Trelawney Town, far from the urban centers of Spanish Town and Kingston. Since 1738 the Jamaican leadership and the Maroons had existed under an uneasy truce in which the Maroons preserved their freedom by capturing fugitive slaves. For almost fifty years the Maroons served as a buffer between the slaves and the planters, preserving white freedom and black slavery. The resistance of Trelawney Town ignited fears that the slaves who comprised 90 percent of the island's population might be "corrupted." Planters worried that slaves would find common cause with the Maroons; some slave fugitives, they knew, presided already as Maroon leaders. Ensuring the neutrality of the smaller Maroon communities in the island depended on a raw display of toughness.

The rebellious Maroons had expected their punishment to take the form of banishment. They anticipated that they would be told to shuttle their families to another part of the large island. But over the course of a few months the planters came to see the resettlement of the "barbarians" within the island as unthinkable. The lieutenant governor of Jamaica, Lord Balcarres, believed the Maroons deserved no reprieve; they had surrendered too late, and only after inflicting heavy casualties on British regulars and the white militia. Balcarres grasped at the chance to remove the Maroons permanently from Jamaica. The Maroons would not be banished. They would be deported—ideally to some remote location from whence they could never return to Jamaica.[1]

By July 1796 the Trelawney Town Maroons found themselves in the North Atlantic colony of Nova Scotia. The lieutenant governor there, Sir John Wentworth, did not turn them away. He hoped to employ them as laborers, "civilize" them as Christians, and, not least, benefit from the generous funds the Jamaican government initially provided for their exile. But Wentworth's ambitions did not withstand the humanitarian agitation that flowed from London on behalf of the Maroons. The Maroons' predicament in Nova Scotia drew the attention of abolitionist evangelicals. Metropolitan reformers soon deemed the Trelawney Town Maroons to be "helpless and injured" subjects in need of rescue. The Maroons' release from the cold climate of Nova Scotia, for which they were presumably unsuited, became a moral and national imperative.

By 1800 Sierra Leone, already established as a settlement for troublesome and discontented blacks, was ready to receive the Maroons.

The colony's founders were expansionist, evangelical antislavery crusaders who hoped that proper white supervision and an influx of black settlers would soon allow Sierra Leone to outshine the slave colony of Jamaica. British visionaries saw the group of free black families, who were accustomed to a tropical climate and diseases and beholden to the British for their delivery out of Nova Scotia, as ideal candidates for colony building. But Maroon loyalty, as the government would discover, did not translate into subservience.

Maroon societies evolved under warlike conditions. They consisted of runaway slaves and their descendants who sequestered themselves in wilderness areas of American plantation societies. By definition they were hybrid communities, made up of multiple African ethnicities. Though their numbers accounted for only a tiny fraction of any slave society, their existence testified to the desire of some Africans to create a free society of their own. Their survival depended on appropriating the military resources of their neighboring slaveholders and the possibilities offered by the local geography. To survive beyond their first formation they frequently relocated to new areas of settlement inaccessible to white settlers. Hence, the larger and more unoccupied the region, the denser its natural foliage, the more impenetrable the forest, the greater chance a Maroon group had of success. Jamaica, 148 miles wide and 52 miles across, with its many frontier areas, provided the essential conditions for the Maroons' continuous long-term survival. A quasi-military organization—makeshift and tattered—kept them together.[2]

To survive in the presence of white society, the Maroons consistently offered their loyalty to the colonists as a counterweight to their African ancestry. The Maroons' leanings toward the British monarch would become part of their complicated relationship of fealty to the empire. They pursued, seized, and sometimes killed slave runaways for white patrons. They elevated their place by adhering to and accepting white customs in unmistakable ways, for example, distancing themselves from field labor because it was the work of slaves. Because some Maroons were former overseers of plantations, they knew close-up the degradations of enslavement. By the 1790s over 75 percent of Maroon men had creolized by taking on the names of their white patrons. The most elite men wore waistcoats and silk stockings and hats with a feather. Adapting their military community to the British rank system, Maroon men used the titles of lieutenant, captain, major, lieutenant colonel, colonel, and general to mark hierarchical relationships. By the 1790s, at least 10 percent of the adult men held military rank.[3]

The Trelawney Town Maroons have attracted extensive coverage from anthropologists and historians.[4] Scholars have written extensively on the continuity of their African lineage, especially their impact on current-day Maroons (part of Heritage studies in Jamaica). These studies, which understand Maroons primarily in relation to white society, depict Maroons either in heroic terms, as freedom fighters, or as tragic, displaced victims of colonial power. By contrast, this book situates the Trelawney Maroons as dispossessed in relation to whites but as empowered *in relation to other blacks.* Like others of African ancestry, the Maroons were denied access to white civil society. But they were not the most oppressed blacks in Jamaica. Their participation in a slave society led them to understand the gradations of nonfreedom associated with race. Armed and granted autonomy, they knew they occupied a place above plantation slaves. They secured their subordinate but above-slave status through their close association with slave-owning whites. Their descendants saw themselves as a free people and expressed no longing for an African homeland. The Maroons adapted to preserve their autonomy and to secure a future for their children that was disassociated from the stigma of field labor.

They drew their values as well as their wealth from membership in the richest colony of the slave-owning empire.[5]

Slavery existed in each society the Trelawney Maroons encountered—Jamaican, Nova Scotian, and Sierra Leonean—but in distinct ways. The stark binary of black and white conceals the divisions not only among whites but also among blacks. In Jamaica, for instance, it was these many gradations of power that made slaveholders insecure and slave society volatile. Non-absentee white proprietors had higher standing than white bookkeepers who maintained accounts. Elite slaves who had deeper responsibilities were often lighter in color than other slaves. A skilled slave carpenter or blacksmith had more status and privileges in relation to a slave who served as a cook or rat catcher. Creolized slaves and whites alike regarded slaves recently arrived from Africa as inferior in manners and language. And a slave washerwoman stood many levels below a head housekeeper. The deported Maroons of Trelawney Town were not simply victims of racism. Many had adopted the racial prejudices of white Jamaican society and considered themselves superior to plantation slaves. Some Maroons owned slaves.[6]

Many works have addressed Caribbean and Latin American Maroon communities on the fringes of slave society. The long and courageous survival of Maroons has also been repeatedly referenced in studies of Jamaica. But no previous study examines the Maroons' settlement in three disparate British colonies, considering their experiences in Nova Scotia and their self-exile to Sierra Leone in an era of Christian humanitarianism and revolutionary upheaval in addition to their experiences in the mountainous interior of Jamaica. This work is the first book-length scholarly study on the relocations of the Trelawney Maroons in the late eighteenth century. By examining the Maroons in motion in three British-run settlements, I capture the possibilities and contradictions of antislavery discourse during a moment of British expansionism. This is the first major contribution of *Almost Home.*[7]

The Maroons' extraordinary transformation from "dangerous enemies" of Jamaica to favored British subjects in Sierra Leone in just four years requires historical explanation. Neither the Maroons' African ancestry nor their rebellious conduct relegated them to the status of permanent inferiority. Their remarkable survival in Nova Scotia and their relocation in Sierra Leone had much to do with the assault on slavery within the British Empire in the aftermath of the War of American Independence. During a moment when slave-owning colonies affected Britons' perception of their own society, the Maroons' precarious fate became a parliamentary issue. It triggered high emotion and demanded attention. Many Britons had never seen an African. Yet, remarkably, virtuous reformers' utterly certain understanding that slaveholders were sinful and blacks sinless drove them to advocate for the Trelawney Town Maroons. Defensive proslavery proponents sought to rationalize black slavery as white guardianship but could no longer do so on moral grounds. In an era dominated by the discourse of gradual abolitionism, the plight of the Maroons, most of whom were women and children, created immediate and resounding sympathy.[8]

The Maroons' odyssey cannot be grasped by studying the local history of Jamaica alone. The island existed within an imperial slave-owning system that was under moral attack. The Trelawney Town Maroons' predicament was as much linked to the paternalistic ideals of British reformers as to the local danger they presented to slave-owning elites. The Maroon war of 1795–96 occurred in the midst of an Atlantic-wide antislavery movement. For almost a decade a committed cadre of organized imperial reformers placed Jamaican slave owners on the defensive. Slave rebels who sacrificed their lives for freedom in the afterlife were contrasted with sinful West Indian planters who tortured blacks to satisfy their opulent earthly comforts. Although the Maroons were not slaves, reformers were too remote from the Caribbean world to grasp the hierarchies among "Negroes"—or to strategically know what best to emphasize. They focused on the cruelties borne by people who carried the stigma of African ancestry. Instead of detesting the Maroon rebels who challenged the white plantocracy, zealous reformers selectively transformed them into heroes. Their devotion to the Maroon cause alarmed Jamaican planters.[9]

The Saint-Domingue rebellion (1791–1804), which had already raged for four years, further traumatized white Jamaicans. Whereas proslavery advocates accused evangelical reformers of fomenting slave rebellion in Saint-Domingue by introducing lofty ideals to blacks who were naturally inferior and unnecessarily violent, antislavery reformers blamed the rebellion on the brutality of slavery, in particular the long hours of field labor, inadequate nutrition, and severe punishments. The rigid terms of slave ownership led both its proponents and its opponents to adopt extreme positions. By the time of the Maroon war, the antislavery forces had gained a secure following in London. The Maroons' deportation arose from the planters' defensive reaction against imperial abolitionism on one side and the nearby Saint-Domingue rebellion on the other.[10]

In Nova Scotia, well-meaning abolitionists transformed Jamaica's dangerous enemies into "helpless and injured subjects," exiled from their homeland by Jamaican tyrants. The Maroons' war against whites and their destruction of plantations were forgotten. As Jamaica had feared, well-meaning abolitionists, eager for a cause to call their own, substituted the Maroons for slaves. They focused on the Trelawney Town Maroons' race and their banishment and nothing else. That the majority of the deported were women and children made Jamaican masters look particularly villainous. The reformers likened the Trelawney Town Maroons' deportation to a Jamaican-ordered middle passage and the Maroons' existence in the cold winters of Nova Scotia to an abhorrent alternative to tropical Jamaica.[11]

British Sierra Leone, founded in 1787, became the abolitionists' dream home for the Maroons, a haven for the "millions [of] yet unborn" Africans. Just as Jamaica was identified as a hell for slaves, Sierra Leone, initially called the Province of Freedom, was projected as a sanctuary for free blacks, a beacon of antislavery in the midst of slave factories and the slave trade. Unlike the sugar colonies of the Caribbean, Sierra Leone would flourish by organizing the labor of free Africans. To establish the settlement, so-called improved blacks from England and the Americas were recruited as colony builders. The arrival of two earlier groups, in 1787 and 1792, had established Sierra Leone as a natural disembarkation for dangerous, unwanted, or unhappy blacks in the British Empire. In 1800 the very Maroons who had preserved slavery in Jamaica were sent to protect the ideals of abolition in Sierra Leone.[12]

It is tempting to narrate the Trelawneys' relocations as primarily a harrowing tale of survival. But to do so would be merely to repeat the narrative that antislavery proponents so successfully constructed. The Maroons' journeys undoubtedly came at tremendous personal cost, but the Maroons were not just victims or simple heroes. I show how a free community of black families negotiated an empire of slavery from three very different vantage points. Deprived of the mountainous terrain that gave them nourishment, shelter, and refuge, the Maroons improvised, making sense of new British contexts and always presenting themselves as trusted military auxiliaries. Their reputation as loyal warriors accompanied them.

During the last years of the eighteenth century, antislavery fervor had reached its most intense pitch yet. Yet there was no reason for the enslaved or ex-slaves like Maroons to imagine that the British Parliament would abolish the slave trade in 1807 and slavery in 1834. The Maroons' adjustments to each British zone must be seen in light of this uncertainty. They were free but not as free as whites; they knew they carried the stigma of African ancestry. They had witnessed the burning alive of rebellious slaves. The Maroons understood intimately the brutality of enslavement and did everything possible to avoid association with a regime they equated with servility and death. The Maroons' moral compromises may strike us as reprehensible two centuries later but we should remember that their alliances with whites protected them and their families from enslavement, sale, famine, torture, execution, and, until 1795, banishment. The Maroons' freedom derived from their attachment to white patrons. Unlike average slaves who died well before their children matured, the Maroons survived. An attachment to a simplistic notion of resistance leaves no room for the Maroons who survived by conserving slavery. Situating the Maroons within a history of loyalism as well as the history of slavery is the second important contribution of this book.[13]

As historians, we have tended to admire resistance and to think of accommodation as a tragic, last-defense reaction. But the endurance of the Trelawney Town Maroons moves me to theorize loyalty more fully. The loyalist framework does not negate the painfulness of their compromise or minimize the severity of slavery in Jamaica. The Maroons' loyalty to colonial authorities afforded them a degree of autonomy, increased their mobility, opened opportunities for deeper contact with whites, in short, it gave them an understanding of the conventions of colonial society. The Maroons gained real privileges in return for their attachment. The positive features of loyalty shaped their world in Jamaica and in exile: the Maroons' nuanced grasp of British norms made their marginal condition more manageable in Jamaica, their sense of imperial obligations and their high self-regard gave them the resilience to resist their conditions in Nova Scotia, and their intuitive grasp of British needs in West Africa helped them in Sierra Leone.[14]

The Trelawney Town Maroons faced and overcame a great deal of racial discrimination. This is an essential part of their experience. Without denying this, my work explores the agency they had in making and remaking themselves in the British world. A close reading of the documentary evidence suggests a great deal of nuance on what "race" meant to the Maroons themselves. This is a story about both racism and agency and, specifically, about the ways in which the Maroons positioned themselves in the British Empire.[15]

The sheer drama of the Maroons' relocations makes for an unprecedented tale: over 150 families were deported to Nova Scotia, suffered through the dreaded winters of that colony, and then resettled in West Africa. At first thought, we can make the mistake of assuming that the Maroons reversed the journey of over 10 million slaves by returning to their ancestral Africa. But we miss too much by placing the Maroons solely within the history of slavery and abolition and not within the framework of immigration and creolization as well. As much as ex-slaves, the Maroons were creolized immigrants. Intimately aware of the power of whites and the debasement of slaves, they accommodated in order to preserve their privileged role, protect their kin, and retain the patronage of white elites. This finding is the third critical contribution of my book.[16]

By the 1790s most Maroons were Jamaican creoles. They were conversant in the English language, adopted British first and last names—and became slave owners. Yet the Maroon community did not follow all the customs of white patriarchal society. As often as they named their daughters Ann and Sally, they named them Nanny—undoubtedly for the heroic Maroon woman who was rumored to defy the Jamaican elite in the 1730s by catching bullets between her buttocks. And the Maroon brothers Captain Andrew Smith and Charles Samuels, for example, did not share the same last name. Some Maroon leaders—captains and colonels—took multiple wives. Maroons also, like slaves, retained distinct beliefs and rituals concerning the supernatural world. Oath-taking, blood-binding allegiance from an earlier African world, held secret and sacred significance for both slaves and Maroons and would be carried from Jamaica to Nova Scotia and then to Sierra Leone. Like immigrants, the Maroons adjusted in order to raise their own status and secure their children's future. Sierra Leone may have been a symbol of hope—the "best poor man's country" for the Maroons—but it was no homeland. Always, they yearned for Jamaica.[17]

Each part of the Maroon story now belongs within the national histories of Jamaica, Canada, and Sierra Leone. Each nation honors the Maroons as heroic ancestors; they remain alive in public monuments, street names, churches.[18] Students, librarians, shopkeepers, and ministers claim descent from the Trelawney Town Maroons. As skillful warriors and undefeated outlaws, they serve as powerful symbols of bravery and tenacity in the face of the worst odds. Over two centuries later, this is the remarkable legacy of fewer than six hundred Maroons.[19]

My work returns the Maroons to the British Empire long before the three nations came into being. It shows that the Maroon societies were shaped as much by their interaction with others of African ancestry as by their relationship to white patrons. It simultaneously places the Maroons within the history of British expansionism, Atlantic-wide loyalism, and black diasporic migrations. It puts together sources spread across three continents—Europe, North America, and

Africa—to explain the Maroons' perplexing interactions with other groups, whites and blacks, free and unfree. The availability and types of sources relating to the Maroons in each region create constraints; we simply do not know enough to develop the Maroons into well-rounded characters. Yet, still, we are left with an intimate record of grief and resilience. Only a thick description of the entire process can recreate the ordeals of the Maroons and show how they adjusted piecemeal to the local circumstances in each British society. The reformers' efforts on behalf of the Maroons created a distinct paper trail in newspapers, assembly records, and parliamentary papers. Career administrators, military commanders, sugar planters, army and naval officers, missionaries, surgeons, and onlookers exchanged frustrated commentary about Maroon beliefs and practices, for example, their naked fear of bloodhounds brought in to capture them; their unwillingness to give up polygamy; their loyalty to their large families; their strategic sensibility under the most taxing circumstances; and their pleas to return home to Jamaica.[20]

The Maroons' tenacity compelled awe and exasperation, similar to the esteem the British would acquire for the Gurkhas of India. George Ross, the Maroon superintendent in Sierra Leone, is typical in his ambivalent regard for the community, expressing a mixture of fondness and disdain by describing one favored Maroon as a "proud troublesome dog." The Maroons themselves have left us their laments, blood oaths, work habits, grieving practices, divided leadership, moments of violent and nonviolent resistance, and a handful of petitions that, taken together, quietly point to routes taken under the most distressful and limited circumstances. As much as outright resistance, a story of accommodation is part of the longer history of slavery.[21]

JAMAICA

(Overleaf): *"Trelawney Town, the Chief Residence of the Maroons" (1800). This etching shows men on horseback attacking Trelawney Town and the Maroons defending it. The Maroons in the settlement had domestic animals like goats, pigs, and chickens. (Courtesy of the John Carter Brown Library at Brown University.)*

1
War

The Trelawney War of 1795 shattered the period of coexistence the planters had reached with Jamaica's six Maroon communities more than fifty years earlier. Following negotiations in 1738 and 1739 a peace treaty had ended the long period of guerrilla warfare between white Jamaicans and the Maroons. Writing in 1790, Captain Philip Thicknesse recalled the successive military failures that had led Jamaicans to sign the treaties. "Such who are unacquainted with that island," he wrote for his English audience, "will be surprised when they are told, that all regular troops in Europe could not have conquered the wild Negroes by force of arms." Thicknesse echoed the remarks made in 1737 by Jamaica's governor, John Gregory, who conceded that diplomacy was most suitable against the dauntless Maroons: "For my part I know but two ways of dealing with an enemy, either by force or treaty; the first we have often tried." The treaties established the Maroons as useful neighbors.[1]

Maroon communities had lived in the northern and eastern mountains since the English takeover of Jamaica from the Spanish in 1655. Early settlers tolerated their presence because the Maroons' numbers were small and they lived in inaccessible, out-of-the-way mountains.[2] In the decades after English conquest, the Maroon population grew, adapting to both the geographical terrain and Jamaican slave society. They combated the superior military technology of the

Jamaicans by relying on intelligence and provisions from slaves. They preyed on plantations and distressed settlers by plundering their homes and carrying away their cattle. Disguising themselves as slaves, they conveniently bartered and sold stolen wares.[3]

Unencumbered by English law or enslavement, the free black rebels proved an elusive and expensive nuisance to Jamaica's expanding elite. The Maroons dissuaded landowners from cultivating frontier areas, and their raids led whites to abandon their settlements. As one commentator put it, "The best and most fertile part of the island was of no service but remained overgrown with woods and shrubs." Most threateningly, the Maroons provided slaves, a growing majority on the island, with an example of how to successfully survive without suffering the misery of plantation labor.[4]

The Maroons' strength derived foremost from their ability to survive in mountainous, wooded areas inaccessible to most other Jamaicans, white or black. They exploited the natural fortification of the island, almost 150 miles of rugged terrain from east to west. One British soldier described the Blue Mountains in eastern Jamaica as "exceedingly steep and high, much broken, split and divided by earthquakes." The barefoot Maroons used "toe fingers" to avoid falling off dangerous precipices. They evaded capture by engaging in ambushes and hide-and-retreat maneuvers. They used an *abeng,* a bugle made from cow's horn, to call out to one another and to arrange meeting places.[5]

Maroon communities buttressed their strength as quasi-military organizations by absorbing skilled and armed runaways. Nearly every slave plantation in the Caribbean employed a blacksmith; when slave blacksmiths deserted to the Maroons, they brought with them the ability to manufacture and repair deadly weapons. In 1743 one settler observed that the Maroons "forge their own iron work making knives, cutlasses, heads of lances, bracelets, rings, and variety of other kinds of necessaries." In addition to their resilience and leadership, their expertise in metalsmithing made them formidable enemies. The treaties temporarily muted their danger.[6]

The colonial government settled with four smaller Maroon communities in the eastern part of the island as well as with the Trelawney and Accompong Maroons in the northern mountains. One contemporary noted that the island had conceded terms to the "wild ones." The treaties mandated that the Maroons live in reserved lands, away from plantations in the largely unsettled interior regions. They had permission to cultivate coffee, cocoa, ginger, tobacco, and cotton and to breed cattle, hogs, and goats. They could not, however, compete with plantations by cultivating sugar or disturb plantations by hunting wild hogs within three miles of a settlement. Later laws would try to prohibit the Maroons from owning slaves. The Maroon leaders' ability to inflict a death penalty was conceded to the white government. The government also appointed two white superintendents to live with the Maroons to ensure that they left their lands only with permission, to hold court for punishments, and to submit a quarterly report on the situation to the government in Spanish Town.[7]

The treaties led to more direct white control but also to some unintended consequences in the long term. The Maroons came into more direct and intimate contact with white society and began to depend on freely granted provisions and favors for their very survival. Their proximity to white culture led to rapid creolization and may have led them to have a sense of superiority over African slaves who arrived in large numbers to replace those who died working in the sugar plantations.[8]

Whites' concessions to the Maroons were structured within a slave system that depended on a system of divide and rule, providing incentives for selected slaves and using coercive authority against the rest. Individual slaves were manumitted if they performed loyal service. Some masters freed their concubines and their children. Slaves were armed at the discretion of their masters. The Maroons were atypical because they operated as separate communities, received land and arms, and entered into a formal, long-lasting multigenerational agreement with the Jamaican administrators.

The resourceful leader who negotiated for the northern Maroons was a Maroon-born Creole named Cudjoe, who was born to Coromantee parents. The political structure of pretreaty Maroon society centered around a chief whose word was law and who was recognized for military and civil decisions he made that were favorable to the community's interests. As described by the British who negotiated the treaty, Cudjoe commanded the greatest deference among the Maroons: "His word is a law to them." Cudjoe ruled with an iron hand; he demanded that the Maroons speak only in English to avoid fragmentation into different African ethnicities. Because of his tremendous influence, the Maroons in the north—the Trelawney Town and the Accompong Maroons—continued to be referred to as "Cudjoe negroes."[9]

The agreement between the Maroons and the colonial government went beyond a legal arrangement. The Maroon leaders, Cudjoe and Quao, his counterpart in the eastern mountains, took a secret blood oath promising allegiance to the British king, George II at this time.[10] Just as they trusted African customs and rites in regard to the afterlife, so the Maroons turned to the king to arm themselves for this life. In part, the Maroons' faith in the protection of a king was a natural extension of an already highly ordered patriarchal community. This ritualistic oath taking, consecrated by both British blood and Maroon blood, created a permanent bond, a kinship, between the Maroons and the British monarchy and entitled the Maroons to a

"Old Cudjoe Making Peace" (1803). The Maroons negotiated treaties with the British government in 1738 and 1739. Old Cudjoe was one of the chiefs who made concessions to the British government in return for the Maroons' freedom. (Courtesy of the John Carter Brown Library at Brown University.)

special audience if and when they should need one.[11] The blood oath ensured that the Maroons' relationship to the king derived its moral legitimacy from a higher spiritual place. The Maroons' rebirth as loyal subjects would incur its own costs, but a dependent relationship with the colonial elite was essential to their survival.[12]

Indeed, the Maroons' attachment to the British king widened their horizons beyond the Jamaican mountains. They came to see themselves as apart from slaves. They were Britain's favored blacks and felt a genuine affinity with the aims of the British Empire. They too identified the French as their enemy. British proslavery proponents argued that the end of slavery would transform slaves into bloodthirsty brutes, longing for revenge and unwilling to live by the rules of colony and empire. The armed Maroons showed firsthand the loyalty of freed blacks.[13]

It seemed to the Jamaican elites that they had little choice but to reach an agreement with the Maroons. Colonial Jamaica lacked an effective white militia, primarily because there were relatively few white men on the island. When white men joined the militia, they effectively abandoned plantations to the discretion of slaves. This situation mandated that white Jamaicans rely on blacks for their defense. But, like the whites, the free black and colored population, which comprised a third of the island's militia, had little military experience or discipline. For their part, the white militiamen balked at serving alongside free men of African ancestry. Nor could the Jamaican elite look to British troops for their defense. British soldiers regarded service in the West Indies with dread; 25 percent of European soldiers in the Caribbean died, more through disease than in battle. Captain Thicknesse remembered that the shipmate who darkly warned, "God knows which of us may slip his wind first," died within forty-eight hours of landing on the island.[14]

In exchange for their autonomy, the Maroons became an auxiliary military force in Jamaica, a "mountain police." They collaborated with the Jamaican slave regime to preserve slavery, patrolling the woods for fugitive slaves and suppressing slave rebellions. The Jamaican frontier—the remote, rugged mountainous areas—henceforth became unsafe for slave runaways. In effect, the treaties turned the Maroons into an internal police force that prevented new outlaw communities from emerging in the interior. In return for their loyalty to colonial authorities, the Maroons received patronage in the form of money, clothes, guns, and cattle. Empowered with these resources, the Maroons charted their own role in the island at a status above that of plantation slaves.[15]

The Jamaican government congratulated itself on the treaties with the Maroons. The single discrete act of signing the treaty had transformed dangerous enemies into loyal slave catchers. In so doing, the islanders had created a standing army at virtually no cost. The treaties hardened divisions between two groups of blacks whose collaboration might otherwise have challenged white rule in the island. With the Maroons acting as slave catchers, thousands of new slaves could be purchased for work in unsettled territory without the worry that they might escape or rebel. Planters such as William Beckford expressed satisfaction with the situation: "The Rebellious Negroes still continue our fast friends & are likely to make very good subjects." He praised the "Negroes in the mountains," who added stability to the island.[16]

The stalemate established by the Maroon treaties of 1738 and 1739 encouraged Jamaica's planters to cultivate the frontier regions. The settlers' confidence in the Maroons of Trelawney Town, located at the intersection of the three parishes of St. James, Trelawney, and St. Elizabeth, allowed plantations in northern Jamaica to dramatically expand. St. James Parish was flooded with white settlers after 1740. The number of slaves increased twenty times, and sugar production grew four times. The Trelawney Town Maroons in turn benefited from the patronage of slave owners. In contrast to the crushing mortality rates suffered by slaves, the Maroons, less susceptible to a fatiguing workload, brutal punishment, and malnutrition, thrived. With at least 660 residents, they were the largest Maroon community in the island.[17]

The treaties established the Maroons as an intermediate group, one whose origin lay in slavery but whose loyalty lay with the masters. Yet even as the truce institutionalized hostility between Maroons and slaves, Jamaicans could not entirely dismiss the Maroons' capacity for disorder. On the one hand, the Maroons' military abilities overawed slave resistance and promoted the steady cultivation of new regions. White Jamaicans benefited from the Maroons' relative freedom in relation to slaves. On the other, the extent of Maroons' loyalty remained in doubt; their military experience could just as easily turn against white society. When minor grievances escalated into full-scale war, the precariousness of their place became evident: white Jamaicans' ingrained suspicion of the Maroons brought tragedy to Trelawney Town.

Tensions began in July 1795, when two Trelawney men, accused of illegally killing pigs, suffered the indignity of being whipped by a slave. The beating was carried out by a slave overseer the Maroons had previously captured as a runaway; adding insult to injury, the Maroons overheard nearby slaves making jeering remarks. The slaves' laughter served as a reminder that, despite their faithful service to slave owners, the Maroons faced the same humiliation meted out to slaves. Outraged, the Maroons forced out the white superintendent,

Thomas Craskell, and demanded that the Jamaican government appoint a leader better acquainted with their "character, disposition, and prejudices." They reminded the planters of their obligation to the Trelawney Town Maroons: "You are our Tattas [fathers], we your children, Our situation and Superiority we have in this Country, we know from our Connection with you; but when we do the duty required of us for the advantages do not subject us to insult and humiliation by the very people whom we are set in opposition to." Taking advantage of the attention they had drawn from local elites, the Trelawney Town Maroons also asked for an additional three hundred acres, as less than 10 percent of the fifteen hundred acres allotted to them in the 1738 treaty had proven arable. The rest either was rock or contained very poor soil. As they awaited a favorable decision from the colonial government, the Maroons threatened war.[18]

Northern planters acquainted with the Trelawney Maroons responded by cautioning moderation. They refused to assign meaning to the Trelawney warnings; the threats, they reasoned, merely expressed annoyance at a personal grievance. Matters would soon cool down. The planters tried to prevent tensions from escalating and to contain tales from spreading south to the colonial government in Spanish Town. When Isaac Lascelles Winn heard that the Maroons planned to assassinate Craskell, he tried to shut down the rumors. The person who spread the gossip, Winn claimed, was "an ignorant credulous bobbling creature on whose report no confidence can be placed." Winn encouraged the government to negotiate "in a way that shall seem to be gracious concessions on our part and favours to the Maroons."[19]

Local elites believed that only a minority faction among the Trelawney Town Maroons was belligerent. It was these younger men who were "ripe for anything." The majority of the Maroons were "kept in awe by the smaller and more violent." Samuel Vaughan, the owner of a coffee plantation two miles from Trelawney Town, remained confident of an amicable resolution weeks into the disturbance. He hoped to quiet the "refractory discontented spirits" among the Maroons and to establish a more secure footing with the loyal Maroons. The island, he explained, had long maintained "respectability" because the "Old Men" among the Maroons had wide influence and had maintained a peace impossible to achieve through either legal mandates or military force. Vaughan referred to the stabilizing effect of Maroon leaders such as the head of the Maroons, Colonel Montague James, who was more aware of the dangers of breaking the customary relations with planters. Working out an accommodation with them, Vaughan judged, would prove to be the best recourse.[20]

Up until this time, neighborhood estates had benefited from the Maroons' proximity. They formed an effective military blockade preventing slaves from seeking refuge in the mountains; many planters considered a small force of Maroons indispensable to the security of their estates. Vaughan asserted that the Trelawney Town Maroons' "frequent scowering of the woods" kept defiant slaves in check. Previously, he recalled, the Maroons had suppressed the Coromantee rebellion of 1766 in the northwest, in Westmoreland Parish. They had "brought in the head or the person of every slave in rebellion in the space of one month." The Maroons, Vaughan may also have known, had shot Tacky, the slave who led a one-year revolt of over one thousand slaves in 1760. Vaughan worried that slave runaways would increase dangerously if the planters lacked Maroon allies: "What check do we have so effectual as the Maroons?"[21]

Because the Trelawney Town Maroons' resistance primarily took the form of threats, nearby planters gauged the potential disruption of a military campaign against the Maroons as more disruptive than capitulating to their demands. The Maroons had earned a reputation as fierce and wily fighters who commanded the mountains as well as the plains below them. Another observer would later emphasize the Maroons' knowledge of "woods and caves" from which "every means employed to drive them out had failed." The Maroons understood their own strength. In the first days of the rebellion, one "bolder sister of a bold and noted Maroon" adopted the title of Queen of Montego Bay. After Kingston, Montego Bay was the largest town in the island; it was also the closest seaport to Trelawney Town. The Jamaican planters feared provoking the enmity of such an audacious and elusive people.[22]

The Maroon woman's adoption of the title of royalty speaks to the complicated nature of Maroon loyalism. The Maroons did not see themselves as hopelessly beholden or permanently subservient to the king. The woman's claim of the position of queen represented as much a bold embrace of power as a desire for integration into the British empire. She borrowed from royalism to imagine a world in which a Maroon queen would rule over the richest slave-owning colony in the empire. The queen, possibly a slave owner herself, would have no reason to abolish slavery in Jamaica, a system that ensured the wealth and status of her island and of her empire.[23]

Jamaica's slave owners also worried that a hardline approach could spin the contest out of control. Their vulnerability was apparent: fewer than 25,000 whites lived with over 250,000 slaves in the island. Some doubted that even an army of 20,000 men, almost the entire white population of the island, could prevent the Maroons from descending from their mountains to destroy their fields and carry away slaves and cattle. Although the Maroon numbers were small—fewer than 300 men in Trelawney Town—their knowledge of the terrain, their access to food sources from their own provision grounds, and, most of all, "the aid they could at pleasure receive from our slaves" were reasons enough to meet their demands.[24]

But the newly arrived lieutenant governor, the Earl of Balcarres, ignored the planters' calls for conciliation. Balcarres, who had reached Jamaica only in April, just three months before the unrest, had no history of dealing with the Maroons. He dismissed the planters' conciliatory approach; he found their tolerance baffling. He complained of the "imperium in imperio" in the parishes of St. James and Trelawney; the overseers and managers in those parishes thwarted his attempts to restore order. Shockingly, they "paid contributions" to the Maroons to keep their properties safe. Balcarres could not fathom why planters were ready to go so far to ensure the loyalty of troublesome blacks. These elites wanted to set their own terms with the Trelawney Town Maroons, who, he complained, exercised "uncontrolled freedom" and possessed "every comfort of life."[25]

Just weeks after the initial unrest Balcarres abandoned the treaty terms of the 1730s, effectively transforming the island's useful auxiliaries into dangerous enemies. In early August his government declared martial law. It issued a proclamation that clearly went against the treaty relationship, framing the Jamaican whites as defensive inhabitants caught in the midst of a "most unprovoked, ungrateful, and most dangerous rebellion." The proclamation announced that the "Maroons endangered lives, liberties, and properties of subjects in the island" and "temporary measures with the Trelawney Maroons are not likely to give any security for the future safety of Jamaica." Balcarres accused the Maroons of illegally driving away their "commander," the superintendent; he reminded them that every path to their homes would be occupied; they would be "surrounded by thousands." Their town would be "burnt to the ground and forever destroyed" unless they submitted immediately to "His Majesty's mercy." Balcarres's exaggerated reaction to the turmoil transformed the Maroons' grievances into a war that raged for eight months.[26]

Balcarres's uncompromising position derived above all from his fear that Jamaica would suffer the same cataclysmic convulsion that had raged in Saint-Domingue since 1791. When the egalitarian ideals of the French Revolution spilled over to the French West Indies, Saint-Domingue's slaves made a violent bid for freedom and self-rule. To the horror of colonial authorities everywhere in the Caribbean and slaveholders everywhere, French slaves destroyed over a thousand sugar plantations and massacred white families. The dangers to Jamaica, which possessed the largest concentration of slaves in the Caribbean only a day's sail from Saint-Domingue, were apparent.[27]

Balcarres's awareness of Jamaica's vulnerability, fueled by rumors of French agents instigating slave revolt in other British islands, led him to move toward exterminating the Maroons "coute qui coute." When he heard testimony, primarily from slaves, that the Trelawney Town Maroons sought not only to kill their obnoxious superintendent but also to encourage slaves to imitate the Saint-Domingue rebellion, he had reason to imagine the worst. Maroons' hostility, he was convinced, "has long been premeditated, and at the instigation of the convention of France whose object is undoubtedly, to throw this island into a state of anarchy and confusion." He was determined to frustrate a potential Jamaican Toussaint L'Ouverture who could unite slaves and lead a rebellion. To Balcarres, crushing the Maroons equated with rescuing the island for the empire.[28]

Balcarres's government also worried about the thousands of refugees from Saint-Domingue and their slaves who had crowded into Jamaica's towns and interior in the first half of the 1790s. It feared not only the ideals of French-owned slaves from Saint-Domingue but also the ideology of French prisoners brought to Jamaica after the British capture of Martinique and Guadeloupe. British imperial ambitions to capture a portion of the French West Indies, meanwhile, had left Jamaica with few troops, vulnerable to external invasion and internal commotion. In an attempt to quell the situation, Balcarres ordered a full-scale eviction of French immigrants along with their slaves in September.[29]

Having no experience of Maroon warfare that had led to the treaties of the 1730s, Balcarres felt confident he could reduce the Maroons in no time. He imprisoned the handful of Maroons who surrendered in response to his proclamation and called troops back from Saint-Domingue to crush the remaining rebels. He saw no reason why his force of fifteen hundred troops, in addition to hundreds of militia, could not bring in some six hundred Maroons, over half of them women and children. He commanded the burning of Trelawney provision grounds to "cut out the heart of the rebellion." He determined to pen the Maroons in the rugged, barren mountains without sustenance so they would survive only as a "band of robbers." And to ensure the cooperation of the local planters, in October Balcarres raised the rank of the British officer George Walpole from lieutenant colonel to major general. As a major general, Walpole ranked above militia officers in every parish and thus had the authority to pursue the Maroon war with or without the consent of northern leaders.[30]

But Balcarres's war did not go as expected. As the crisis dragged on from weeks to months, the lieutenant governor began to understand something of the nature of Maroon warfare. After British soldiers burned the Maroon town in mid-August, the Trelawney Town Maroons dispersed but did not surrender. They hovered, ambushed small groups, and disappeared, without offering a chance for attack. Each encounter left eight to twelve white men dead or wounded, with few Maroon casualties. A nightmarish guerrilla war ensued. Daily, the

Maroons attacked and killed the troops and militia who blockaded their cockpits. In September, when two revered British colonels died in ambushes, Balcarres knew that the "danger to the island is not less than it was." The hatred of some Maroons became evident in the desecration of a white officer's body. After Colonel Fitch of the 83rd Regiment was shot, a Maroon woman—perhaps the so-called Queen of Montego Bay—reportedly cut off his head, "ripped open his belly, and put his head into it while the corps was still warm." At least some Maroon women were warriors. In October Balcarres reported that the Maroons were nowhere close to surrender and had, in fact, taken an "oath to spare no white person whatsoever." He struggled to describe the drawn-out contest to his superiors.[31]

The soldiers found it impossible to access the Maroon enclaves. The troops had destroyed the Maroons' provision grounds and dislodged them from Trelawney Town, but the Maroons remained stubbornly ensconced in the impassable wooded interiors. As Balcarres would write, "The Maroons retreated into a country of rocks beyond description—wild and barren into which no white person has ever entered." Aware of the large rewards offered for their heads, the Maroons remained especially vigilant, difficult to track and capture. A British force more than five times the number of Maroon men could not compel their submission. Balcarres worried that Maroons hiding in the mountains, like Polish robbers he had read about, would give "employment to some [British] regiments for years."[32]

Morale slumped. But Balcarres had gone too far; there was no turning back. Planters who had previously opposed the war now sided with the government. The tenuous nature of the collaboration between planters and Maroons became apparent. Although the planters had expressed gratitude for the Maroons' protection of slavery and had tried to avoid escalating hostilities, they soon saw advantage in

"The Maroons in Ambush on the Dromilly Estate in the Parish of Trelawney, Jamaica" (1801). The hilly, dense forests occupied by the Maroons made it difficult for British soldiers to defeat them, thus prolonging the Maroon war. (© The British Library Board [Maps.K.Top.123.59].)

the Maroons' extermination. The planters saw benefits in taking out their temperamental armed neighbors who never acquiesced to full subordination. If the government could root out the Maroons, the planters were ready to be rid of them.[33]

The massive number of newly imported African slaves in Jamaica undoubtedly led to the planters' cooperation with the tactics of the colonial government. During the 1790s the threat of Maroon unrest spilling into slave rebellion loomed especially large. Jamaica had taken advantage of the turmoil in Saint-Domingue to increase its sugar exports, and greater sugar production demanded increased labor. The island had imported the largest number of slaves in the island's history. In 1793 alone, over twenty-five thousand Africans were added to the population, magnifying the potential of slave resistance. Some of the planters' dread of slave rebellion stemmed from the presence of thousands of "new negroes"; long-settled whites knew greater resistance came from unincorporated slaves with no familial ties in the island.[34]

The treaties of 1738 and 1739 had not fully eliminated planters' apprehensions about a slave–Maroon alliance. No Maroon was known to have helped slaves rebel, but if Maroons decided to rebel, Jamaican planters felt certain that they would look to slaves for food and information. Surely they would try to encourage them to rebel. Driven by this anxiety, Jamaican authorities continued to regulate relations between Maroons and slaves. Planters especially worried that the connections Maroon men formed with slave women could overrule their loyalty to whites. As one contemporary noted, a slave who "connected himself with a woman whose brother, sister, or other relations were fugitives would probably be tempted to remit his pursuit of them, and even to favour their concealment." A succession of laws enacted over the mid-1700s but enforced haphazardly attempted to define the terms of interaction between Maroons and slaves. In a clumsy effort to limit the intimacy between the two groups, social gatherings between slaves and Maroons were restricted to daylight hours.[35]

The Maroon war unleashed Jamaican masters' paranoia about a united black assault on their world. In August 1795 an account from a slave named Harry revealed the potential of a blood alliance between slaves and Maroons. When Harry was captured by the Maroons, the Maroon leader, Captain James Palmer, gave him "three cuts on the wrist and caught the blood in a calabash intending to make him drink it the next noon and swear not to return to his master but to go about to get people to join them." A vision of slaves silently hatching a plot to end their masters' rule, joined by blood to the unconquered Maroons, was the recurring nightmare of Jamaicans.[36]

Planters took brutal measures to deter slaves from seeking out the Maroons. Consider the case of Commodore, a slave who gave up his life in a desperate bid to challenge the plantocracy. A "negro driver," Commodore, the property of James McKean, was accused of rebellion and conspiracy. He had captured four slaves and threatened to "chop their heads" if they did not join the Maroons. The four slaves escaped and determined to wreak vengeance. Commodore, it appeared, had a longer history of runaway attempts. Twice before, he had attempted to escape by "putting to sea in canoes" with "parties of other negroes." The planters had seen enough. They authorized his immediate hanging and ordered "his head afterwards to be cut off, and placed in the most public situation." Commodore's head would remind slaves of the futility of resistance.[37]

Other slaves took advantage of the war to vent their animosity toward the Maroons. The treaties of the 1730s had succeeded in setting not only Maroons against slaves but also slaves against Maroons. In August slaves stood before the colonial government and testified against the Maroons, alleging that they had sought to join the French to burn Jamaica. In a cruel twist, slaves sought protection from white slave owners against Maroon kidnappers. Abraham testified that three Maroons came to him while he and four other slaves were working and ordered them to "desist from work and go with them." When they resisted, the Maroons asked them if they knew about their "quarrel with the backra's [white people]." The Maroons told them that the backras had destroyed their lands. If the slaves went with them, they could get the "better of the backra's," and they "should live very easy and should have their freedom." But the slaves refused. The Maroons, armed with guns, cutlasses, and knives, threatened to cut off their heads, and the slaves purportedly had no option but to go with them. When the Maroons slept at night in the "deep wood," the slaves, including Abraham, ran away to the estate. One slave who went with the Maroons, Aberdeen, did not return.[38]

Slaves touched by the Maroon war became acutely vulnerable to suspicion from slave masters. Both voluntary and involuntary return were fraught with danger. Unable to imagine why runaways would flee fugitive status to return to a life of permanent enslavement, white Jamaicans assumed that slaves who returned must be spies. One slave was shot without questions. A more fortunate slave named Jamaica, the property of John Reid, had an opportunity to explain how he found his way back. Jamaica told Reid that he knew the path to "Backra country and find his master." His reasons for returning to his white master were clear. In his unwillingness to stay with Maroons, he may have expressed the sentiments of the slave majority: Jamaica "would not have a Negro for a Master." For Jamaica at least, Maroons offered only another kind of enslavement.[39]

Like Abraham and Jamaica, some slaves negotiated their freedom by collaborating with slaveholders, just as the posttreaty Maroons had done for decades. In exchange for freedom, they led the Jamaican militia and British soldiers to the "different haunts" of the Maroons. They served as spies and reported on the Maroons' morale as well as the conditions of the families. In November the newly free slave Zell reported the resolve of the Maroons who refused to submit to whites;

they would "suffer their heads to be taken off and their bodies to rot on the ground." They were short on provisions and gunpowder but had safety in the cockpits. Zell escaped at night when the Maroons went off to bury a young man who had died from a ball "which passed through his arm and entered his body." Using information supplied by slaves like Zell, British regulars and the Jamaican militia subsequently destroyed Maroon retreats, sometimes confiscating swords, helmets, and pistols.[40]

The Maroons' practice of sacred rites persisted during war. Their resistance to forsaking burial even in such dire circumstances hints at their strong beliefs about the afterworld. They honored the memory of a young warrior by carrying him to a burial ground worthy as a resting place. The meaning they attached to the interment mattered enough that they risked Zell's escape. In the most extreme circumstances the Maroons' reservoir of spiritual faith guided them to honor kinship ties—in this life and the next. Family and kinship remained of enormous significance.[41]

Balcarres had correctly predicted that the Maroons' dire circumstances—the lack of food and gunpowder—would dissuade large numbers of slaves from joining them. Reduced to despair by famine and ill equipped to support their wives and children, they could hardly provide a haven for runaways. In September one contemporary observed that the destruction of the Maroon lands had "reduced them [Maroons] low in the eyes of there [*sic*] negroes." In October an article in the *Royal Gazette* noted triumphantly that the Maroons "have no magazine, or place of security, left them, where to deposit their plunder." Just as important, the anonymous author remarked, the Maroons could no longer offer a place of refuge for runaway slaves: "They have no prospect to hold out to runaways, but that of being reduced to the same situation as themselves." Worse, the runaways carried measles into the Maroon community, creating dire stress. As the Trelawney Town Maroons struggled to survive the war, the potential for a slave–Maroon alliance receded.[42]

In fact, the Maroons' desperation alienated slaves. The Maroons' only chance of avoiding starvation was through plundering well-guarded estates or raiding slave provision grounds. Jamaican estates commonly included hills of poor-quality sugar land where slaves could plant crops like corn and plantain for their personal use or surplus sales. Although this land legally belonged to the estate owner, slaves guarded the provision grounds as their own preserve. Maroon depredations that diminished the food available to slave families created resentment.[43]

Impressionistic evidence suggests that the Maroons turned away from regarding slaves as potential blood brothers in relatively short order. The unpredictability of slaves' allegiance compromised their situation. The Trelawney Town Maroons had learned that slaves could return to plantations and plot to destroy them for their own rewards. Or that retaken slaves could reveal secret information about Maroon retreats to protect their slave families. The large number of runaways who entered and left their retreats created risk and forced the Maroons to find new hiding places. In November a runaway slave named Clark joined the Maroons while another one, Covey, ran away from them the same day.[44] Curiously, the Maroons and the slave masters confronted the same problem: neither had means to authenticate the slaves' true allegiance. Both groups knew that slaves' support would determine the outcome of the war.

Rather than exposing the weakness of the white ruling minority, the Maroon war revealed the surprising stability of a mature Afro-Caribbean slave society. The colonial state's policy of dividing slaves and Maroons was proven effective. The island experienced no massive convulsion like that in Saint-Domingue. Few slaves who deserted their masters sought an alliance with the slave-catching Trelawney Town Maroons. The vast majority of slaves, having families in the island, fearing violent retribution from masters, and harboring doubts about freedom inside the Trelawney community, stayed on their plantations. The colony's fears notwithstanding, black collaboration, or the "combination between Maroons and slaves," did not materialize.[45]

As Jamaican masters patrolled slaves' conduct, the colonial government turned to ensuring the loyalty of the three smaller Maroon communities in the eastern part of the island. They feared that the Trelawney Town Maroons' ability to hold out for months against professionally trained soldiers sent a message that whites were weak. Since the beginning of the unrest Balcarres was distraught that Maroons at Scot's Hall, Moore-Town, and Charles-Town would find opportunity in the unrest. French agents could conspire to turn them against the islanders. In September Balcarres observed that these Maroons were "by no means staunch." In the same way they had compensated slaves for their loyalty, the Jamaican government rewarded Maroon communities for their neutrality. The Maroons at Moore-Town received a cow and ten gallons of rum every two weeks during the seven months of martial law. Balcarres knew that the news of the destruction of the Trelawney provision grounds had thus far kept the communities quiet and saved the island from a chain of insurrections by Maroons. Suspecting the Maroons' distrust, he downplayed his role and elevated the British king as their leader, "the father of all good and loyal Maroons."[46]

In his short time on the island Balcarres grasped the reverence the Maroons held for the British monarch. By contrast, the Maroons regarded the colonial administrators—governors—as poor standbys. The Trelawney Town Maroons would fiercely fight against perceived maltreatment by the governor and his friends but stand proudly loyal to a faraway British king, imagined as merciful and all-powerful. Balcarres knew his approach had the desired effect on the attending Maroons. As he reported, "When I speak, they hear the speech of the King." Balcarres's strategic use of the royal voice stood in for the benevolent king imagined by the Maroons.[47]

The Maroons of Trelawney Town and the Accompong Maroons of St. Elizabeth shared ties of proximity and kinship, and it may have surprised the Jamaican planters that the Accompong Maroons, the second largest Maroon community in the island, stood ready to kill their neighbors. Within two weeks of the unrest the Accompongs renewed a compact with Jamaican authorities to baptize all their children. Sixty men from Accompong Town promptly offered military assistance against the Trelawney rebels. The Accompongs looked to the Jamaican planters to reward them for their military service and to protect them from the Trelawney Town Maroons. They requested a company of militia to guard their wives and children when they left to fight for the Jamaican planters. In return, the community received a gift of five hundred pounds. Accompong casualties left a long chain of unsupported dependents in the care of the Jamaican government. One Accompong colonel's death left seventeen children, five boys and four girls by one wife and six boys and two girls by another. As it did to the families of militia men, the government offered compensation to the families of Accompongs killed in battle. Accompong deaths on behalf of Jamaican whites affirmed the Trelawney Town Maroons as a particularly ungrateful and difficult lot.[48]

By late 1795, despite assistance from the Accompongs and British regulars, the Trelawneys remained elusive. The difficulties of pursuing them into the woods recalled the experiences that had led to the treaties in the first place. Eyewitness accounts conveyed the same awe of

Maroon fortitude as Captain Thicknesse had recounted following the battles of the 1730s. The quickness of their movements, along with their knowledge of the terrain, made them almost unconquerable. Because they lived by shooting wild hogs and wild fowl, they had become "marksmen beyond credibility." They fired from trees or points of rocks inaccessible to whites, and they rarely missed. Attacking their hideaways was dangerous and unlikely to succeed. The Maroons concealed weapons as well as kin in retreats impossible for men to discover.[49]

A frustrated Balcarres gave up on using troops and militia to bring in the Maroons. In December the colonial government, with approval from the planters, resolved to use canine auxiliaries, bloodhounds, to save the island from the Maroons.

2
Bloodhounds

By putting an immediate end to the Maroon war the planters hoped to preempt a looming imperial humanitarian intervention on behalf of the Maroons. What Lieutenant Governor Balcarres feared was that antislavery sentiment would interfere with his ability to deal with the Maroons as he saw fit. The *Somerset* decision of 1772, which criminalized the return of Africans to slavery in the Caribbean colonies against their will, had set a legal antislavery precedent in Britain. In the 1780s and 1790s continued abolitionist challenges in Parliament threatened to turn the planters' world upside down. An influential group of lobbyists, humanitarians, and evangelical Christians focused attention on the shamefulness of Caribbean slavery to the British Empire. Ex-slaves like Olaudah Equiano and evangelical parliamentarians such as William Wilberforce condemned the physical mistreatment of slaves, who faced long hours of field labor, inadequate nutrition, severe punishments, and high mortality rates. These reformers regarded slave rebellions as a natural and justifiable response to the inhumanity of slavery. The planters feared that reformers in England would equate the Maroon war with slave revolt and use it as a pretext for urging more imperial regulation on slavery in the Caribbean.[1]

Unfortunately for the Jamaican planters, the Maroon war coincided with a deepening, Atlantic-wide aversion to slavery. Economically, in an era of increasing industrialization, slave labor came to be regarded as inefficient and costly in relation to the flexibility of wage labor. Morally, slavery came to signify the incarnation of evil, repugnant to the dignity of civilized nations. A group of evangelicals emerged as one of the most powerful pressure groups in late eighteenth-century England. These saints printed pamphlets about and circulated images of the atrocities of slavery—suicide, rape, disease, and death—especially in Jamaica. One slave trader who had turned abolitionist, John Newton, went so far as to describe black rebels as patriots! To Wilberforce, the member of Parliament (MP) for Yorkshire and one of the most eloquent and persistent antislavery proponents, abolition became an all-consuming duty, a cause that drove him for over forty-six years. Thomas Clarkson, a professional abolitionist in England, gathered incriminatory material from slave ships and spoke passionately against slave ownership. Between 1787 and 1794 he covered thirty-five thousand miles on tours in Britain, lecturing about the brutality of enslavement. Wilberforce, Clarkson, and others combined their fervent efforts to work toward a single clear-cut goal: the end of the slave trade.[2]

The complications brought on by the antislavery movement and the Trelawney Town uprising came at a fraught moment for Jamaican planters. Although sugar production in the 1780s had recovered from the disruptions caused by the War of American Independence, the British economy was moving away from the Caribbean, toward Asia and Africa. The older Caribbean colonies like Jamaica faced the risk of becoming less relevant to broader British interests. The Saint-Domingue rebellion, while illustrating the threat of slave rebellion, unexpectedly gave Jamaica the occasion to raise its sugar production. The planters could not allow well-meaning reformers from without and a group of black rebels from within to ruin their chance to shine once again.[3]

Yet the Jamaican planters could not compel the Trelawney Maroons to surrender. By December 1795 the Maroons, surrounded by British soldiers, had retreated. The Jamaican militia's numbers had been increased by the addition of trusted slaves, who sought to discover and destroy the Trelawney haunts and retreats. And still the Maroons remained.

The onset of the dry season, which lasted from late winter into early spring, created new anxieties among the Jamaican elite. As the rains ended, planters thought less about how diseases would weaken their military strength and more about harvesting their crop. This was the time for cutting, loading, and transporting sugarcane to the mill. It was the time when white militia and slaves, along with carts and cattle, were most needed in the fields. But martial law prevented whites from returning to supervise the harvest. One overseer, Thomas Barritt, worried about havoc in his estate if whites' military duty continued during crop season: "We shall be much puzzled how to take [the canes] off and there will be great pilfering going on, as well shall be obliged to trust much to the negroes." Without oversight or order, slaves would remain idle or, worse, carry off supplies.[4]

Even deeper unease loomed with the arrival of the dry season: the Trelawney Town Maroons might torch the planters' sugarcane fields. As early as July, when the unrest began, one planter had warned, "We live amongst stubble, fully dry, and a few incendiaries might easily put it in a blaze." Flames would race through the canes. Since plantation buildings abutted cane fields, the burning canes would likely also destroy sugar works and houses. Balcarres, in fact, worried so much about the coming dry season that in October he was almost ready to offer concessions to the Maroons. A handful of Maroons could not massacre whites, as was happening in nearby Saint-Domingue, but they could engulf the island in flames. Other planters expressed fears that the Maroons might set fire to untended plantations.[5]

In desperation, Balcarres and his assembly turned to using dogs—not just any dogs but trained Cuban bloodhounds bred specifically to track down and feed upon human flesh. These bloodhounds were known to be ferocious, their only aim being to seize and devour their prey. They would follow the Maroons' scent and spread terror. As one contemporary remarked, "A Naked Maroon may brave us under cover of the woods but a gang of Dogs will make him very faint hearted." Balcarres and his allies hoped the dogs would force the Maroons to capitulate, showcase slaveholder invincibility, and deter a Saint-Domingue-like conflagration in Jamaica. The government saw no other means of gaining an upper hand in the war. Force and military skill were not enough, and the dogs' awesome reputation for brutality was sought after, not shunned.[6]

In using bloodhounds, Jamaican planters were taking their cues from the Spanish in nearby Cuba. According to one account, Havana had almost entirely avoided black unrest with the assistance of three hundred dogs: "There is no such being known in Cuba as a Maroon." Since September, a month after Balcarres's war began, Jamaicans had considered raising "a Corps of Dogs." One gentleman noted that a gargantuan military force had not reduced the Maroons; now "stratagem must be substituted for strength." By chance he had met a Spanish captain who mentioned that the Indians along the Mosquito Shore alarmed the Spanish in the same way that the Maroons plagued the Jamaicans. The dogs, which could sense the silent approach of Indians, had reduced Spanish casualties and resulted in the taking of Indian captives. Two hundred dogs enabled the Spanish to turn the Mosquito Shore into a peaceful region. There was no reason they would not be just as useful in Jamaica. They would signal the "lurking retreats of the enemy" and put whites on alert against ambushes which otherwise proved fatal.[7]

With the coming of the dry season, the Jamaicans finalized negotiations with the Cuban government for the use of the dogs. Meanwhile, the economic costs were adding up. Isaac Gibbs, the overseer of a cattle pen and coffee plantation in Trelawney Parish, lamented the destruction "from the horses galloping through the plantation and breaking down the bushes." Another overseer, Joseph Tucker, abandoned his plantations in St. James Parish when Maroons threatened his life. A contemporary pointed to the larger problem: the military consumed both "slaves and stock [provisions]," leaving plantations untended and ill equipped to meet the needs of the residents. Plantations could not possibly recover if the war continued much longer.[8]

On November 27 Don Guillermo Dawes Quarrell, a lieutenant colonel in the Jamaican militia, reached an agreement with the Cuban government. The Jamaicans would rent 104 dogs, accompanied by 40 chasseurs (keepers), who would "practice every means necessary to pursue and apprehend with our dogs, [the] said rebellious negroes." The keepers asked for and were promised additional bounties for any Maroons captured independently of the hounds.[9]

Having reached an agreement, Quarrell turned to the details of transporting the dogs the ninety miles to Jamaica. He bought muzzles and chains for the dogs; for the keepers he purchased cattle, for barbeque. He hired an interpreter, Joseph Zeny, to mediate between the demands of the mercenary keepers and the Jamaican government's needs. The contract committed the dogs and the keepers to three months in Jamaica.[10]

Both the dogs and their keepers had murderous reputations. One contemporary historian, Richard Dallas, described the violent

"The Mode of Training Blood Hounds in St. Domingo, and of Exercising Them by Chasseurs" (1805). A French soldier positions a slave in front of a pack of caged bloodhounds. The violent image suggests an antislavery perspective. (The Library Company of Philadelphia.)

"A Spanish Chasseur of the Island of Cuba" (1803). A man with two muzzled dogs and a sword passes an encampment. Cuban handlers (chasseurs) were hired by the Jamaican government during the Maroon war. (Courtesy of the John Carter Brown Library at Brown University.)

training the dogs received for their primary mission, namely, attacking black rebels:

> On coming up with a fugitive, they bark at him till he stops, then they crouch near him, terrifying him with a ferocious growl if he stirs. In this position they continue barking to give notice to the chasseurs, who come up and secure their prisoner. . . . At home the dogs are kept chained, and when walking with their masters, are never unmuzzled, or let out of ropes, but for attack. . . . [Their] coat, or skin, is much harder than that of most dogs, and so must be the whole structure of the body, as the severe beatings he undergoes in training would kill any other species of dog. . . . The chasseurs beat their dogs most unmercifully, using the flat sides of their heavy muschets [machetes].[11]

As the Jamaican government had anticipated, the dogs transformed the complexion of the war. Whites and blacks cleared the streets and shut their doors with the arrival of the bloodhounds, who were deemed "wild and formidable." Even the military commander, Major General George Walpole, found it necessary to return to the safety of his chaise upon the sight of the dogs. Of the 104 dogs, only 36 were completely trained. Whereas the trained dogs knew to bark at their prey and await the keeper before making the final capture, the untrained ones flew at the throat of their quarry and did not let go until the victim was cut in two. Rumors spread of an "unfortunate accident" in which one got loose from its keeper and "worr[ied] an old negro woman." Presumably, an untrained bloodhound assaulted her.[12]

In partnership with the Jamaican government, the Spanish chasseurs staged theater to terrorize the Maroons. They cut the throat of a bullock and allowed the dogs "to plunge their heads to drink the blood" and "push each other about covering themselves with blood and dust." They trusted that the slaves who witnessed the scene would carry the accounts to the Trelawney Town Maroons. They were right.[13]

Within four days of their arrival on the island, the bloodhounds ended the stalemate between the planters and the Maroons. No doubt both slaves and Maroons had heard rumors of dogs hunting down black fighters and eating black families in nearby Saint-Domingue. One recaptured slave, Quamin, confessed that the hounds had convinced him and another slave, Bernard, to leave the woods and return to their owners. The mere prospect of the hounds induced the Trelawney Maroons to repair to the negotiation ground. The proximity of snarling dogs accomplished what military forces had failed to do in nearly four months. As one historian would remark almost ninety years later, "The Maroons were a brave race and had no objection [to] fighting—as long as they had only to fight men."[14]

On December 21 the Trelawney Town Maroons signed a treaty with Walpole—before the troops deployed the bloodhounds. The Maroons agreed to surrender and to return runaway slaves in exchange for resettling in another part of the island. Most critically, Walpole provided a secret assurance, on oath, that they would not be deported from the island. Just as the Maroons had demanded that slave allies take the blood oath as a promise of loyalty during the war, so they obliged Walpole to take a secret oath to end the war. Walpole remained silent on the rituals, but it would soon become apparent that he felt morally bound by the oath. Balcarres and his assembly ratified both the treaty and Walpole's secret oath. Hostilities were suspended three days after Christmas as the military prepared to receive over six hundred Maroons.[15]

During the next weeks the Trelawney Town Maroons, having no choices left, surrendered as a people. The men came alone and conferred with Walpole for two or three days, then asked permission to return to the mountains to bring out their kin. Walpole permitted them to leave, even though he knew some would never return. He understood the factors that drove the Trelawney Town Maroons' mode of surrender. The Maroons were "as mistrustful as possible" and "each man is desirous that the other should make the experiment before him." Each wanted his neighbor "to try the white faith first." Few were as eager as Robert Fowler, who begged "he may have a gorget, with some inscription to shew that he was the first who made peace with the white people." Fowler's wife was pregnant, and his concerns for her safety may have overridden other worries.[16]

In an age in which British officers—outsiders to slave society—manifested growing moralistic tendencies toward those caught in war, Walpole showed compassion for the Maroon soldiers. His oath may have committed him to quasi-kinship ties with some Maroons. He requested shoes for barefooted men. As a sign of respect he let Maroon men who had surrendered retain their arms. Walpole sympathized with the Maroon families' plight. He observed that many were hindered by sick or injured family members they could not leave behind. Walpole observed that many made "three or four trips backwards and forwards for their children." Most returned within a few days, late at night, with their families, sometimes carrying children on their backs. Walpole supplied provisions for the women and children who surrendered. Some trusted Maroons supervised others who had surrendered. But by December 30 only sixteen Maroons had surrendered. On January 1, the agreed-upon date for surrender, only five more reached Walpole.[17]

Balcarres soon grew impatient with the pace of the surrender. Since September 1795 each of his dispatches to the secretary of state, the Duke of Portland, and the secretary of war, Henry Dundas, had promised to quickly terminate the war. With the surrender dragging on, he risked appearing incompetent and inadequate. Starting in January, Balcarres applied increasing pressure, ordering Walpole to deploy the bloodhounds "until their inefficacy is proved." He was suspicious of the Maroons' intentions; their duplicity, he wrote, was no match for British "strength in truth and openness." The island would have no security until "such time as these quick-silver rebels are under lock and key." Balcarres also demanded that Walpole send the surrendered Maroons to military barracks, where they would be under guard—why place trust in Maroons when British regulars were available to assume oversight of the captives?[18]

Walpole stalled. He assured Balcarres that a delay did not mean failure. Without directly defying Balcarres's orders, Walpole postponed deploying the dogs. The noisy barking and rattling chains already terrified the Maroons, who "begged so hard" for more time to retrieve their families from the woods. Walpole's resistance to their use was as much strategic as it was humanitarian: he doubted whether the dogs could survive the long march to the cockpits without water. To his mind, the dogs were a more effective threat than a weapon. To Walpole, Balcarres's distance from the scene of war had impaired his judgment on the matter of the hounds: "There will always be a difference as to thinking between those on the spot and those at a distance: representations never strike the same as ocular and even auricular demonstrations."[19]

In mid-January, when Walpole could no longer ignore Balcarres, he finally began his march with the bloodhounds against the Maroons. He put aside his distaste for canine operations to comply with Balcarres's repeated orders. But he kept the dogs with their keepers in the rear of the troops, muzzled and leashed, resolutely refusing to use them. Instead, he hoped the mere sighting of the hounds would compel the Maroons to surrender. And indeed, within two days most of the Trelawney Town Maroons surrendered. Walpole reported that he had in his possession 400 Maroons, 130 of whom were men. He insisted that his conciliatory approach had led to their surrender. In fact, he reported, the Maroons were already on their way to meet the troops before he went in with the dogs. The Maroons submitted because they trusted him and his oath; Walpole denied that the bloodhounds' furious pursuit had forced capitulation.[20]

Walpole's paternalism extended to individual Maroon men. He doubted that the military could have achieved the peace without cooperative Maroons because there was "little chance of any but a Maroon discovering a Maroon." Accustomed to their role as intermediaries to whites, some Maroon leaders brought in runaways and other Maroons to Walpole. One trusted Maroon, Colonel Thomas Johnstone, supervised the conduct of surrendered families and prevented Maroon men from drinking too much rum. Johnstone represented the austere morality of some older Maroons. Walpole wrote that he and Johnstone "at present are very great friends." In February Johnstone, acting for Walpole, persuaded another six arms-bearing Maroons with some women and children to surrender.[21]

More than Johnstone, Captain Andrew Smith emerged as the intermediary between the Maroons and the British military. In January 1796, when the Maroon war seemed almost over, Smith volunteered to find the Maroons who had not yet surrendered. As he told Walpole, "Sir, we can bring them out as easy as to kiss your hand." He advised Walpole on how best to pacify the families who had surrendered. He recommended that the Maroons be kept under strict armed supervision until "their eyes should grow tame." They were quite wild, he said, and would remain so till "they are used to white people." In his loyalty to Walpole, Smith played the role of junior officer to his superior. He allied with the empire against other Maroons to gain preferential treatment for his large family. His decision was rewarded many times over: Smith remained a favored subject in Nova Scotia and in the early days after arrival in Sierra Leone.[22]

However much he sympathized with the surrendered Maroons, Walpole aggressively pursued the stragglers through February. He had long feared that even if only a few Maroons remained in the hinterlands they would foster a continuous state of rebellion: "If you destroy them to five, those five will be a rallying point for more runaways to resort to, and thus the war be perpetuated for years." But still, Walpole refused to countenance the use of bloodhounds. The dogs, he explained to Balcarres, could only scent a recent step; in that the Maroons were deep in the woods, the chances of capture remained small. The divisions between Balcarres and Walpole on the question of the dogs echoed two months later in the House of Commons. In Jamaica the issue had revolved around the hounds' efficacy; in London the debate concerned the slave owners' humanity.[23]

As Jamaican leaders had suspected, antislavery members of Parliament found the use of the bloodhounds against the Maroons inexcusable. In the same way that they had challenged the moral premises of slavery, they now denounced canine warfare as a stain on the British Empire. In debates held in March 1796 these MPs constructed a sympathetic portrait of the Maroons as a "useful race" that had faithfully served the planters for decades. They contrasted the loyal Maroons with the menacing image of bloodthirsty hounds who ate human flesh to torture the Maroons into submission. At least one bloodhound had reportedly lost control in Jamaica: he "flew at and fastened" upon a soldier's wife while she was holding a child in her arms. Only the quick action of soldiers, who killed the dog with bayonets, had prevented the woman's certain death. The MPs linked the Jamaicans' depraved conduct toward the Trelawney Town Maroons, which had led to an attack against a white woman, directly to slavery. Only the wicked institution of slavery could induce British subjects to treat free men so inhumanely. The Jamaicans had shamed the British nation, blotting and staining its ideals.[24]

The fact that British subjects, British soldiers, and British officers had followed the brutal precedent set by the Spanish during the conquest of Mexico horrified the antislavery MPs. Like Spanish soldiers who "split a child in two or cut up an Indian in quarters" as a feast to the dogs, the Jamaicans had offered black rebels as bait to the hounds. Regardless of the war's origins—with or without French instigation—the British "had no right to pursue them [Maroons] with bloodhounds." The British nation should be disgusted with itself, the MPs argued, for repeating the cruelties of the Spaniards.[25]

The evangelicals in Parliament equated the Maroons with slaves. As in the case of slaves, the Maroons' natural inferiority required paternalistic care and Christian teaching. Wilberforce, for example, blamed the Maroon war on the indifference and insensitivity of the Jamaican planters. The war would never have occurred, he observed, if white Jamaicans, during their 140 years among the Maroons, had preached "the blessings of Christianity." If whites had been properly acquainted with the "principles, habits, and manners of the people who surrounded them," the Maroons would "neither have been ignorant or cruel." He lamented that the Maroons had no lobbyists in the House of Commons to plead their case.[26]

Indeed, some MPs made heroes of the Trelawney Town Maroons, establishing a long tradition of glorifying the Maroon war. These MPs called the Maroons "a handful of brave men" who began an insurrection out of pride. Unwilling to be whipped for stealing hogs, these "independent people preferred death to ignominious punishment." Like other so-called savages, their "passions were strong and their resentment of injuries indiscriminating." The Jamaicans should have offered friendship to these people; had they done so, the Maroons' passions would have moved toward infinite gratitude. Their "noble resistance" did not merit extermination.[27]

The antislavery MPs faced opposition from both their proslavery peers and the Jamaican planters. A proslavery essay from Jamaica, read in the House of Commons, disputed the idealized portrayal of the Maroons. It defined them as dangerous enemies who deserved brutal reprisal. The essayist observed caustically that "[of course Mr. Wilberforce would shrink from] hunting human flesh and blood with bloodhounds." But Jamaica had lost half a million pounds and many fine soldiers to the Maroon war. The island had grown exhausted from the battle with the Maroons: "You could scarcely credit that 500 of these fellows could so long withstand upwards of 5,000 troops. . . . [T]hey get into their interior parts of the mountains and 'tis impossible to get at them." The essayist urged Wilberforce to consider the deaths and damage caused by the war before condemning the "speedy extirpation of [the Maroons]."[28]

The proslavery MPs similarly defended the use of the dogs as the only means of maintaining public order in the island. Surely the Jamaicans were justified in protecting themselves against robbers and murderers, just as Englishmen protected themselves against brigands who infested English forests. Bryan Edwards, an MP who was a planter and historian, justified the use of bloodhounds on the basis of the terms of the 1738 treaty. The Jamaican Assembly had been unfailingly kind to the Maroons over the past decades, he argued, "conceiving the highest opinion of their utility." Yet the Maroons had refused the lieutenant governor's demand to submit peacefully. A report in the *Times* alleged that Edwards claimed that the Maroons were cannibals who deserved no mercy.[29]

Secretary of War Dundas, a longtime friend of the West Indian planters and a supporter of his fellow Scotsman Lord Balcarres, also endorsed the use of the bloodhounds. Indeed, he had known of the Jamaican government's plan to employ them since September 1795, a month after Balcarres's war had begun. Dundas favored a gradual end to the slave trade instead of the immediate abolition proposed by more radical elements. The Maroon insurrection, he argued, had led Jamaica to a state of alarm and danger. The Maroons descended at midnight to commit the most "dreadful ravage and cruelties upon the wives, children and property of the inhabitants." The island had suffered great distress; the militia was constantly in arms. The dogs, he contended, were trained merely to "seize and retain" black rebels, not to "tear and mangle them." As proslavery proponents would distinguish paternalistic from tyrannical slavery, Dundas distinguished between humane and inhumane use of canine combat.[30]

Planters justified canine warfare in the identical way they defended slavery, that is, as necessary to the security of their world. During the 1780s and 1790s Jamaica's planters responded furiously to the reformers' allegations of cruel treatment of slaves. In 1788 Simon Taylor complained about high-minded moralists who were "so willing to represent us as Devils incarnate." He dismissed the abolitionists as "mad enthusiasts," "miscreants, fanaticks and villains." Planters like Taylor blamed an unbalanced sex ratio and individual cases of mismanagement for the slaves' low fertility. At the same time, the Jamaican Assembly tacitly conceded to accusations of maltreatment of slaves by passing legislation that protected them from planters' tyranny, at least on paper. Gradual changes to the slave system, they hoped, would pacify reformers and allow them to avoid further scrutiny.[31]

Jamaican planters claimed that a state of public emergency justified the use of canines. In so doing, they were not reenacting Spanish brutality but defending the property of British subjects. During the early years of conquest, in the late 1400s and early 1500s, the Spanish, in order to rob and plunder, used dogs to attack the Indian inhabitants, the peaceful proprietors of the land. Jamaicans, on the other hand, had borrowed the dogs for "their own *defence,* and for their own protection." They did not embrace the dogs to acquire territory, like the Spanish, but rather to maintain territory by every possible means. Indeed, only "terror, excited by the appearance of the dogs," had led the Maroons to surrender. They implied that psychological terror was an acceptable mode of warfare.[32]

To justify their use of the bloodhounds the Jamaicans cited the wide use of elephants and horses in other parts of the empire. If "Asiatics" used elephants in their battles, and if the British cavalry used horses, why "shrink at the idea of hounds?" Indeed, if lions and tigers had the docility of elephants, military men could well have used them. Most important, the Maroons were not "an unarmed and innocent race of men" like the Native Americans; they were a "banditti of assassins." Expressing tenderness for such an enemy translated into "cruelty to all the rest of humanity." A brutal stance had to be taken against men of such stealth.[33]

One Jamaican summarized the chain of circumstances that mandated the bloodhounds. They were a "necessary defence and protection against rebellious savages" who committed crimes against a government to whom they owed allegiance. Furthermore, without the dogs, "Jamaica would have been a scene of general conflagration and ruin in a few months." The excessively dry season made the fields so combustible that a spark of fire would in a few hours consume three to four plantations. The grass was too parched by heat. If the blaze raged out of control, it would be impossible to keep it from consuming the entire island. Seeing the success of the Maroons, slaves, "with a view of independence," would have been emboldened to join them. The dogs were "not brought in to devour and suck the blood of the unhappy Maroons" but to protect the island for the empire. And except for some "unfortunate accidents" not a drop of blood was shed.[34]

Asked to respond to the abolitionists' allegations, Balcarres too defended his actions as a form of Jamaican self-preservation. He reiterated the argument about the danger the Maroons presented to Jamaica, for they possessed a country "[into] which no European ever dared to penetrate." Their "skill and ability in planting ambushes" made it impossible to crush them by "ordinary means." Whereas Walpole, attempting to avert canine warfare, had represented the plight of Maroon families sympathetically, Balcarres constructed a scene of Maroon stealth to champion the use of the hounds.[35]

In a calculated effort to augment Jamaica's defense, Balcarres added the sanction of racist beliefs to the sanctions of necessity. He compared the Maroons not to slaves, whose bondage elicited sympathy, but to Native American groups in North America. Let Britons, he remarked, waste no tears on the Maroons, for the Maroon enemy was like no other the British had known. The Maroon men and children were akin to barbarians from an alien world: "In a war a Maroon savage goes through his exercise with his hair plaited, his face besmeared, and his body painted the colour of the ground or foliage; he conceals himself; when discovered, he twists and turns to avoid the enemy fire; he throws his arms in the air with wonderful agility and when represented victim falls, the children run forward and with their knives close the scene." Using hounds against such a species of men was warranted.[36]

The bloodhound debates in Parliament threatened to destabilize the stalemate between the Caribbean slave owners and imperial humanitarians. Meanwhile, the government had shipped the Trelawney Town Maroons to the south, close to Spanish Town, where a verdict about their future would be announced. The Jamaicans would decide the punishment of a people regarded alternately as incendiaries, assassins, and savages. Resettling them inside the island, as neighbors, was not viable.

3
Deportation

For seven weeks, starting on March 1, 1796, the Jamaican legislature deliberated how best to protect the future of the island. It arrived at a decision without consulting the military commander, George Walpole, who had negotiated directly with the Maroons and encouraged them to surrender. Neither did it seek counsel from London. In a decade when revolts and conspiracies in the Greater Caribbean averaged nearly four per year, Jamaicans had managed to isolate the Trelawney Town Maroons and to prevent a longer, bloodier war. They wanted no outside interference in their local affairs.[1]

The Trelawney Town Maroons' surrender had no effect on the mountainous terrain that kept the Maroons mobile and whites feeling unsafe. A community that had withstood the assault of thousands of militia and British regulars for months could again escape to inaccessible retreats, baffling Jamaican efforts to conquer them. The island included uncultivated frontiers that were especially difficult to patrol and protect when British troops were preoccupied by the war in Saint-Domingue. In 1808 one visitor memorably captured the island's geography by taking a sheet of writing paper, crumpling it between his hands, and then placing it on the table. This he called the "best description he could give of the face of the interior of Jamaica." As war had shown too well, only a Maroon—or bloodhounds—could discover another Maroon.[2]

In employing the Cuban dogs, the Jamaicans had crossed the Rubicon. Their use broke the tacit 1738–39 pact between white society and the Trelawney Town Maroons that established an uneasy coexistence. As one member of the Jamaican legislature stated, the Trelawney Town Maroons would never forget the bloodhounds brought in to hunt them down, closing off the possibility of a "cordial reconciliation." An eyewitness summarized the anxiety of Jamaica's decision makers: Maroons who appeared "silent and peaceable" secretly planned to wreak vengeance; they could destabilize the island by "stirring up revolt and insurrection among the slaves." Ensuring peace required isolating the Maroons from the slave majority.[3]

Although slaves had not joined the rebellious Trelawney Town Maroons en masse during the war, Jamaican leaders worried that Maroons would seduce slaves and overthrow slave society. Part of whites' paranoia came from their difficulty in distinguishing recent slave runaways from Maroons. Raw British recruits mistook slaves for Maroons and sometimes killed the wrong men. Some slaves deliberately tried to "pass as Maroons." To guard against such confusion, the December 1795 treaty stipulated that Maroons must turn in all runaways. But the government knew that the Trelawney Town Maroons had not abided by this condition. At least two men, Harvey and Williams, known fugitives, surrendered "in the character of Maroons." Balcarres feared that as many as 25 percent of those who surrendered were slave runaways and not part of the Trelawney community. These runaways stood ready to face any punishment meted out to the Maroons to avoid being reenslaved. Here was terrifying proof that a slave–Maroon alliance remained viable.[4]

Other examples of black alliances during the Maroon war fueled planters' nervousness. Jamaican proprietors had difficulty isolating slave culprits from Maroon ones, especially when they acted in concert. White planters knew already that some slaves exploited the war to seek vengeance. In November 1795, when fields lay destroyed, planters could not isolate the incendiaries. When a cocoa field lay in ruins, the slave named Jamaica testified that "he no know if Cudjoe Negro [Maroon] do it or not." Some slaves joined Maroons to burn their masters' plantations and kill overseers. In one case of a white who was killed, "seven very young Maroons" along with "several runaway Negroes" proved responsible. Intimacy between Maroons and slaves challenged the very basis of slave society.[5]

As Jamaican leaders deliberated the fate of the Maroons, they found further reason to doubt peaceable coexistence with the Trelawney Town Maroons. On Balcarres's orders, British ships carried surrendered Maroon families from the northern port of Falmouth to Port Royal in the southeast. Some Maroons suspected foul play and tried to take over the ship. In this failed attempt, the government saw the first signs of vengeance. As reported in the newspaper, "One of the ruffians, it is asserted, was detected in an attempt to communicate fire with a flint and steel, to a train of gunpowder leading to a magazine." These Trelawney Town Maroons suspected betrayal and stood ready to die even before hearing the legislature's sentence.[6]

Some Jamaican planters, meanwhile, had begun to realize the potential profit that lay in removing the Maroons permanently from Trelawney Town. As much landholders as manufacturers, they grasped the value of Maroons' land. Military action against the Maroons had revealed unexplored regions. As the surveyor James Robertson observed, the Maroon war "hath been the cause, from the various operations of the army, of discovering and examining many places." Balcarres estimated the value of the produce of Trelawney land at more than forty million pounds. The Jamaican legislature echoed him: the Maroons' removal would lead to the "augmentation of the value of property which is likely to take place" in the lands around Trelawney Town. In late April a contemporary affirmed Jamaica's gains when he wrote that property in the island had "acquired a degree of security which it NEVER heretofore had."[7]

Both the governor and the general celebrated their victory over the Trelawney Town Maroons. In late March 1796 the Earl of Balcarres announced, "Thus has ended the nation of the Trelawney Maroons." Unintentionally, Balcarres acknowledged the tight-knit bonds that made the Maroons a unique people. Major General Walpole echoed Balcarres. "Content yourself my lord with this reflection," he wrote, "that the island, by firmness and humanity together, had been saved without a single cane destroyed; and at a time when the slaves were set agog by Mr. Wilberforce." Walpole's reference to the abolitionist Wilberforce attested to the encouragement slaves drew from antislavery agitation. The island had won a double victory, over both the Trelawney Town Maroons and the antislavery reformers who encouraged violent liberation. An ardent patriot, Walpole brooked no tolerance of upheaval in British lands. He celebrated breaking the Trelawney Town Maroons' sway because the Maroons had dared to assault British people and British property in the midst of a larger Anglo–French war. No matter the cost, he would not lose British Jamaica to the French enemy.[8]

Walpole offered his own advice as he awaited the legislature's decision. First, he recommended that some Maroons "be dispersed about as free citizens, like the people of color." Manumitted slaves, many of them fathered by slave masters, lived among whites in nonrural areas of the colony. In Walpole's eyes, the Trelawney Town Maroons who surrendered—especially older Maroons, along with Maroon women and children—could be integrated into this mixed-race urban world.[9]

Walpole oversimplified the white–black divisions in Jamaican society. Jamaica's blacks maintained hard divisions among themselves; although less than 5 percent of the colony comprised ex-slaves—the Maroon communities and the free black and colored population—the two groups did not intermingle. Indeed, some free blacks betrayed the Trelawney Towns during the war. Unlike the Maroons, who lived a separate existence, the free and colored people tried in every way possible to merge into white society. In multiple individual petitions, they repeatedly asked for a higher status in the island, for civil and political rights equal to those granted to whites. But Jamaican laws vigilantly restricted the mobility of these free people. In 1711 Jamaican whites excluded the free blacks from employment in public office; in 1713 they forbade them to manage estates. Twenty-two years later, in 1733, they deprived them of the right to vote, and in 1761 they prohibited them from purchasing land in excess of the value of two thousand pounds Jamaican currency and from inheriting property beyond that amount.[10]

The Jamaican government, determined to preserve a strict racial distinction, in 1792 again rejected the demands of the free black and colored population. Emboldened by the Saint-Domingue rebellion, free blacks petitioned as a group for the first time, for the same legal rights as whites so they could defend their families as well as their property in slaves and land. These men asked to "have the same privileges . . . as our free born subjects of England." They argued that they had no security against whites invading their properties or assaulting their families because they could not bear testimony against the whites. They insisted they had always considered that "obedience and protection were reciprocal." They ended by reminding the legislature that they, like free whites, possessed "estates in land, slaves and stock" which also required protection. Like Jamaican whites, the free blacks measured their success by counting the acres they owned in land and the numbers of their slaves. But the collective petition that peacefully protested the terms of white rule had not received a hearing: the dangers of an empowered free black population had become all too apparent in light of Saint-Domingue. Four years later, in 1796, despite all evidence to the contrary, Walpole's proposal raised the disturbing possibility that vengeful Trelawney Town Maroons would instigate already-inspired free blacks toward rebellion.[11]

Balcarres supported mixing the smaller communities of non–Trelawney Maroons among the free black population. In his opinion the Maroons of Charles-Town, who had shown a "most refractory and disobedient spirit," and who now gave "oaths of allegiance to His Majesty" on their knees, presented no risk. Jamaicans could tolerate and incorporate these humbled "Maroon tribes." The Trelawney Town Maroons who surrendered after January 1, by contrast, required special handling. Early in the Maroon war, Balcarres's government had endorsed the integration of rebellious Trelawney Town Maroons who were ready to relinquish their land and to merge with free blacks. Jamaican law stated the following: "It shall be lawful for any Maroon negro or negroes to appear in person" at the courts and "declare that he, she, or they are desirous and willing to give up any right he or she or they may have to any part of the lands which have been granted to the Maroon negroes, and that he, she, or they are desirous and willing to reside in any other part of the island except in any of the Maroon-towns." In November 1795 at least thirty Maroon women and children accommodated themselves to the white government. Balcarres accepted their allegiance as authentic and singled them out as a favored people; these Maroons would escape punishment. Balcarres refused, however, to extend this grace to the Maroons who had endured the war—and the bloodhounds. They had come in too late.[12]

Walpole's second proposal also showed his misunderstanding of Jamaican society and the planters' paranoia. He advised enlisting Maroons in a British Company of Rangers. Given the small number of whites, free black and colored men already served as defense for the colony in white-supervised militia units. But unlike Walpole, the Jamaican planters questioned the ultimate loyalty of all blacks: what would they finally defend, the liberty of slaves or the property of whites? Admitting Maroons, some of whom had already killed white soldiers and officers, into a British military corps that served across the West Indies remained unthinkable to slave owners. They resisted imperial calls for slave-soldiers who could absorb "wild enthusiastic and pernicious doctrines" and instigate slave rebellion in Jamaica. Saint-Domingue showed the ruin possible in Jamaica.[13]

Yet Walpole's recommendation to outfit Maroons was consistent with imperial thinking about the utility of black troops. Few white soldiers became truly seasoned for service in the tropics; almost seventy thousand of them died in the West Indies between 1793 and 1815. The defense of Jamaica, which was never attacked, cost eight thousand white lives. Blacks provided a solution for the shortage of British troops and the growing military needs of the empire in disease-ridden locales. Whereas the Jamaican planters focused on the uncertainty of black loyalty, Walpole, like other British decision makers, focused on the hardiness of the black body.[14]

Contemporary wisdom held that the black body could naturally endure a tropical climate and tropical diseases. As one concerned Briton observed, whereas "the European soldier would sink with fatigue and perhaps contract a fatal disease by an ordinary European march," people of African ancestry would feel "rather exhilarated than oppressed, by the solar blaze." Given their natural constitution, blacks would experience an arduous climb as recreation and not as toil; they ascended and descended the steepest and most slippery mountain ridges without losing their breath using the "flexibility of the muscles of the toes and feet." If a trained European soldier acted an able seaman and skilled aeronaut, a black soldier naturally resembled a shark in water and an eagle in flight, suited to fight and survive in his natural habitat. Far from weakening slaves, the institution of slavery made black bodies more robust and taught black men the habits of preservation—"to endure nakedness" and "to live on a mere pittance"—optimal for military service. The Maroons, experienced guerrilla fighters inured to the heat, qualified as ideal soldiers in the British West Indies.[15]

Walpole's suggestion foreshadowed what became a global military strategy by the end of the eighteenth century. What had seemed inconceivable just a few years earlier became routine for the British military in the West Indies: regiments of loyal British slave-soldiers guarded against insurrection by plantation slaves. And like free blacks, slave-soldiers stayed loyal to white society. A favored military status persuaded them that the advantages of accommodation were much greater than the cost of rebellion. The island planters could not imagine the British West Indies that would shortly emerge: a region that depended on importing slaves and a growing slave army. By 1800 the proven loyalty of black soldiers would grant the Trelawney Town Maroons who surrendered a military opportunity denied to them by Balcarres in 1796.[16]

On April 20, 1796, the legislature ignored Walpole's advice and confirmed the Maroons' worst dread: it ruled to banish the rebels from Jamaica forever. Balcarres and the assembly justified their decision in narrowly legalistic terms: by coming in weeks after the stipulated date of January 1 and not turning in the slave runaways who had joined them, the Maroons had broken terms, and the government had no obligation to honor the treaty. As Balcarres emphasized, the Maroons had not surrendered so much as capitulated. The island, however, would nevertheless compensate them by offering generous terms of deportation. The Trelawney Town Maroons would relocate to a country "in which they would remain free" and would receive suitable clothing and necessaries for their voyage. Jamaica would cover the costs of transporting them as well as fund their settlement elsewhere for a "reasonable time." The price of this agreement was permanent exile from Trelawney Town. The assembly confiscated the fifteen hundred acres of land the Maroons had gained by treaty in 1738.[17]

Walpole was aghast. Belatedly, he realized that Balcarres's order to ship the surrendered Maroons to Port Royal foreshadowed the legislature's decision to exile them from Jamaica. The passage from Trelawney Town to Port Royal had marked the Maroons' first relocation. Balcarres had worried that those who surrendered would escape Walpole's reach and give the island "the slip." He had gathered the Maroons in one place and imprisoned them in ships so they could be disposed of readily. Balcarres would do anything to protect the island—and his reputation in the eyes of his king and his country. Like many of the sixty-five hundred other Scots who traveled to Jamaica in the last fifty years of the eighteenth century, Balcarres was determined to achieve success and high acclaim.[18]

Walpole saw no reason to banish a broken people. He called the ruling an injustice to the Maroons, a "foul crime," both immoral and illegal. It betrayed the oath he had personally given the Maroons in the king's name; he had assured them that the "white people would never break their faith." The Trelawney Town Maroons had suffered enough by the devastation wrought by the war. He reassured Balcarres that the Maroons would never again rise against the Jamaican planters; they had been too "severely and effectually chastised." Urgently, he reminded Balcarres of the risks of exiling the Maroons. In the absence of the Trelawney Town Maroons, northern planters, "gentlemen of the first landed property," would remain "insecure," as no other "barrier" existed between the mountains and the lowlands to stop slave runaways.[19]

Too late, Walpole knew that the local government had exploited him and the treaty in a meaningless ploy. In December, when Walpole made his promise, the government feared an endless guerrilla war with the Maroons. Despite their lack of clothing, salt, and gunpowder, the Trelawney Town Maroons had fought hard for four months. Far from capitulating, they conspired to find a new refuge in the interior of the island where they could prove even harder to capture. But to the canny Jamaican planters the treaty was only a diplomatic feint, not a promise. As Balcarres explained to Secretary of War Dundas at the end of January, "Notwithstanding I had ratified the treaty, I had not the smallest confidence in their sincerity and every preparation was made to continue the war with unabated vigour."[20]

Balcarres never intended to reconcile with the rebels. He calculated that the Maroons would neither come in by January 1 nor surrender all the runaways they held. He shrewdly used their lack of compliance to justify banishment. Though small in number, an armed black community had dared to challenge the white regime in a moment of war. That they were unconnected with worldwide revolutionary forces mattered less than the damage they had inflicted on the island. The slave owners knew that Jamaica had the slave majority necessary to maintain a full-scale war of violent liberation. To the planters, the Trelawney Town Maroons' reincorporation into Jamaican society was unthinkable.[21]

Even in the face of the legislature's ruling, Walpole continued to search for suitable alternatives for the defeated Trelawney Town

Maroons. Unable to garner support for the full community, he did his best to save the Maroon families who personally assisted him. Balcarres, having won the larger victory, offered concessions as an "indulgent Father would treat his child." He allowed a Maroon child, Johnny, to stay in the island if Accompong Town would adopt him. He gave permission to Captain Andrew Smith's family, his wife and children, to remain in the island. He granted the same favor to the Maroon families of Captain James William Dunbar and Captain Williams. As much as possible, Balcarres wanted to quiet tensions and hush the Maroon affair. But when Walpole proposed carrying Smith's brother, Charles Samuels, to England, Balcarres balked. No Maroon would leave for England under his watch.[22]

Colonel Montague James, the head of the Trelawney Town Maroons, remains surprisingly invisible in the Maroon war sources for Jamaica. The testimony of the slave man named Jamaica identifies James as "a very old man who gave orders, who is grey-headed and when he says, 'to day no for walk,' they don't stir." Walpole mentioned him various times, and, indeed, he was present when Walpole took the secret oath in December 1795. But the colonel, deeply suspicious of the consequences, was ambivalent about coming to terms with the government. As Walpole noted, "Old Montague is, as far as I can guess, the obstacle to peace, as much as he dares." Montague James played a role for the Maroons equivalent to that Lieutenant Governor Balcarres did for the whites of Jamaica. But unlike Balcarres, who commanded military and legal authority though royal appointment, Montague James's influence derived from his military reputation, the customary respect given to him by younger Maroon men, and his ability to preserve strong bonds within the community. Because the colonel's authority depended on diplomacy with Maroon captains as well as with Walpole, his cautious approach may have frustrated both sides.[23]

On June 6, 1796, the Trelawney Town Maroons were taken away from their land and their kin under close guard. Of the 568 deported, 167 were arms-bearing men; the remaining 401 were women, children, and the aged. The island had shattered the strength of the most powerful Maroon community. Some who had not taken an oath to live as subordinates within white society remained in hiding. A few others, too sick or wounded to move into the transport ships that conveyed the others away from Jamaica, stayed on. In November 1796 7 remaining Trelawney Maroons, reduced to a sorry state, petitioned the Jamaican legislature for provisions and support. They had inherited the lot—poverty—of the free black population. Having no land, they needed government welfare to sustain themselves.[24]

Since part of the point of banishing the Maroons was to discourage slaves from running away or fomenting rebellion, the local government also punished, sometimes horrifically, runaway slaves who had participated in the rebellion. As if the banishment of the Trelawney Town Maroons did not serve as a sufficient sign of white power, Jamaicans used the 34 runaways to impart a further warning to Jamaica's slaves. They sentenced Bernard, the property of John Gray, to be hung and to have his head cut off and placed on the mill house of the estate. Two weeks later 3 more slaves suffered the same fate on the same day: Jupiter, the property of Peter Francklyn; Sampson, the property of Robert Fowler; and Joe Harvey, a mulatto slave owned by the heirs of John W. Harvey. They sold another slave, Pope, out of the island. The government simultaneously offered favors to slaves who had lost family members and body parts while suppressing the rebellion. Cato, Samuel Vaughan's slave, remained a faithful guide during the campaign against the Maroons. Cato was killed in an ambush in December; some planters believed he was murdered in revenge for the intelligence he had provided. Cato's sons, William and Francois, received ten pounds in annuities for the rest of their lives. Another slave, Cudjoe, who led a company of black men, was given his freedom, a badge of honor, and a lifelong annuity of twenty pounds. The Maroon leader who negotiated the 1730s treaties was also named Cudjoe: the Maroon Cudjoe received his freedom in exchange for turning in slave runaways in 1739; the slave Cudjoe received his freedom for turning in Maroons in 1796.[25]

Twenty-one members of the assembly had supported deportation, while thirteen opposed. The problem of slave defiance had dominated the debate over the Trelawneys' fate in the legislature. Those who ruled for banishment observed that neither the end of war nor the capitulation of the Maroons had brought peace to the island. Slave escapes continued in numbers alarming to Jamaican masters. In January 1796 at least 150 runaways remained in the woods. In March, even as the legislature deliberated, a new body of rebels hid, armed with firelocks and cutlasses—they included 24 Maroons and 8 runaway slaves. Those who opposed deportation, meanwhile, worried about a Jamaican future without Trelawney slave catchers. They too found ample justification for their stance and blamed Balcarres for a foolhardy punishment, detrimental to the safety of the island.[26]

In the first days of June, before the Maroons sailed away, there were reports of runaways who associated "for rebellious purposes" in the Trelawney region.[27] By this time the government had no scenting hounds to track or catch them.[28] In the aftermath of the deportation Jamaica suffered new convulsions. Intended to showcase the futility of slave opposition to white society, the removal of the famed slave catchers did precisely the reverse. As group runaways escaped into the mountains without fear of being recaptured by the fearsome Trelawney Town Maroons, slave owners recognized that the deported Maroons had served a useful function. Four months after their exile,

Thomas Munro from St. James Parish lamented their banishment, for they had "added to the security of the colony."[29]

Two years later, tensions in northern Jamaica, now bereft of Maroon slave catchers, approached the boiling point. Runaways who "associated themselves for rebellious purposes" stalked the Trelawney region. In 1796 Balcarres had observed the confidence of the Trelawney Town Maroons. When they descended from the mountains and demanded what they wanted of white proprietors, no one dared "refuse them any thing they ask." Two years later, runaways conducted themselves in the same fashion. The new estates that planters had established around Trelawney Town since 1796 worked against the whites: they provided ample food to "any number of banditti." One planter, William Green, noted the higher risks presented by slave runaways over Maroons. Male fugitives could pillage estates anywhere on the island because "they have no wives or children to attach them to one place, like the Maroons." He condemned Balcarres for the foolhardy banishment: "The danger we are now threatened with is much worse than occasioned by the Maroons."[30]

The decision to exile the Maroons had long-lasting consequences for the Jamaican legislature, even beyond the expense of dealing with slave runaways and internal criticism. The government's action drew the ire of British antislavery reformers, who focused their full attention on yet another wrongdoing of West Indian planters. It started in April 1796, nine days after the announcement of banishment, with Balcarres's acceptance and Walpole's simultaneous rejection of a sword gifted to each by the Jamaican legislature. Ashamed of the part he played in betraying the Trelawney Town Maroons, Walpole did not touch it. The Jamaicans' sentence, he wrote, deliberated in the "lock-up privacy of a chamber, broke with the terms of the treaty, and shamed British justice."[31]

News of Walpole's clash with Balcarres reached England within weeks, became widely publicized, and stayed in the news. As one paper reported in August 1796, "We hear that Walpole declines accepting the sword. Difference of opinion [with Balcarres] as to the observances of the articles made the Maroons the cause." And as Walpole had hoped, his protest earned the Maroons an audience in Britain. The murmurings against banishment compelled the British government to order a copy of all the correspondence related to the Maroon war. These proceedings, in turn, brought the Trelawney Town Maroons to the attention of the House of Commons, which discussed the issue for the next four years. Effectively, antislavery proponents used the Maroons' banishment to put Jamaica and its slave owners on moral trial.[32]

As they had with the bloodhounds, abolitionist proponents used banishment to draw attention to the Maroons' predicament. The association between slaves and Maroons—both of African ancestry and both perceived as sufferers—could not be avoided. Antislavery sympathizers equated the Trelawney Town Maroons with slaves and the slave owners with evil, while expressing sympathy for the Maroons. The tension between abolitionists and antiabolitionists echoed some of the exchanges between Walpole and Balcarres during the last months of the war. Both sides agreed that blacks required moral oversight. But they disagreed about black character: Did blacks merit pity, like children? or did they require harsher measures, like banishment, suited for savages? A new era of humanitarianism favored the former. In November 1795 one metropolitan newspaper described the "Maroon Indians" as a heroic group who "preferred death to a return of bondage."[33]

Abolitionism was a battle for the hearts of the public, but the Jamaicans refused to allow the Maroons to become beneficiaries of humanitarians or to assist in ending the slave trade. Over the next year Balcarres continued justifying the banishment as a moral act. He knew that "humanity, benignity, and mercy" stood as ornaments of the British Crown. He had not crushed a poor, helpless people, as "Gulliver did the flames of the Palace of Lilliput." Instead, he waged a defensive campaign against enemies who carried on a "war of extirpation" and who had taken an oath "to spare no white person whatsoever." Jamaica used transportation as a merciful sentence, one that lay in between execution and imprisonment. Only those who had rebelled would leave the island. Many well-behaved Trelawney members had received the opportunity to stay instead of being "sent off with their friends and relations." The government had generously provided "sufficient provisions, proper clothing, and other necessaries for their comfort and support" during their passage away from the island. Moreover, the Trelawney Town Maroons left as a free people. Like proslavery advocates who emphasized the benefits of food and shelter for slaves, Balcarres focused on the conditions, not on the fact of banishment.[34]

Taking a chapter from antislavery rhetoric, members of the legislature argued that compassion led them toward deportation. Once the Maroons had been placed on board ships in Port Royal, the "temper of the island was so justly irritated against those Maroons that it would have been unsafe to have relanded them." Balcarres lied and claimed that the Maroons had recognized the hostility of white Jamaicans and "were most impatient to leave the country." He had only honored their desire to leave. Moreover, the great scarcity of provisions in the island had necessitated sending them hastily to another port. By sending them abroad, Balcarres argued, Jamaica protected the Trelawney families from starvation.[35]

Over time, the debate with respect to the injustice of the Maroons' banishment mutated into an Atlantic-wide discussion that pitted the morality of two British agents, Walpole and Balcarres, against one another. In 1798 the Jamaican government finally won its battle against Walpole by vilifying his character. The Jamaican agent, Robert Sewell, cast Walpole as a two-faced do-gooder. He triumphantly produced evidence of Walpole's duplicity before Parliament. In December 1795 Walpole had expressed contempt toward the Trelawney Town Maroons: he suggested that the Maroons should be settled in towns where "their access to spirits will soon decrease their numbers and destroy their hardy constitution which is nourished by an healthy mountainous situation." How could the House of Commons trust Walpole when he advocated a slow extermination of the Maroons through intoxication? Walpole offered no excuses.[36]

Looking back from the perspective of the 1820s, the Reverend George Wilson Bridges accused Balcarres of sentencing the Maroons to cruel retribution. An eyewitness to the frictions in the island, he bemoaned the internal convulsions that shook the island for years after the Trelawney Town Maroons' relocation. He lamented that the Maroon war was "begun without cause, prosecuted without glory, and terminated, if not dishonorably, at least without effect." The proximity to Saint-Domingue led Jamaicans to magnify a minor disturbance into war and to deport black collaborators who might otherwise have kept peace in the island. Balcarres, who "possessed the iron temper of a soldier, without the art of prudence of a General," had left Jamaica in a state of permanent volatility.[37]

The Maroons, for their part, revered Walpole and shared Reverend Bridges's later distaste for Balcarres. Their precarious position, based on white patronage rather than legal protections, had become evident: a single-minded governor's paranoia had cost them exile. The Trelawney Town Maroons cursed Balcarres as a vicious Scottish governor. The Maroon captain Andrew Smith "true beg massa King for no send any of dem poor Cotch Lord for Gubner again." No military Scot met them upon their arrival at their destination in Halifax, Nova Scotia, chosen as a convenient temporary landing place because it was a reasonable distance away. Instead, they faced the Anglican paternalism of Sir John Wentworth, who saw in the Maroons an opportunity to redeem his own soul.[38]

NOVA SCOTIA

(Overleaf): *"View of Halifax from Georges Island" (1801). Georges Island was located in Halifax harbor and served as a naval base. Here, Halifax is portrayed as a peaceful but well-protected city. (© The British Library Board [Maps.K.Top.119.79.a.])*

4
Conversion

In late July 1796, on a "glorious day of warmth and sunshine," three large transports brought 549 Trelawney Town Maroons to the harbor of Halifax. Some Maroons left valuable land and well-furnished homes in Jamaica while others carried their property—slaves—with them. The Maroons came with two white superintendents and 25,000 pounds of Jamaican currency as reparation. No one knew how long the refugees would stay in Nova Scotia. Instructions regarding their final destination had not arrived.[1]

The civil and military leaders of Nova Scotia—Lieutenant Governor Sir John Wentworth, the British commanding officer; Prince Edward Augustus, who at the time was commander in chief of the British forces in Canada and was later to become the father of Queen Victoria; and Admiral John Murray—disembarked the Trelawney Town Maroons without waiting to hear from London. In meeting the prince, the Maroons, the deported enemies of Jamaica, became the first group of blacks to directly encounter royalty. Neither Wentworth nor the prince had reason to fear the Maroons' military background: unarmed and weary families, many of whom were sick and enfeebled from being imprisoned in transport ships for four months, hardly posed a danger in an environment alien to them. Two-thirds were women and children. Halifax was a garrison and could answer misbehavior with military force.[2]

As it had in Jamaica, the ongoing war between France and Britain created urgency in the British Maritime colonies, in a way that, in Nova Scotia, worked in the Maroons' favor. Nova Scotia was in dire need of military laborers; just a year earlier Wentworth had requested two hundred men for repairing fortifications. Because their livelihood was supported by the government of Jamaica, the Trelawney Town Maroons could meet Nova Scotia's labor needs at no cost to Wentworth's government; they would receive wages for their labor but these would come out of Jamaican funds. Ready to benefit from the Maroons' labor, Wentworth and Prince Edward ordered them to come ashore to build the fortifications in Citadel Hill to guard against a French attack on the city. Confining the Maroons for an even longer period in the crowded vessels would have led to sickness and deaths, diminishing the numbers of potential workers.[3]

The Maroons' arrival during the harvest season made them particularly valuable to the colony. They could take the place of the white workers laboring on the fortifications, who clamored to return to their farms. In a colony where families grew food for subsistence and the growing season was short, the absence of men from farms, especially between April and July, could mean dire results. The Maroons' availability would save white families from wrenching scarcity in the winter.[4]

In 1796 the Maroons' appearance of submission inspired confidence. As Prince Edward noted approvingly, "It is but justice to them to say that they conduct themselves in the most orderly and obedient manner, and that whatever may have been their former errors, they now seem fully determined to do their utmost to merit His Majesty's favour and forgiveness." The Trelawney Town Maroons earned goodwill. They reassured Wentworth that they regretted the war and had only sought self-preservation. Yet memories of the bloodhounds that had created terror and compelled their surrender had not faded. In September Wentworth heard them mention Spanish dogs "as objects of terror." When he inquired further, they reassured him that they had "never suffered by or even seen them." Preoccupied with his own agenda, Wentworth accepted their studied humility: "I rather think they are ashamed of being frightened by them, and that they would now be esteemed a ridiculous Scarecrow."[5]

No one suggested reenslaving the Maroons, although the hardships of a northern climate had not prevented African slavery in Nova Scotia. Slave ads in newspapers and wills showed the wide acceptance of the institution among the populace and the elite. Britain also legally protected slavery in British North America in 1790, encouraging the importation not only of household utensils and farming implements but also of immigrants who owned slaves. Most slaves toiled side by side with their owners in farms and shops or on the docks. White settlers used slaves to clear stumps, cultivate fields, fell trees, and build homes and barns; slave women did domestic chores and minded white children. The smaller number of slaves in Nova Scotia did not blur the racial divide; as in the United States, deeply ingrained racial prejudices precluded black people's chances of integrating into Nova Scotia's civic society. Slaves as well as free blacks received harsh indications of their servile place: public whippings for small offenses were the most visible and painful reminders.[6]

Yet white Nova Scotians imagined themselves as a people apart from West Indian planters. Criticism of slavery and the slave trade appeared in Nova Scotia's magazines and newspapers. Antislavery debates in the House of Commons also circulated widely. Long essays delineated the disposal of slaves in the West Indies in minute detail. Slave buyers, the essayists declared, eyed slaves at auctions, seized them with their hands, and used handkerchiefs and sometimes ropes to tie them together. When some slaves fled the scene in fear, they were "hunted down and retaken." The essays condemned slave purchasers as bargaining for bodies with the "ferocity of brutes." Nova Scotians portrayed West Indian slaves as being worked to death, always hungry, and inhumanly punished by evil, power-hungry tyrants. By contrast, Nova Scotia appeared humane: the prevalence of black servitude and racism in its midst did not compare to the callousness in the Caribbean.[7]

No slave code existed in British Nova Scotia in the eighteenth century. During the 1780s and 1790s courts in Nova Scotia, drawing support from slave runaways and the voices of sympathetic whites, ruled against slaveholders. An incipient antislavery movement in the 1780s, charted by immigrants such as the Scottish Presbyterian minister James McGregor, challenged the injustice of black enslavement, and the prevalent thinking in the Maritimes moved in the direction of antislavery. Although these sentiments did not lead to a large-scale evangelical movement as they did in Britain, they affected the sensibilities of influential whites. Legal opposition to slavery, however, did not equate to social and political equality with blacks, and racism persisted long after slavery faded away by the late 1810s and early 1820s. Still, Wentworth may have been likely to look upon the Maroons more as free blacks than as slaves.[8]

Yet, surprisingly, Wentworth distinguished the Maroons sharply from the black Loyalists. In 1796, when the Maroons arrived, approximately three thousand free blacks lived in the colony—but in scattered locations distant from Halifax. Disillusioned by racist treatment, unfair wages, and rocky soil, over one thousand had left for the British West African settlement of Sierra Leone in 1792. The black Loyalists' self-imposed exile just four years before the Maroons' arrival in Halifax naturally invited comparisons. Wentworth insisted that the two groups were absolutely distinct. The black Loyalists, recent ex-slaves "who lacked every idea of providing for themselves or having any property," could not adjust to freedom. They suffered because they arrived with thousands of white Loyalists with whom they competed for lodging and place. They struggled because local administrators lacked local knowledge in settling inhabitants. Wentworth's prejudices stood apparent when he wrote, in 1793, that British charity had encouraged black Loyalists' "idleness and profusion." He had opposed the loss of black Loyalists because "transporting the black people from hence to Sierra Leone diminished useful laborers and the supplies of small provisions and vegetables they brot [*sic*] to the market." British handouts, not the humiliating conditions they endured, had created dissatisfaction. Wentworth dismissed the black Loyalists as immoral and indolent but upheld the Maroons as a people ready for redemption. He would come to regard the Maroons, in effect, as the black version of the indigenous population, the Mi'kmaq.[9]

Within weeks, Wentworth received permission from the secretary of state, the Duke of Portland, to settle the Trelawney Town Maroons permanently in Nova Scotia. The duke sidestepped Major General Walpole's concerns about the injustice and illegality of the Maroons' expulsion from Jamaica. The duke had tried to prevent the deportation, but Jamaica had acted without awaiting orders. He now hedged. He sent news of imperial approval to settle the Maroons in Halifax "for the present." Pragmatically, the duke encouraged their use in military works: "Consider whether some of the young men may not be applied usefully on the works now carrying on for completing the defences of the province." Wentworth had already put the duke's recommendations into effect. Other details of the Maroons' settlement the duke left to Wentworth and the two accompanying Jamaican superintendents, Lieutenant Colonel William Dawes Quarrell and Captain Alexander Ochterloney.[10]

The question of the settlement of the Maroons caused disagreement between Quarrell and Wentworth. Quarrell, who had rented the bloodhounds and voted against the Maroons' expulsion as a member of the Jamaican Assembly, advised Wentworth to disperse the Maroons over remote areas in Nova Scotia. As Quarrell related to the Jamaican agent in London nearly six months after the Maroons' arrival in Nova Scotia, "Nothing but dispersal and that pretty extensively promises a proper disposal of them." Quarrell proposed segregating them: a hundred should remain near Halifax, while a hundred should be sent to remote locations in Nova Scotia, a hundred to slave states in the United States, and a hundred each to Bermuda and the Bahama Islands. Quarrell also suggested consigning the most "peevish and discontented" Maroons to a place far from Nova Scotia, that is, Sierra Leone, which black Loyalists had reached in 1792. Prince Edward promptly offered transportation to relocate these incendiaries across an ocean.[11]

Quarrell, like other Jamaicans, blamed the war on the Maroons' sense of superiority and exclusivity. He echoed the Jamaican councilor Bryan Edwards, who regretted that the 1738 treaty had kept the Maroons segregated from colonial society; it had encouraged "keeping them a distinct people" and "introduced among them what the French call an 'esprit de corps.'" This sense of unity had allowed them to sustain resistance for eight grueling months. Quarrell hoped that the breaking up of the Maroons would lead to their incorporation with other inhabitants and weaken their sense of being a separate people. He also ambitiously hoped the Maroons would facilitate a trade relationship between Nova Scotia and Jamaica: the Trelawney Town Maroons could cut timber and catch fish and ship both to the West Indies; in return, Jamaica would send its produce to Nova Scotia.[12]

Yet Wentworth decided against dispersion. He disregarded Quarrell as a mere Jamaican accountant; having forty years' experience in "settling people," he saw himself as managing and directing the Maroons' settlement. Wentworth, the oldest of three children born to the richest man in New Hampshire, was nothing if not ambitious. He was the former governor of New Hampshire and was one of approximately thirty thousand white Loyalists who entered Nova Scotia to escape the punishment of the victorious rebels to the south. Most Loyalists were farmers, artisans, and shopkeepers and came nowhere near his status. Recently granted a baronetcy, he seized upon the Maroons to push the colony toward greater agricultural competence and even prosperity.[13]

Wentworth took advantage of Quarrell's confinement to bed in late July and early August by violent attacks of fever. Using the money supplied by Jamaica, Wentworth, within two months of their arrival, moved the entire community of Trelawney Town Maroons to Preston, across the harbor from Halifax and some six miles to the northeast. As Wentworth reported to the Earl of Balcarres, "These people are settled in a little village near the town: this was a happy and cheap purchase as it furnished houses for them which could not possibly have been built in time for this season." Wentworth went so far as to house fifty Maroons in the outbuildings of his farm. He boasted that he lived with them without a sentry. The distribution of men, women, and children selected to live with him remains unknown, but we do know that Wentworth fathered a child with a Maroon woman.[14]

Preston, previously a settlement of black Loyalists and now mostly abandoned, offered multiple conveniences. It would serve as training ground for farming; here, the Maroons, as tenants, would acquire a "knowledge of agriculture and discover inclinations and exertions to support themselves." Maroon men would sell the fruits of their labor, potatoes and turnips, along with firewood to the nearby marketplace in Halifax. The soldiers stationed in Halifax would benefit from much-needed provisions, and the settlers could utilize surplus Maroon labor to build fences and construct homes. Most of all, the Trelawney Town Maroons would live within Wentworth's jurisdiction but "separate from the [white] inhabitants." Quarrell, when he got over his sickness, witnessed a fait accompli.[15]

Wentworth's vision for keeping the Maroons together in a single site drew from his association of the Maroons with the Mi'kmaq. Wentworth first encountered this indigenous community when he arrived in Nova Scotia after the rebels' victory in the War of American Independence. In 1783, at the age of forty-six, he secured appointment as the surveyor general of Nova Scotia. He undoubtedly received help in the position from the Mi'kmaq as he traveled west to east, reserving regions with white pine trees suitable for masts on British ships.[16]

During his nearly decade-long post as surveyor general, Wentworth also witnessed the constraints imposed on Mi'kmaw ways. The massive immigration of Loyalists disrupted the aboriginal–imperial balance that had sustained relations in the colony for decades. Previous British-sponsored settlements by Germans, Highland Scots, and New England planters had remained confined to the coastal areas and to farms along the Bay of Fundy. But the scale of the immigration as much as the Loyalists' demands touched every region in Nova Scotia and would compel the Mi'kmaq to change their ways of using the land.[17]

The Mi'kmaq had coexisted with Europeans for almost two hundred years. Before the British entered the region in 1710, a small number of French settlers had lived side by side with the Mi'kmaq: French Jesuits converted many to Catholicism, and the French settlers paid tribute to the Mi'kmaq in the shape of annual presents of arms, ammunition, food, and clothing. The British recognized the political and religious ties that existed between their French enemy and their inherited aboriginal subjects. Multiple treaties signed between 1726 and 1760–61 indicate acknowledgment by the British of the Mi'kmaw position; diplomatic ties with the Mi'kmaq were viewed as essential. During the war with France in 1744–48, the Mi'kmaq sided with the French against the British; they also helped defend Louisbourg in 1758. In 1783, after more than seven decades of British control of the region, a Hessian soldier observed the aboriginals' casual observance of Catholic ritual in French: on hearing bells from the church, they crossed themselves and said, "Au nom de Dieu, du père, du fils, et du saint esprit." The close ties between the Mi'kmaq and the French, combined with a scarcity of Protestant settlers and soldiers, precluded British domination over the area.[18]

All of this changed with the sudden arrival of thousands of American Loyalists. Earlier treaties did not protect the Mi'kmaq from this massive demographic shift. Endemic respiratory ailments and outbreaks of typhus and smallpox swept the region. Moreover, the displaced Loyalists saw themselves as entitled to rewards for the sacrifices they had made on behalf of the empire. The Loyalists, many of whom had traveled to the Maritimes from the southern colonies of Georgia and South Carolina, viewed the aboriginal nations who wandered across their own countryside as vagrants and inferiors. The peripatetic life of the Mi'kmaq, which the immigrants exploited, became intolerable after aboriginal land became British property. In one instance a leading Loyalist proposed regulations so that "every Indian shall be obliged to Stay att his Respective place of River and Not be Running from one place too an Other." To secure against the mobility of the Mi'kmaq, some advocated that they carry a pass when outside of an allotted area.[19]

By 1796, when the Maroons arrived in Nova Scotia, the numbers and the ambitions of the American settlers had begun to overwhelm the Mi'kmaqs' way of life. The Loyalist immigrants did not want Mi'kmaq neighbors. As one settler, Edward Barron, put it, "I do not mean to have an Indian Town at my Elbow." As Loyalist settlers set fires to clear land, they destroyed the slow-growing moss and thereby destroyed the game that fed on it. Eager to settle in their new homes, the Loyalists grabbed land along rivers for agriculture, for the building of sawmills, and for fishing. As wildlife and fish became less plentiful, the customary Mi'kmaq means of earning a livelihood became difficult to sustain. When the Office of Superintendent of Indian Affairs lapsed in 1784, no one protected land for the Mi'kmaqs' use or prevented the newcomers' unfettered claims to the land.[20]

Wentworth knew the damage a small group of Mi'kmaq forces could inflict on settlements if they were provoked. He also undeniably felt sorry for the distress the aboriginals endured with the massive influx of Loyalists. The "poor savages" had suffered because the extension of roads and settlements had "driven off wild beasts" and deprived them of hunting. They had lost their means of subsistence by the "augmenting settlements of His Majesty's subjects." Only "a royal and just charity" would benefit them: they needed "potatoes, meal, fish, bread and clothing" to survive. Indeed, with the help of continuous subsidies, Wentworth hoped the Mi'kmaq "in a very few years" would support themselves. In December 1796 he noted that by his criteria the Mi'kmaq had already improved: they wore English clothes and began to understand the meaning of the word "property." He saw himself as their protective and kindly patriarch. In an era of antislavery that radiated out to color the sentiments of military officers, colonial administrators at every level, and well-intentioned Christian settlers, he would not be the last.[21]

Wentworth had long pitied the aboriginals' losses in the wake of white colonization. His paternalistic compassion for the natives grew out of his years in New Hampshire. In 1770 he expressed his sentiments: "I most sincerely pity these poor people and shall heartily rejoice to have them under my protection, to have an opportunity of rendering them the benevolence due to Humanity, which I fear has been too much neglected toward Indians in general wherever Europeans have come." Other Loyalists shared his view. In 1783, when Jonathan Odell made the Maritimes his new home, he envisioned living with a transformed indigenous group, men involved in cultivation and farming, not hunting. He equated hunting with diversion and leisure, not with labor. Odell put the matter succinctly: "If they [Indians] are ready to learn, we are willing to teach them . . . all the methods of agriculture by which an unfailing Subsistence is secured to all civilized and industrious Planters." But the Mi'kmaq resisted becoming a supervised society.[22]

In the wake of the migration of Loyalists, Mi'kmaq families stubbornly held on to customary sites with spiritual and cultural histories. Their resilient cultural framework enabled them to adapt to a mixed economy, combining older practices of seasonal migration with wage work. Despite suffering material deprivation and becoming politically marginalized, they did not rush to become the sedentary farmers visualized by a faraway imperial government. They preserved what white settlers called "roving practices" and sought to participate in economic activities that enabled them to survive while maintaining their rounds of hunting, fishing, and gathering. Some Mi'kmaq bands accommodated the new regime by growing potatoes and keeping pigs, cows, and sheep.[23]

Wentworth's repeated requests for funds for the Mi'kmaq wearied the imperial and local government, especially when he exceeded the two hundred pounds sent annually. If white settlers struggled for subsistence, why should the aboriginals be given a handout? Wentworth assured the home government that the expense for the Mi'kmaq would go down after the restoration of peace. He used aid only as a temporary quieting tactic. Yet, in 1798, when the French threat had subsided, he continued to lament the "indigent and distressful situation" of the Mi'kmaq. Their native country lay destroyed through "progressive occupancy, culture and improvement." But Nova Scotia's Assembly had had enough. Its members viewed the aboriginals as a nuisance. Despite Wentworth's opposition, it determined to cut all aid to the Mi'kmaq: the less civilized could support themselves by hunting or fishing whereas "civilized" aboriginals could procure a living by cultivating land. Continuing charity only encouraged the Mi'kmaqs' "indolence and supineness"; their distress proceeded from their "unwillingness to labor." By 1800 the Nova Scotian Assembly ruled that the Mi'kmaq merited treatment no different from that of transient paupers.[24]

Wentworth could not overrule the determined imperial and local objections to supporting the Mi'kmaq. However, in 1796 Jamaican funds allowed Wentworth to experiment with settling the Maroons—and adding his signature to the age of reform. Wentworth and, indeed, some London newspapers seemed to regard the Maroons not only as *like* the Mi'kmaq but possibly as indigenous themselves. During the Maroon war London's newspapers expressed confusion about the Maroons' origins, reflecting muddled thinking with respect to indigenous people in the growing empire. Were the rebels more similar to the Mi'kmaq or to Africans? or were they something in between? Another report from March 1796 described them as "the remains of the aborigines and of the Spanish and other negroes." In Wentworth's first estimation the Maroons stood closer to the Mi'kmaq and hence merited the same paternalistic benevolence. Like others influenced by romantic ideals of colonization, Wentworth regarded the aboriginals as noble savages: a community to be admired for their endurance, pitied for their sufferings, and pacified through gift giving. In 1796 he created a similar fantasy of savage innocence around the Trelawney Town Maroons. They could become law-abiding farmers if properly civilized and Christianized.[25]

From the beginning, he did not view the Maroons as being dangerous to Nova Scotia. He never thought to shackle or imprison the Maroon families; he viewed them as victims of Jamaican slaveholders' paranoia, just as he viewed the aboriginals as victims of European conquest.[26] Almost as zealous as the evangelical Wilberforce, Wentworth hoped to bring the Trelawney Town Maroons under his wing. Wilberforce had upbraided Jamaican slave masters for the war: if acquainted properly with the "principles, habits and manners of the people who surrounded them," the Maroons would "neither have been ignorant or cruel." The slave owners, too ready to utilize the branding iron and the lash, could not become custodians of free blacks. Like Wilberforce, Wentworth blamed the Maroon war on white Jamaicans who had neglected to school them on Christianity and English laws, customs, and civilization. The Maroons had to remain in one group in part because it offered the best path to civilizing them: dispersal would require a Christian teacher for every family, and Jamaica would have to incur heavier expenses.[27]

Wentworth constructed a utopia of peaceful coexistence between whites and Maroons sealed by Anglican teachings. He did not dismiss the Maroons as unredeemable and lowly. He saw his chance to transform them into a godly community of grateful farmers. Wentworth showed his high esteem for Maroon families: "They are remarkably clean in their persons, houses, cloathing and utensils, and very healthy." They worked harder than "an equal number of more enlightened white people from any part of Europe or America." They showed deep attachment to their wives and children. Wentworth praised their potential as good colonizers.[28]

The first steps in realizing the Maroons as a black peasantry entailed instruction in farming and religion. In 1790 the *Nova Scotia Magazine* painted a glowing portrait of the small-scale, self-sustaining farmer: "No class of men is more useful or respectable in society—none more independent or happier." The essayist, Columella, proclaimed, "I glory in the name of the farmer." By meeting the subsistence needs of the whole community, farmers supported expansion in the realm of commerce. Only through the assistance of the farmer's plough could British ships sail across the globe. In 1796 the planter Bryan Edwards's hopes for Maroon colonization in Nova Scotia followed this thinking. He anticipated that the Maroons' removal from a "former wild and savage way of life" would produce a new people: a "useful body of yeomanry." Wentworth echoed Edwards. In time, he believed, both the Mi'kmaq and the Maroons would submit to the rhythms of agricultural work.[29]

But Christian teachings were also essential. Wentworth would not have agreed to settle the "six hundred pagans" in Nova Scotia "without a faithful establishment for their instruction in the Christian religion and in reading and writing the English language." Only through these means could "any people be reclaimed and fitted for living in a British colony." Christianity would domesticate the Maroons. The church would change them from the "Maroons of war and hunting [to] those of peace and patient industry"; they would soon lose the "self importance" derived from their migratory customs. Within a month of the Maroons' arrival, Wentworth noted that "it will be of the most serious importance, both civil and religiously considered, to instruct these poor people in the Christian religion and to teach their children to read and write and common cyphering for which I find them both capable and much disposed."[30]

Successful colonization required a rite-of-passage conversion, and this could happen only in a single site. In the long run, Wentworth felt, dispersion would be more costly and conversion cheaper for the empire. Like the bishop of Nova Scotia, the Reverend Charles Inglis, Wentworth linked faith in the Church of England with attachment to the empire. Just as white youth imbued with the principles of loyalty to their king and country would be more likely to remain loyal to Britain—and much less likely to emigrate south for greater prosperity in the United States—Maroon families would establish attachments to their land and the mother country through exposure to the church. Christian teachings would "disseminate piety, morality and loyalty among them." The Maroons would resist becoming "dreadful instruments in the hands of designing men." They would refuse to side with the French enemy in times of crisis.[31]

Just two months after their arrival Wentworth executed his Christian vision for the Maroons. He appointed the Reverend Benjamin Gerrish Gray to minister to them. Services would ensue on the second Sunday in October. The Maroons, he believed, would be "more easily reformed" than an "equal number of more enlightened white people from any part of Europe or America." At the same time, he authorized a Maroon school and appointed a fifty-nine-year-old fellow Loyalist, Theophilus Chamberlain, as teacher. Chamberlain, a graduate of Yale University, had served as a Congregationalist minister in Connecticut and taught at the Latin School in Boston. A member of the Society for Promoting Agriculture in Nova Scotia, Chamberlain had long explored ways to stabilize Nova Scotia: he studied methods of preparing hemp and making oil-compost and of choosing the best seeds for wheat. He would now devise a strategy on how best to domesticate the Maroons. As a former teacher to "Indians in the wilderness of America," Chamberlain met Wentworth's qualifications.[32]

The sources do not reveal the extent of Chamberlain's influence over the Maroons. We know that his position provided a safeguard for at least one Maroon woman, Elsy Jarrett. Jarrett, who was pregnant, first complained to Chamberlain about a "thumping" from "Barnet." She was likely referring to Captain James Barnett, who, along with the Maroon captains Andrew Smith, John Jarrett, and Charles Shaw, was key to the Preston group and would cosign the Maroons' petitions to England for removal from Nova Scotia. Chamberlain's punishment of Barnett, if any, is lost to us.[33]

Wentworth's vision for fitting the Maroons for British Nova Scotia followed earlier schemes for converting indigenous people. He envisioned transforming their manners and morals to make them more conformable with English occupations, burial practices, and, most of all, marriages. The Trelawney Town Maroons should abandon the hunting of wild hogs and pigeons and settle into an agricultural mode of life. They should stop "festive excesses" at interments and desist from burying their dead near their dwellings. The men should renounce polygamy and accept the rites of a Christian marriage. The steady inculcation of Christian principles would "accomplish a reformation on their head and affect the manners of the rising generation." The old Maroons would carry their customs to the grave, but the newer generation would adapt to English ways.[34]

Wentworth's hopes for the Maroons' conversion appeared realized when one group of Maroons broke off from the main settlement in Preston less than one year after arrival and asked for committed Christian guardianship. But Wentworth knew that the breakup arose from tensions internal to the Maroon group and not from his evangelical efforts. The splintered group settled in Boydville, twenty miles from the main group in Preston. The Preston Maroons included the loyal Maroon captain who had assisted Major General Walpole, Andrew Smith, and the Maroons' leader, Montague James. The man whom Smith had treated "with great contempt" during the Maroon war, Captain John Palmer, led the Boydville group. In July 1797 Wentworth quietly reported the results of his program to the duke: "One family of twenty-eight people, led by a noted captain, removes this day to a separate estate, at his own earnest request, to settle for life." Wentworth had not supported a separate establishment of Maroons, but preexisting tensions among Maroons left him no choice.[35]

Long-standing rivalries, difficult to cull from the sources, divided the two Maroon groups. George Fowler, who had asked for a gorget to memorialize his loyalty to whites, went with Palmer. The tensions among the Trelawney Town Maroons broke families: Charles Samuels, Andrew Smith's brother, joined Palmer in Boydville. Existing evidence does not explain the divisions among the Maroon officers, but they likely did not occupy equal status within Trelawney Town: they may not have shared the same African ethnicity, some may have been born in Jamaica and others in Africa. Those born in Jamaica may have regarded themselves as superior to the African-born. Some may have derived a sense of superiority because they had a lighter complexion than others. Captain Andrew Smith appears to have had great fluency in English, which may have afforded him opportunities and access denied to other Maroons.[36]

As he had in Jamaica, Andrew Smith emerged as the favorite of white officials. Wentworth charged him to do what he could "in reconciling the Maroons to the country" and in exchange gave Smith a "good house" in nearby Dartmouth." For a small annual salary, fifty pounds, Smith became responsible for the boats that carried provisions between Preston and Halifax six days a week. Along with Smith, Charles Shaw, another Maroon captain, manned the store in Preston that supplied the families.[37]

But as the Maroons' condition in Nova Scotia deteriorated that first winter, Smith's intermediary position made him an "object of general execration" among the Trelawney Town Maroons. Walpole received news of the "utmost rancor and revenge" expressed against Smith. Some Maroons regarded Smith as a mercenary and a traitor. As Smith related his situation in his letter to Walpole, "He is very much blamed by the rest of the Maroons for deceiving them with promises and of having received money from you to betray them." As he faced the wrath of many disappointed Trelawney families he was consumed by fear and "wept like a child."[38]

Smith felt trapped; he believed he would be killed even if he could return to Jamaica. He begged to leave Nova Scotia to serve under Captain John Hale, the secretary to Prince Edward, or Captain Alexander Ochterloney in "whatever country it may [be] his lot to live in." His family's dire situation in exile left him anguished: "He did not think white people could have used him so after what he had done." Smith had refused to avail himself of the opportunity to stay in Jamaica because Lord Balcarres would not make the same exception for his siblings. Now it was too late. As Wentworth wrote, a "resolute acute family" who possessed influence and "great knowledge of the island" could not be readmitted to the island.[39]

While Smith lamented leaving his home, another Trelawney Town Maroon, Martin Sewell, found a means to join his community in Preston via Roatán Island in the Bay of Honduras. Sewell had escaped the worse fate of the Saint Vincent Caribs, who, in April 1797, sailed toward Roatán following a violent war with white settlers. The Caribs were a mixed-race people, descended from an intermixing of

Indians and Africans. Since the British acquisition of Saint Vincent in the 1760s, the Caribs had presented formidable opposition to British settlers' goals for sugarcane cultivation. Their resistance came to an end when over five thousand were forced to embark and leave Saint Vincent. Fewer than half survived the journey to Roatán.[40]

Roatán, a 30-mile-long island nominally British since 1742, lay 444 miles southwest of Jamaica. Although closer to Jamaica than to Nova Scotia, it was more remote from the British Empire. It served as home to British soldiers and sailors and to indentured servants—as well as a slave majority—who made their living from the logwood industry. The British government benefited from trading in logwood in the island without incurring permanent expenses in warships, standing armies, and forts. The Caribs, furnished with tools, seeds, and other supplies, were abandoned in this frontier zone without any long-term plan for their future.[41]

The Caribs' exile created an example of a path not taken in the case of the Maroons. The Caribs reminded the duke of the much cheaper dispensation of a troublesome people. By choosing Nova Scotia over Roatán as a destination for the Maroons, the Jamaicans had incurred undue costs and built unwarranted sympathy. The Caribs' deportation, the duke explained, showed that dangerous rebels did not have to be relocated inside His Majesty's dominion but could be supported as a bearable overhead cost in Central America, where they would neither elicit compassion nor require expense. The expense of realizing Wentworth's paternalistic mission was averted.[42]

Surviving handwritten copybooks hint at Wentworth's die-hard vision for the Maroons in Preston. Maroon boys copied rules of conduct, such as "Good Manners Always Procure Respect." They recited the catechism, the Lord's Prayer, and the Ten Commandments perfectly. Wentworth described one fourteen-year-old, John Tharpe, who learned to write in eight months. Another boy, John Morgan, twelve years of age, possessed "traits of the most wonderful genius and avidity for instruction." In his correspondence with the Duke of Portland, Wentworth enclosed the two boys' copied hymns as "some specimens of progress."[43]

From Wentworth's perspective, the Maroons' military experience presented no threat to his civilizing agenda; indeed, he counted it as a bonus. Once again Wentworth likened the martial experience of Maroons to that of the Mi'kmaq. In September 1796, fearing an attack against Halifax from a French squadron, Wentworth contemplated receiving assistance from both groups. In October he exulted that the Maroons would be "decidedly good men against any enemy." He compared the Maroons to the Mi'kmaq because both could maneuver skillfully in hilly terrain. The men had experience in guerrilla warfare against European armies and could assist British soldiers. British riflemen would supervise "Maroons or Indians in the wood or difficult rocky country." One hundred and fifty aboriginal men could be "very serviceable" in repelling an invasion. An equal number of Maroon men would serve the same role. Wentworth imagined that each group would serve as a "useful and faithful corps" in case of invasion. And Maroon soldiers, like Mi'kmaq men who could be enlisted to fight on behalf of British interests, came cheap. They would receive compensation in the form of presents and provisions rather than pay or pension. They would not permanently burden the resources of the imperial government.[44]

Yet the same characteristics that made the Maroons and Mi'kmaq ideal allies made them potentially dangerous enemies. Men with talents suited to frontier warfare could terrify adversaries but also proved harder to discipline and control. This worry existed especially with respect to the Catholic Mi'kmaq. Too few to pose a threat on their own, the Mi'kmaq, allied with the French, could cause havoc. In 1793, during Britain's war with the French, the Indian superintendent, George Henry Monk, resumed office. Wentworth instructed Monk to issue provisions to those who appeared most wretched or who showed proper humility and to look for signs of "democratic French practices among the savages." Wentworth's sympathy for the Mi'kmaq extended only so far: he referred to them as a "restless savage people" who would work to Nova Scotia's advantage only if supported—"fed and lightly clothed." But Wentworth stood ready to exploit their attachment to their families to ensure their allegiance in times of war. Holding wives and children captive would serve as "pledges for their fidelity." At least temporarily, Maroon and Mi'kmaq men would be induced to side with British interests.[45]

Wentworth knew the Maroons as people of African, not aboriginal, ancestry. Multiple times he inquired of Portland if Nova Scotia could receive an additional allowance for the Maroons from funds destined "for the civilization of negroes." Still, he held the Trelawney Town Maroons as a people apart. He did not wish Nova Scotia to lose the Maroons, whom he saw as inherently more malleable than the black Loyalists. He viewed his charity toward the Maroons—like that toward the Mi'kmaq—as nurturing allegiance. His aims would succeed because he gave personal attention to the distressed people. He met the Mi'kmaq individually, "examined their respective distresses, instructed them in their loyalty, and received engagements of their fidelity and ready appearance." Under his direct supervision, the Maroons too would become useful settlers. They came with funds, they would be converted, and they would stay. He would not spoil them. He visited the Preston Maroons regularly and did his utmost to "establish their happiness."[46]

Wentworth regretted the expressions of racial prejudice in the Maritimes. But as slavery moved toward a slow "extinguishment," he optimistically noted that "distinctions actually painful to these people are gradually dying away." His scheme for the Maroon settlement would further this goal and draw the approbation of abolitionists. In a short time they would be "so much more happy and contented than they ever were, that their condition will satisfy Mr. Wilberforce or any other reasonable philanthropic patron of the black race." Here, Wentworth sought praise from British monitoring his experiment. He went so far as to assure the Duke of Portland that the Maroons could not "be prevailed on by any persuasion to return to Jamaica." The duke was taken aback: Wentworth's reports exceeded his every expectation.[47]

But Wentworth conveyed the pacification of the Trelawney Town Maroons too soon. The Jamaican councilor Bryan Edwards had regarded the Maroons' conversion to Christian teachings and incorporation into farming society with skepticism. The "conversion of savage men," he observed, "from a life of barbarity to the knowledge and practice of Christianity, is a work of much greater difficulty than many pious and excellent persons in Great Britain seem fondly to imagine." Edwards's racist observation unwittingly acknowledged the independence and pride of the Trelawney Town Maroons. An assimilated and grateful group of Christianized Maroons did not materialize. Jamaican funds and Wentworth's Christian zeal could not compel the exiles to forsake their dreams.[48]

5
Winter

The Maroons endured neither their banishment nor the cold in silence. After the first cold season, reputed to be the worst since the founding of Halifax, the Maroons, with direction from well-meaning benefactors, began a crusade to leave the colony. Winter favored their claims. Despite humanitarians' conviction of inner human equality, no one on either side of the Atlantic believed that all races had equal tolerance to a cold climate. From the moment the Maroons stepped ashore in Halifax, British sympathizers insisted that blacks could not endure a frozen climate for which they were constitutionally unsuited; they would thrive only in a tropical climate like that of Jamaica. The same Britons who had associated Jamaican bloodhounds with the mangling of Maroon bodies linked the severe winters in Nova Scotia to suffering and starvation; transplanted black people would wilt and die. As one correspondent lamented, "Conceive if you can the feelings of a West India constitution, in such a climate." Wentworth's grand plans stood no chance against the cold and wet of a Maritime winter.[1]

Remarkably, in their preoccupation with climate, the London authorities and humanitarians treated the Maroons like uprooted refugees, not like the dangerous enemies of the British state that they were, adversaries who had fought and killed white settlers in Jamaica. Like voluntary immigrants, the deported Maroons could not simply be dropped into the Nova Scotia climate; they would have to be acclimatized. People who promoted voluntary immigration to North America for white settlers had long emphasized the positive correlation between successful settlement and a temperate climate: newcomers fared best in a land where the climate matched the environment of their homes. One contemporary noted, for example, that English emigrants should, when settling in the United States, avoid the heat of the southern states and settle only in the northern regions. "A sudden and violent change should if possible be avoided," he wrote, and "newcomers should be exposed to no great excess of heat or cold, beyond what they have been accustomed to bear."[2]

The concern with Nova Scotia's climate did not originate with the Maroons' arrival. British humanitarians had raised questions about black people's intolerance for Nova Scotia's winters over a decade earlier. In 1786, when English reformers like Granville Sharp considered destinations for relocating poor blacks from England, Nova Scotia emerged as a possibility. These reformers knew that black Loyalists had emigrated there after the American Revolution. But they explicitly rejected Nova Scotia for this purpose. A handbill from May 17, 1786, announced, "It has been mediated to send blacks to Nova Scotia but this plan is laid aside, as that country is unfit and improper for the said blacks." Curiously, the philanthropists who proposed to resettle poor blacks never discussed the climate in England: only Nova Scotia stood symbolic of frozen possibilities. Instead, the handbill celebrated the benefits of the "grain coast of Africa," considered the "most pleasant and fertile countries in the known world." In 1787 over four hundred of London's black poor were relocated to Sierra Leone; this was the colony to which more than one thousand black Loyalists from Nova Scotia would flee five years later.[3]

Promoters of settlement in Nova Scotia forcefully touted the hidden benefits of the cold for white settlers, at least relative to the fatal heat of the West Indies. Over two decades earlier, upon visiting Nova Scotia, a British officer acknowledged the harsh winter: "Climate is perhaps the greatest natural evil attending this country." Yet he reassured his audience that the autumns were "serene and moderate" and the winters came "by degrees." Even better, a remarkable summer followed the long, severe winters. Although short, the summer stayed "wonderfully productive and vegetation stronger and more rapid than in most other parts of the world." Moreover, Nova Scotia was not peculiar in its winters. Along the entire Atlantic Coast sudden transitions from heat to cold were to be expected. Once these areas were peopled, the climate would become more moderate, as was understood to have been the case in the United States. But implicitly these discussions assumed white colonization.[4]

The removal of the Jamaican Maroons from tropical Jamaica to the much more temperate coast of Nova Scotia elicited immediate concern from a public that assumed black people could die in one cold season. The association of tropical climate with black bodies, already deeply rooted, became reinforced by the black Loyalists' emigration to Sierra Leone in 1792. By and large, commentators attributed the black Loyalists' emigration to the unbearable winters. In December 1797 a newspaper in Boston expressed concern for the painful cold the Maroons must surely endure. The following month one in New York City alleged that two Maroons had died upon drinking cold water. The essayist cautioned, "Persons from warm latitudes should be cautious of taking large draughts of water in northern climates." Anonymous publications in London's newspapers noted that the cold climate was uncongenial to the Maroons' constitution. Nova Scotia seemed an unsuitable place for blacks, albeit convenient for Maroons owing to Wentworth's enthusiasm and the lack of convenient alternatives.[5]

Although Wentworth dismissed the concerns as "lamentably misguided zeal," he found himself on the defensive. From the first, Wentworth's primary correspondent in the British ministry, the Duke of Portland, requested specifics about the Maroons' survival in a severe climate. Portland asked, Would Maroons fare any better in the cold than black Loyalists? Portland assumed that refugees from a tropical climate should naturally be repatriated to a region with a similar climate. As early as July 1796 he had suggested that the unhappy Maroons be relocated from Nova Scotia to Sierra Leone.[6]

By the time the Maroons landed in Nova Scotia, the center of gravity of the free black experience had shifted to West Africa, and both Portland and Wentworth knew it. During the 1780s and 1790s—as in no other time in British imperial history—the focus on the upper Guinea Coast united men interested in colonization, expansion, antislavery, and morality. A British West African settlement could add to the tropical produce of the British Caribbean, with one crucial difference: Sierra Leone would be the world's first West African colony committed to antislavery principles.[7]

The early visionaries of Sierra Leone linked colonization to transplantation. It is no accident that a botanist, Henry Smeathman, suggested the peninsula of Sierra Leone for British explorations in West Africa. The eighteenth-century age of botanical research overlapped with the era of imperial expansion; both shared in the zeal for improvement and reform. The prevalence of botanical language, with its focus on the right environment (soil and climate) for transplanted seeds, would become convenient shorthand for discussions of transplanted people.[8]

Commercially minded men hoped that new colonies in West Africa would replace the "old thirteen" colonies lost in 1783. The African colonies could serve as a source of new raw materials and become a market for British manufactured items. Most investors in the Sierra Leone Company hailed from middle-class backgrounds, particularly in business. Englishmen from multiple regions and occupations—merchants from London, gunsmiths of Birmingham, clothiers of East Angola, cotton producers from Manchester—all sought a market for their products in West Africa. Britain's economic ties to the region had grown over the course of the eighteenth century. In 1720, 65 ships left London, Liverpool, and Bristol for African ports; by 1772, 175 ships sent exports worth £866,000. With the right encouragement, explosive growth seemed reachable. Still, the colony occupied a small area just eighteen miles long and twelve miles wide on the coast of a rugged, mountainous peninsula.[9]

In the era of antislavery, reformist aims overlapped with commercial ones. Many who legislated to end the slave trade saw an opportunity to launch a settlement premised on free black labor. Their example would advance abolitionist principles and be a model to Africans, Europeans, and West Indian slave owners. Uncivilized and un-Christian African slave traders would witness an example of a flourishing settlement based on Christianity and the fruits of free labor. European nations would behold an experiment in British humanitarianism. Jamaican planters would witness agricultural success that did not require the slave labor that stained the British character in the Caribbean.[10]

Still, contemporaries knew that Sierra Leone was no tropical paradise. In 1796, in fact, even the Jamaican planters rejected it as a dumping ground for the Trelawney Town Maroons. Across the Atlantic, whites knew the high fatalities in the region resulting from malaria and yellow fever. The colony was a deathly place, too punishing even for Maroons. The Maroons' superintendent, William Quarrell, who had voted against their banishment, discouraged the Trelawney

Town Maroons' transportation to Sierra Leone because he knew that settlement to be "unhealthy in the extreme" and "unlikely to succeed." He recommended abandoning only the most troublesome Maroon men in Sierra Leone, presumably to die.[11]

By 1796 the situation in Sierra Leone was dire. Britain's war with France in 1793 brought a large withdrawal of imperial interest and also of naval support from the Upper Guinea coast. Worse, the French invaded the colony in September 1794, burning much of it to the ground. Robert Sewell, Jamaica's agent in England, understood the miserable state of the colony after the French attack. In September 1796 he discouraged the Maroons' relocation from Nova Scotia to West Africa, unwilling for them to settle in "a land of so much bitterness and war as I took Sierra Leone to be."[12]

A Court of Directors, absentee founders based in London, governed Sierra Leone. The directors included the evangelical reformer Wilberforce as well as his cousin the banker-merchant Henry Thornton, who saw no contradiction between colonization and humanitarianism. These directors, for their part, feared the Maroons, who were in effect deported rebels, and would not risk destabilizing their new settlement. They observed that it was "totally inconsistent with the security of [our] settlements in Africa to admit the landing on any part of the coast under their direction any of these people." In response to discreet queries about the Maroons' potential settlement in their colony, Sierra Leone's directors offered an ultimatum: the colony would accept the Maroons, but they must arrive in Sierra Leone at different times, with no more than twenty families landing at a time. Small numbers of dispersed newcomers could be absorbed, whereas larger numbers would entail expense and vigilance.[13]

Sensing Portland's unease about the Maroons, Wentworth offered a rationale for keeping people of African ancestry in Nova Scotia. He dismissed the cold as being deleterious to black health. In a letter to the duke written just one month after their arrival Wentworth addressed the climate directly: if black people were "well fed, warmly cloathed, and comfortably lodged, I have always found negroes directly from the hottest coasts of Africa have grown strong and lusty in the winter and that they did not suffer by it." His careful ministrations would eclipse any disadvantages of climate. In October 1796 Wentworth lamented that the black Loyalists' distress five years earlier was blamed on "the only causes which had been really friendly to them, viz. the climate, in which they were still healthy, although poor and almost naked." The winters, he observed, "excited apprehensions and universal competition" among all inhabitants and led to misery for whites and blacks alike. Exaggerated "zeal and affection" expressed at the blacks' plight had led to their unfortunate removal from the colony.[14]

Wentworth was partially right. The focus on Nova Scotia's weather had proven a convenient, if mistaken, shorthand to explain British failure to adequately provide for black Loyalists in the 1780s and early 1790s. Well-meaning abolitionists had not blamed Nova Scotia's governor, John Parr, or white Loyalists for their repressive treatment of free blacks. In fact, Wilberforce recommended avoiding a conversation with the governor on the "ill usage the blacks had received," as this would "nettle" him. Faced with the unmistakable reality that white racism was undermining the black Loyalists' ability to start over in Nova Scotia, Wilberforce and his evangelical friends sought only to extend benevolence to them. The abolitionists sought moral guardianship over the free blacks, as Wentworth later would over the Maroons. They evaded challenging the racial status quo in Nova Scotia and focused on rescuing the blacks from winter.[15]

Significantly, none of the black Loyalists themselves identified the climate as an obstacle to their staying in Nova Scotia. In 1791 John

Clarkson, the white agent who led the black Loyalists to Sierra Leone, recorded their desperate circumstances in Nova Scotia in a tiny notebook. They complained of being forced to work as day laborers, sharecroppers, indentured servants, and, in the case of children, apprentices. They told him that "whites seldom or ever pay for work done." Others tired of living on "white men's property." Some received lower wages than promised for their work. "It is a common custom in this country," they said, "to promise a black so much per day and in evening when his work is finished" to renege on the commitment. Black children received no pay when they worked in white households; whites had already compensated black parents by providing children with lodging and food. Black Loyalists portrayed a dismal picture of unchecked servility and racism. Yet the imperial memories of their emigration remained linked to blacks' inability to adjust to the frigid climate.[16]

Wentworth went to preposterous lengths to succeed where Governor Parr had failed. In October 1796, when he learned that four Maroon families wanted to leave immediately for a warmer climate, he grew alarmed that their clamors would affect the remaining Maroons and end his project. In response, he fabricated what the Trelawney Town Maroons would find in Sierra Leone: he told them that the coast of Africa was colder than Nova Scotia and that they would die upon arrival there. Indeed, he cautioned them that native Africans, who had heard rumors of their intentions to relocate there, "were beginning to dig graves for them."[17]

At the end of the Maroons' first winter, Wentworth minimized the cold as an impediment to their successful settlement in the North. He reported that the Maroons' survival in Nova Scotia boded well for their capacity to stay permanently. In April 1797 he wrote, "They have got through the longest and most severe winter known since the settlement of the province, with less difficulty and more comfort than could have been expected." People of African ancestry could thrive in Nova Scotia. They suffered "no real detriment from the climate" and would settle in due time. Wentworth determined to keep the Maroons and the Jamaican funds that came with them in Nova Scotia.[18]

The Maroons possessed physical strength and could serve usefully as farmers, cheap laborers, and military auxiliaries. A long line of imperial thinking about black bodies as brawny and capable of high exertion shadowed the Maroons. The Jamaican councilor Bryan Edwards had praised their "bodily perfection," saying it was higher than "any other class of African or native blacks." Their demeanor was "lofty," their walk "firm," and their muscles "prominent and strongly marked." Every movement, he observed, displayed a "combination of strength or agility." Wentworth would follow in this vein. The Maroons' food preparations, he noted, should surely cause indigestion—they immersed "unkneaded dough and all sorts of fish and meat into hot ashes"—yet this had no effect on their "powerful constitutions." Black constitutions were "Herculean"; the Maroons could thrive in Nova Scotia even better than whites. Nova Scotia's treasurer, Michael Wallace, did his part to circulate the myth of the indestructible black body. Judging from his observations, he avowed that the "constitution of the Black species are stronger than the whites and better calculated to endure labours and hardships." This belief did not imply that white people were weak. Rather, it showed that black bodies were extraordinarily, unnaturally robust.[19]

His reassurances about the winter notwithstanding, Wentworth encountered close scrutiny from British reformers, who viewed the Maroons' rescue from the cold in the same terms as freeing slaves from tyrannical masters. Contradictory accounts from Nova Scotia, some submitted by the Maroons themselves, filtered into London and challenged Wentworth's optimistic reports. The Maroons wanted to leave, and their trust in General Walpole, the commanding officer in Jamaica who had never endorsed their deportation in the first place, may have predisposed them to have faith in British officers sympathetic to their circumstances. The Trelawney Town Maroons related their "utter discontents" to the "gentlemen of the army and navy and passengers going to England." Some Maroon families pleaded to be returned to Jamaica. Captain Andrew Smith worried about his family's survival in Nova Scotia. If his family of eighteen, including four wives and eight children in addition to his father and brothers and sisters, could not relocate to a warmer climate, they would surely perish. In June the weather continued so wet and cold that potatoes rotted in the ground. It was already too late in the season to replant them; they had no seed potatoes in any case.[20]

In their letters to well-wishers in England the Maroons lamented their absolute dependence on the colonial government. For the majority of the year the season precluded them from procuring the basic necessities to sustain themselves and their families. Tropical fruits and roots like yams, bananas, cocoa, and cayenne pepper did not grow in a cold climate. Nor could they hunt wild hogs. They had no means to obtain staples: rum, sugar, coffee, and cocoa. According to the British military commander, Prince Edward, who absolutely refused to visit them, their stories of hardship created undue sentimentality. Indeed, the Maroons' misery aroused compassion and encouraged bystanders, especially soldiers, to offer whatever assistance they could manage. In January 1797 a Nova Scotian recounted the Maroons' painful condition. The Trelawney Town Maroons never left their houses, sat close "around their stoves," and lived "a most melancholy and pitiable existence." Their misery, his report stated, counted no less than the abuses borne by slaves.[21]

Upon receiving news of their anguish, Walpole represented their plight in the House of Commons. He had entered Parliament in 1797 and remained in the House of Commons until 1820. In April 1797 Walpole raised the matter of the injustice suffered by the Maroons by focusing on the unsuitability of the Nova Scotian climate. He worried that the Maroons had been taken "from a tropical climate to freeze and perish in Canada." Humanity, he argued, required that Parliament inquire "why a whole People should be removed from the hottest climate under the Torrid Zone to the very coldest region of the habitable world." He expressed his desire "for their removal to a warmer climate." Eyewitnesses' correspondence, along with the verbal evidence of senior officers such as Walpole, questioned the morality of the Maroons' banishment to a frigid climate.[22]

Critics of Wentworth's experiment, however, worried about more than the cold climate. The mounting expense of keeping the Maroons in Nova Scotia earned the hostility of the Jamaicans who footed the bill. Wentworth's vision for the Trelawney Town Maroons had not come cheap. By all accounts, his mode of settling them was excessive. He appointed an army of caretakers—not just a chaplain and a schoolmaster but also a doctor, a clerk, and two boatmen—to manage the Maroon families. He requisitioned all variety of goods for their permanent colonization: clothes and thimbles, shoes and shoestrings, tobacco and soap, shovels, axes, nails and knives, and garden seeds for carrots, parsnips, onions, beets, rye, and wheat. Metal buttons should be "large and a quality fit for laborers." Wentworth kept his own fashions in view as well. In the same request he saw fit to order for his own table "plain ivory handle knives." He requested they be "fashionable and good." He billed it all to Jamaica.[23]

Jamaicans, predictably, viewed the high costs with dismay. At first Jamaica complied. The legislature had granted £25,000 for the

Maroons' support in April 1796 and voted to give more in December 1796, August 1797, and again in December 1797. But by 1798 the Jamaican legislature balked; it opposed further requests. Wentworth, William Quarrell charged, had no control over the Maroon establishment. Jamaica had already spent more on "rebellious sanguinary Maroon negroes" than the British government had provided to white American Loyalists in three years. The Maroons, much smaller in number and, from the government's perspective, less worthy, hardly required extravagant and endless assistance. Jamaica would henceforth provide £10 per Maroon until July 1798 and nothing after that.[24]

From the beginning, Quarrell had been convinced that nothing short of coercion would subdue the Maroons. He regretted that their stay in Nova Scotia had led to idealism. The Trelawney Town Maroons had gone from "ferocious banditti" to an "unfortunate people" to an "innocent poor deluded people" and finally to "good settlers." He had known that the sentimental approach employed to transform the Maroons would diminish the long-term chances of arriving at an efficient solution for them. Indeed, he recalled, when he had beaten an insolent Maroon man in April 1797, some Nova Scotians judged him harshly as a "monster of barbarity."[25]

The Jamaican government offered several justifications for its refusal to continue supporting the Maroons in Nova Scotia. In banishing the Maroons from the island, the Jamaicans claimed, the colonial government had complied with instructions received from Britain. In January 1796 the Duke of Portland had advised the Earl of Balcarres to do whatever was necessary to "incapacitate them [the Maroons] from contriving further mischief." This, Balcarres noted, pointed to transportation, the only mechanism that secured the island against the possibility of a second insurrection. The Jamaicans had chosen Nova Scotia as a convenient landing place because it was a reasonable distance away; they had not chosen it as the "*final* station of the Maroons" and hence would not bear the heavy costs of the Maroons' adjustment to that climate. The island opposed supporting dangerous criminals and their descendants for generations. The Trelawney Town Maroons, the Jamaican legislature protested, comprised not a "loyal and favored people" but a group of "atrocious delinquents," deported for taking up arms against His Majesty's government.[26]

Wentworth had long seen Jamaica's gratitude as his due. He reminded Lieutenant Governor Balcarres that the islanders had no cause to complain about any expenses incurred for the Maroons. The exiles, after all, had been a "continual terror" and "enormous expense" on Jamaica. They brought with them "uncultivated savage manners of a warm inland country." Without his oversight, some of them could have escaped and returned to Jamaica to incite another revolt. Any funds he requested to keep them in Nova Scotia paled in comparison to the reduction in risk to the island. Indeed, relocating the Maroons to any other British zone would mean the same expense unless the British government provided them with arms on the "coast of some warm climate to conquer and possess it." But in that situation they would have either died or murdered others "to make room for themselves." Jamaica had left undone the work of transforming the Trelawney Town Maroons into British subjects; Nova Scotia required compensation for directing this undertaking.[27]

As the Maroons' fate lay undecided between the Jamaicans and the Nova Scotians, the Duke of Portland lost patience. He advised Wentworth to support the Maroons as expeditiously as possible. He prohibited Jamaica from prescribing a definite limit to maintaining them or for relieving themselves of the Maroons' burden by laying it upon the people of Nova Scotia.[28] In his opinion the imperial government had no reason to assume responsibility for the Maroons' costs. It had never explicitly authorized their relocation to another British zone or agreed to subsidize them.

Wentworth stalled. Instead of dismissing the winters as an absolute detriment to the Maroons' settlement, he emphasized their inexperience with the cold to justify the costs of their upkeep. In 1797 he observed to Portland that white settlers too required time to adjust to Nova Scotia. He asked for patience: "Europeans who are used to climate and its mode of agriculture and labor were longer supported and still longer assisted in forming settlements to maintain themselves." Wentworth blamed British sympathizers for dramatizing the Maroons' situation in Nova Scotia; he trusted his experiment would succeed with sufficient time and funds.[29]

Shrewdly, Wentworth reminded the British authorities that Nova Scotia's weather suppressed the risks the Maroons supposedly posed to British slavery. Winter acted as a civilizing force by suppressing the disorderliness associated with a tropical climate. In April 1797 he claimed not only that the Maroons were thriving in the cold but also that the weather tempered their rebellious instincts. Wentworth reminded both the Jamaican legislature and the imperial government that the Trelawney Town Maroons would be a dangerous people in any of the West Indian islands. They could not live among slaves without corrupting them or instigating a slave revolt. Only in Nova Scotia, "where they are subjected by the climate," could they be isolated and pacified and do "no material harm." A year later he repeated the claim: "I am fully persuaded that these people are situated in the only part of the world where they can do no mischief." The Jamaican legislature had no "reasonable cause of complaint." The climate substituted for the slaveholders' tight rein, forced dependence on white government, and muted any danger the Maroons might pose.[30]

Until the last months of 1797 Wentworth trusted his program of Christian conversion would succeed. The Maroons' discontent with the cold was temporary. The Maroons included many older people, who did not know how to labor in this province. The younger people would soon "fall into the habits of the country and the climate," while the older class would "drop away." The Maroons already showed signs of acclimatization: they weighed two-thirds more than when they arrived from Jamaica, so "fat and lusty" had they grown.[31]

Wentworth also boasted of the Maroons' growing numbers. Like nothing else, evidence of increasing population would refute concerns about the Maroons' unsuitability for Nova Scotia. The climate promised health and longevity. The allegations about the effects the cold would have on the Maroons proved to be false, as they survived the winter unscathed. Forty-nine Trelawney Town Maroons had died since the group's arrival in Nova Scotia, but most of these deaths were of the aged, infirm, and infants. Some, he acknowledged, had lost fingers and toes to frostbite, but "none have lost more than a joint of a toe or finger and but few of these." Had the Maroons been more willing to wear shoes and stockings, he averred, they would not have suffered so. Whatever sickness they experienced arose from a lack of exercise, and they kept their homes at "fever heat." Wentworth submitted optimistic reports on the Maroons' overall health. In May 1797 he reported 532 Maroons as "healthy as any sett of people on Earth." Only one Maroon woman's situation remained dangerous, but she had shown signs of sickness long before leaving Jamaica. Thirty Maroon women were "big with child." One boy suffered from rheumatic complaints, but summer would improve his condition. Wentworth communicated the increase in the Maroons' numbers to London: by September 1797, 542 persons; by April 1798, 559.[32]

Options other than Nova Scotia had existed for the Maroons; Wentworth, who now blamed the Maroons for their failures, at the same time defended his opposition to these alternatives. One planter from Georgia, for instance, had offered to take the Maroons, presumably as servants, not slaves. But Wentworth explained that he could not have allowed the Maroons to trespass international borders without approval from the governments of the United States and Britain; approval from the slaveholding United States would not have been forthcoming. Moreover, he suspected that Jamaica would not have wanted the Maroons so close by, particularly in Georgia, where known French and Spanish emissaries stood ready "to disseminate rebellion" and seized every chance at exciting it. Wentworth had protected Jamaica by keeping the Maroons in Nova Scotia. In time, they would have proliferated as a "distinct black peasantry." If only both London and Jamaica had supported him in his endeavors, Nova Scotia—and not Sierra Leone—would have showcased a model colony based on free black labor.[33]

The Duke of Portland read the ever-growing pile of correspondence with dismay: how had a small group of rebellious black families created so much commotion? In 1799 a series of clandestine petitions written by the Maroons reached the attention of British humanitarians, revealing Wentworth's protracted failure to convey the reality of the Maroons' circumstances. The endless discourse on winter had covered up a more disturbing set of local circumstances.[34]

6
Resistance

The Maroons' objections to Nova Scotia had gone beyond their sharing of the dire situation with local sympathizers and military officers. Within months of their settlement in Preston, the Trelawney Town Maroons showed, through acts of passive resistance, their unwillingness to become paupers in Nova Scotia. Their noncooperation, they hoped, would mean a return to Jamaica, or at least relocation to a region where they could sustain themselves and their families without dependence. They could never thrive as farmers in Preston. Instead, as they had in Jamaica, the Trelawney Town Maroons offered their military experience and their loyalty to protect British interests. They obstinately rejected Wentworth's project.[1]

In December 1796, less than six months after entering Halifax, the Maroons launched a campaign of opposition. They ceremoniously vowed to resist engaging in cultivation in Nova Scotia. Through resistance to planting, the Maroons hoped they could avoid the fate of living as dependents in Nova Scotia forever. According to an eavesdropping carpenter named Cox, the Maroon "captains and principal men" entered into "solemn engagements" to be guided by Alexander Ochterloney, one of the Jamaican superintendents. The Reverend Benjamin Gray described the moment as a "dreadful religious ceremony wherein the parties mutually bound themselves to encourage and support alone the scheme of removal from this country." The Maroons carried the tradition of the blood oath with them.[2]

The Maroons' covenant with Ochterloney, another secret oath, was the first indication of resistance. Ochterloney echoed the Maroons' impressions of the winter: Nova Scotia was "cold, barren and fit only for bears and moose to live in." He had accompanied the Maroons from Jamaica and knew well their military potential. Better than farmers, the Maroons could best serve British expansionist goals in Africa and Asia by forming an auxiliary army. As General Walpole had earlier, Ochterloney proposed to embody the Maroons in a regiment; he would lead them in British ventures in the Cape of Good Hope or in India. The Maroons would share in the plunder of every town and village attacked and once again enjoy the kind of life they had cherished in Jamaica. Their military victories would expand Britain's claims in new territories around the world. Ochterloney encouraged the Maroons to ask Wentworth for arms, ammunition, provisions, and ships to carry them to places where they could support their wives and children by "making room for themselves."[3]

The Maroons' staunch loyalty to the British Empire could not be missed. In June 1797, almost a year after their arrival, Captain Andrew Smith offered Maroon men as trusted military auxiliaries against the French in Nova Scotia. Young Maroon men would demonstrate to Prince Edward that they were a "brave and loyal people" and would "die in defense of him, our King, or his good Family." Smith expressed his hatred of the French. If the French invaded Halifax, "by Heaven cold as the weather may be we will warm them every step of the road they take towards [the city]." In the ultimate show of loyalty to the British cause, Smith christened his son George Walpole. The next generation of young Maroon Walpoles would also fight to defend the British Empire in any part of the globe.[4]

The outcome of the ceremonial pledge with Ochterloney shocked Wentworth. Within a few days of the making of the pledge, all of the Maroon men scattered within three or four miles "laid down their axes, and refused to strike a blow" to cut another tree. The Maroons determined "not to work—not to plant—not to repair their houses—or help build others—not to send their children to school—not to go to church—lest these things keep them here." In April 1797, when the Maroons ideally would have begun cultivation, there was no sign of work. Wentworth and his coterie of Maroon caretakers noted the event as a "strange phenomenon," one calculated to oblige the Nova Scotian government to relocate them.[5]

At first, Wentworth dismissed the Maroons' compact as both inconvenient and preposterous. But the Maroons' resistance cost the colony precious planting time. Their refusal to cultivate resulted in an "unpleasant sort of suspension, inconvenient in our short summers." One week's worth of breaking ground in April counted for as much as three weeks in the heat of the summer.[6]

Even though Wentworth himself had advocated a military role for the Maroons, he had envisioned that role as being temporary, a convenient and cost-effective stop on the route to civilization. A permanent military position for the Maroons within British regiments was as unthinkable to Wentworth as it had been to Jamaica's slave owners. Weakly, he turned to demographics and Ochterloney's evil-mindedness to reject the feasibility of the military plan. Too many Maroon women and children—double the number of men—made the idea of a Maroon regiment inconceivable; the government would be left with the burden of supporting large families. Far from benevolent, Ochterloney was an active and enterprising opportunist who "*has his fortune to make.*" In Wentworth's eyes, Ochterloney was an ambitious fraud who exploited the Maroons' fears of the cold climate to promise them an elusive escape. Ochterloney wanted possession of the Maroons, Wentworth claimed, "for the sake of the means afforded for their support." In contrast to Ochterloney, who promoted the Maroons' predatory desires for his own mercenary ends, Wentworth, in his self-portrayal, was the true humanitarian.[7]

In May 1797 fears of a French naval attack compelled attention to the Maroons' noncooperation. An internal convulsion would distract Nova Scotia's military and prevent an adequate defense against the French. Wentworth attempted to quiet the Maroons and increase his sway by offering a remarkable concession. Addressing himself directly to the Maroon officers whom he regarded as most influential, Captain Smith and Colonel Montague James, Wentworth asked the Trelawney Town Maroons to give Nova Scotia a fair trial of twelve months. If, in May 1798, they still clamored to leave, he would write on their behalf to London. This would allow ample time to make arrangements for their relocation before the onset of the next winter. Wentworth exacted concessions: "You are to exert your best endeavors to cultivate and improve the buildings and estate whereon you now reside and occupy and that you will faithfully obey and execute my orders and directions." In June, Wentworth showed relief: the Maroons had "unanimously approved" his recommendation for trying another year. Wentworth expected that his concession would lead them to turn seriously to the task of cultivation.[8]

But the second Jamaican superintendent, Quarrell, who knew the Maroons better, doubted the authenticity of their agreement. He opposed the concession. Wentworth had encouraged the Maroons to believe that an alternative to Nova Scotia stood feasible. Quarrell suspected that, given the opportunity of leaving in another year, the Maroons would wait Wentworth out instead of improving the land allotted to them. They now had no incentive to cultivate the poor soil.

In a moment of panic motivated by the French threat, Wentworth had compromised too much.[9]

Whatever the accuracy of Quarrell's assessment, Wentworth's bargain had bought time for his experiment with the Maroons. Wentworth removed the troublesome Ochterloney from the Trelawney Town Maroons and appointed Captain Alexander Howe of the Royal Nova Scotia Regiment as superintendent of the Maroons in the summer of 1797. A longtime resident of pre-Loyalist Nova Scotia, Howe had spent earlier years in Jamaica and apparently had a "happy talent of attaching inferiors to him." Howe, like Wentworth, discounted the cold as an obstacle to the Trelawney Town Maroons' adjustment. Whereas the humanitarian activists compared the Maroons' distress to the black Loyalists who had left for Sierra Leone, Howe compared the Maroons to the two thousand black Loyalists who had remained in Nova Scotia. He too validated the Maroons' suitability in a cold climate. If blacks from Virginia and South Carolina, also regions with warm, sultry climates, survived in Nova Scotia, so could the Maroons. Howe supported Wentworth in believing their settlement required time. The machinations of Ochterloney had deprived Nova Scotians of a full year of Maroon-produced crops. With proper guidance, the Maroons would become valuable cultivators in the colony.[10]

Still, Howe could not compel the Maroons to accept Nova Scotia. They insisted it could serve only as a "temporary rendezvous" and not their final home. The land in Preston could not yield sufficient food; disbanded soldiers as well as "some hundred" black Loyalists had previously abandoned the rocky soil. Moreover, because the Maroons included so many large families, with large proportions of children and the old, "the greatest exertions on the lands at Preston" by younger men would not have made them independent. Some witnesses recognized the difficulty Maroons faced in settling in Nova Scotia. How, one contemporary wrote, "could a Maroon, the father of a family, with three or four wives, and perhaps a dozen children, look forward to their support?" Maroon men's unfamiliarity with farming implements was obvious: "The plough is unknown to him, and equally so is the scythe, the sickle and the spade."[11]

But the Maroons' lack of experience in tilling rocky soil only partially accounted for their noncooperation. From the beginning, the Maroons resisted becoming the black peasantry Wentworth envisioned. They equated a life of cultivation with enslavement and exploitation. They suspected that the lands they cleared and cultivated "would not be theirs but given to white people." When it came time to work in fields, they pretended to have a pain in the stomach. They attributed any sickness to the cold climate and the want of West Indian fruits and used any reason to stay in bed. Instead of picking stones and clearing land to plant oats and potatoes, they sought more profitable employment through making hay, packing fish, loading ships, and working at wharves; the children picked fruits and sold them in Halifax. Ready to earn for work by task, the Maroons resolutely evaded work that paid by the day. They boycotted jobs "without pay equal to a whiteman." They spoke of Jamaica as "nothing short of a paradise." Preston they accepted only as interim quarters.[12]

The Trelawney Town Maroons rejected the consolation of religion and mocked Christian teachings. This may, in part, have been Ochterloney's doing; in 1797 he provided rewards of liquor and food—and cockfighting as entertainment—to those who avoided the church. He convinced the Maroons that the king paid white parishioners for sitting still in church; by not paying the Maroons, Wentworth had cheated their families of obligatory compensation. With Ochterloney's encouragement and "Maroon wit," the exiles had turned to "scoffing at all the ceremonys, dutys, and instruction of religion." In 1798, as British statesmen learned with embarrassment, Captain Howe had followed in Ochterloney's footsteps, but in reverse. Whereas Ochterloney had paid the Maroons not to attend religious services, Howe paid every four Maroons who attended church a bottle of rum the next day. Without the bribe, he claimed, they would have pursued entertainments like "cockfighting, gambling, and debauchery." The Maroons' activities undoubtedly fulfilled social needs and relieved some of the tensions and resentments of being in Nova Scotia. Colonial administrators took un-Christian shortcuts to appear to be in conformity with Wentworth's vision.[13]

White administrators exploited the vulnerability of Maroon women as well. The extent of their involvement became evident when the pro-Wentworth and anti-Wentworth factions attacked each other for immoral conduct. The pro-Wentworth Captain Howe accused his predecessor, Quarrell, of entertaining "eight or ten Maroon girls . . . for his own and [his] friends [*sic*] entertainment." Ochterloney fared no better. The Maroon schoolmaster, Theophilus Chamberlain, accused the superintendent, Alexander Ochterloney, of keeping "five, or six, and often more" of the "finest Maroon girls, constantly in his house, and several of them in his bed chamber" not only for his own use but also for his "religious friends and assistants." Ochterloney, according to Chamberlain, ran an Ottoman-like seraglio. The anti-Wentworth British officer Captain John Hale had relations with Maroon women and "kept [one] as mistress publicly in his House, for seven or eight months." This same woman, Wentworth knew, had cut off Colonel Fitch's head in Jamaica. Wentworth, as noted earlier, also engaged in such exploitation. At the age of at least sixty he had relations with a Maroon woman, who bore him a son.[14]

Wentworth's attempts at Christianizing the Maroons failed abysmally. In June 1798 Howe voiced his disappointment: "Our religion had never been inculcated in the minds of the Maroons in Jamaica." Reverend Gray concurred: "It is not so easy a thing to eradicate from the mind those attachments which early habit and constant practice have endeared to it." The Maroons' caretakers had noted the differences that set the Trelawney men apart from the white and black residents in Nova Scotia: their dedication to supporting multiple wives and extended families, their festive celebrations during burials, their boisterous enjoyment of gambling and gaming. They doubted the Maroons' willing incorporation into a British and Christian world. In June 1798 John Oxley, the surgeon to the Maroons, admitted that the "present generation will ever be Maroons."[15]

By 1798 Wentworth had lost patience and faith in the Maroons. Other caretakers followed his lead. The Trelawney Town Maroons had exploited the government's benevolence with no compunction, they claimed. Using the excuse of the cold climate, they played while the government fed them. And no efforts at coercion worked. As Chamberlain noted, "The Maroons here have been reasoned with, been persuaded, urged, and bribed to go to work and been punished for not working; and various methods have been tried to induce them to it." In September 1798 Chamberlain tried cruelty: he withheld provisions from the Maroons for four days, from Sunday to Wednesday. Only after they had made satisfactory promises to cooperate did he give them food. He exulted to Quarrell, "We are finally getting the better of a little mercenary clan that don't lie half as snug as they imagine."[16]

John Fraser, the surgeon for the Maroons who had replaced Oxley in 1798, provided the rationale for the carrot and stick approach. Fraser trusted the strategy would compel work from the "lazy, the intemperate, and the turbulent." Outside of discontinuing food allowances, no method existed to rouse the Maroons "from their indolence and pernicious determination." Of course, provisions for the aged, sick, widows, and orphans should not cease. Fraser had lived twenty-one years in the colony and was convinced that the land at Preston could generate more food than the Maroons produced. He lamented that rumors of starvation excited a "misplaced compassion" for the Trelawney Town Maroons. The Maroons, strong and capable of exertion, only needed incentives to reconcile themselves to their new home. Fraser too reverted to the stereotype of the Herculean black laborer.[17]

Wentworth's efforts to civilize the Maroons came to an abrupt halt in January 1799, when he confronted direct and sustained critiques of his handling of the Maroon situation from the Duke of Portland. The London ministry had grown tired of mediating between politicians in Nova Scotia and Jamaica on the subject of the Maroons while facing accusations of inhumanity at home. It turned to a solution for the Trelawney Town Maroons that would quiet abolitionists, reduce expenses, and benefit the empire. In January 1799, three years after he had first entertained the notion, the duke directed the Sierra Leone Company to supervise the Maroons' reestablishment in West Africa. Unlike Nova Scotians, who received the Maroons unannounced, Sierra Leone's founders would have time to form a "pre-concerted plan" for their settlement.[18]

The company's willingness to accept a group of Jamaican rebels appears surprising in light of their purported desire to civilize and convert Africans. The Maroons, a community of polygamous non-Christians, hardly qualified as ideal settlers if British goals in West Africa were to be realized. But the need for immigrants who would lay absolute claim to land had become clear. In May 1799 Sierra Leone's governor emphasized the importance of situating the Maroons in "a place we don't occupy but have." In the absence of a group of British-supervised settlers, the land would inevitably revert to the natives, regardless of the labor and expense spent on cultivating the land and building on it. Only through permanent settlement could the company's right be preserved. Unsupported by military power, written treaties mattered less than diplomacy through annual presents, and the latter meant little without actual occupation.[19]

The duke's determination to relocate the Maroons was forced by a series of secret petitions that Maroon sympathizers had carried to England. Collectively, the petitions succeeded in circulating a narrative of the Maroons' frailty, even paralysis, in Nova Scotia. The petitions incited charged discussions in the House of Commons, received as they were during the decade when Parliament debated the harsh conditions of the slave trade and the high mortality of slaves. In January 1799 the duke received a letter from a sympathizer in Nova Scotia who lamented that the Maroons remained "incapable during several months of the year of making any exertions that can contribute to their support & maintenance." Winter, it seemed, incapacitated the Maroons. The petitions exposed Wentworth as a fraud and pronounced his scheme doomed.[20]

The first Maroon petition, addressed directly to General Walpole, arrived in London in April 1797. It was carried in confidence by Captain Hale. Signed with an X by the Maroons' leader, Colonel James, it expressed the Maroons' unshakable confidence in Walpole: he had provided the Trelawney Town Maroons with "positive assurance of not only sparing our lives but our not having removal from the country." Deferentially, James asked Walpole to find an alternative for their "miserable situation." The Maroons had "experienced knowledge of his goodness" and trusted that his "kind interference" would benefit them.[21]

Subsequent petitions, submitted secretly despite the Trelawney Town Maroons' May 1797 bargain with Wentworth, moved toward a stringent, accusatory tone. In the second petition, of June 1797, the Maroons portrayed themselves as involved in a defensive struggle and accused the Jamaicans of betrayal. The Trelawney Town Maroons held that "false representations of malicious persons" had induced them to take up arms against their "beloved friends and countrymen." The Maroons had surrendered "as far as the nature of circumstances and our situation would admit of." Yet in violation of that treaty they had been transported and legally merited reconsideration and ultimate removal. They faced the "utmost wretchedness" because Nova Scotia posed too huge a contrast to their "native climate." They wanted foremost to return home to Jamaica. Otherwise, they pleaded to go to "some warmer climate" where they could support their wives and children.[22]

The next three petitions appealed to an authority higher than Walpole. The Maroons directly addressed the secretary of state, the Duke of Portland. Written in August and November 1797 and in August 1798, the requests summarized their earlier complaints against Jamaica. They blamed Jamaica for "scandalously violating" the peace treaty. They took advantage of the discourse circulating on the unsuitability of the cold for black families: they wanted to live in a climate "more congenial to our habits." The cold killed their families. The "poor distressed Maroons" could survive only in "some warmer part of the globe." But in these later petitions the Maroons boldly singled out Wentworth as a liar. He had misrepresented their willingness to endure the climate of Nova Scotia. Any reports by Wentworth were "so far void of truth that the very idea of it makes us shudder." The Maroons did not mention their own defiance in Nova Scotia: their resistance to cultivation and to Christian conversion. Their focus remained on Jamaicans' unlawful actions and Nova Scotia's uncompromising winters. They represented themselves as free subjects waiting for benevolent imperial compensation—like black Loyalists.[23]

In January 1799 the Maroons recognized that their best chance of being relocated was to focus totally on the harshness of Nova Scotia's climate. A petition, signed by Captain Smith, Captain Charles Shaw, and four other captains, directly addressed the House of Commons, which they called "the seat, fountainhead of law, equity and justice." They referred to themselves as "Maroon exiles" and conceded that their expulsion was "just in some degree." Yet both Jamaica and Nova Scotia misrepresented them as troublemakers, to "blacken the Maroons beyond their natural hue." They knew they could not survive in their present situation. No people who had lived independently in the West Indies could tolerate a life of dependence in Nova Scotia: "Such a phenomenon is nowhere to be found in nature, such incongruities and such antipathies do not exist either in the moral or physical world, as a West Indian to be reconciled to Nova Scotia." If they could not live in a climate "congenial to their natures and constitutions," they stood ready to receive "death in its most awful shapes, the latter they prefer to a residence in Nova Scotia." The code words for freedom became West Indies; for independence, hot weather; and for death, Nova Scotia.[24]

In the spring of 1799, as the Sierra Leone Company considered Portland's request, Wentworth completely lost control of the local situation. The Maroon petitions influenced public opinion, raised specific inquiries, and placed Wentworth on the defensive. They also emboldened some Trelawney Town Maroons to adopt a stance of bold defiance. The Maroons' refusal to cultivate and fence land increased the expense of supporting them—money that neither Jamaica nor Britain would provide. But on April 10 the Maroons' defiance led Wentworth to turn, for the first time, to military retaliation. At the first sign of resistance he followed the protocol set by his appointees in previous years: he withheld food and accused the Maroons of "disobedience and obstinate perverse idleness." Confronted with starvation, the Maroons did not back down as they had in previous years: they threatened to slaughter cattle to feed their families. As the situation spiraled out of control, Wentworth called up fifty men from the Royal Nova Scotia Regiment to stand duty in Preston.[25]

Wentworth's paternalism had always come with restrictions. He had long supported withholding provisions to compel the Maroons to work; by his estimation, cruelty mixed with kindness would lead to the desired results. But some of the Maroons' caretakers had feared the consequences of withholding food from the exiles. Maroon men could break open stores, kill cattle, and take whatever they wanted rather than "be starved into compliance." But until 1799 no open defiance broke out. Atlantic humanitarians, as the Maroon leaders knew from experience, supported peaceful measures, not violent protest. The violence of the Saint-Domingue rebellion had not won praise from antislavery advocates. The Maroons knew from a long education how to placate whites' fears and play up to their egos. The change in tactics in the spring of 1799 indicated an internal fissure in the Maroon community in Preston and perhaps the depth of its desperation.[26]

The Trelawney Town Maroons' open resistance drew sympathy from commanding British officers stationed in Halifax. Like General Walpole, the Irish brigadier general John Murray regarded them as a wronged people. He disliked Wentworth and opposed his starvation tactics. Whereas Prince Edward had absolutely refused to hear the Maroons' complaints in person, Murray met them personally. Without consulting Wentworth, Murray withdrew soldiers that stood guard over the Preston Maroons. As he had decried Ochterloney's influence in 1797, so Wentworth criticized Murray's interventions in 1799. Again, Wentworth cursed the breakdown of authority over the

Maroons as caused by "bad advice and advisors" who overwhelmed his scheme. If the Maroons stopped receiving encouragement from humanitarian meddlers—"if all hopes of removal were absolutely taken away"—they would become useful settlers. But in an era of antislavery, political agitators, military officers, and evangelical reformers temporarily formed a cohesive group. They would not allow the Maroons to vanish from view. The Maroons inched one step closer to leaving Nova Scotia.[27]

A confounded Wentworth tried to identify the cause of the Maroons' open challenge to government orders. The troublemaking superintendent Ochterloney had long since left the colony, and no one could readily identify the "baneful influence of Mahiavelian [*sic*] politicians." No philanthropic machinations from England led to the explosion of tension. Wentworth conceded the hand of Maroon leaders: the Maroon families who had survived best working small jobs in Halifax remained the most troublesome, the "worst disposed." Although "healthy, stout and robust," they indulged in rum and refused to lay a finger to the fields. Wentworth put aside his dream of converting the Maroons into contented farmhands; his colony did not need more turbulence.[28]

By the summer of 1799 Wentworth resorted to dire warnings in order to exonerate himself and to condemn the Maroons' conduct. The Maroons' discontent, Wentworth wrote, had nothing to do with him or with their circumstances in Nova Scotia. Rather, it came from their wish to "be placed in a situation where they may ravage and pillage with impunity." In Jamaica the Maroons' unwillingness to cultivate land had led to subsidies and then to plunder; Sierra Leone would face the same expense because the Maroons "will be no better disposed to earn their own subsistence [there] than in Nova Scotia." The Maroons, savage to the core, could never be rehabilitated. He issued a dire warning to the Sierra Leone Company: it must exercise "great circumspection, vigilance and power" over Maroon men and boys to maintain internal discipline. The greatest risk came from five troublemakers: "two Jarratts, two Shaws, and one Harding." Eight families were "proud, turbulent, and savage." Ominously, he pronounced, "I fear the Sierra Leone will find them ungovernable." The Maroons' strategy of noncooperation had defeated Wentworth—and left him furious.[29]

Wentworth mocked the ideal of setting the unruly Maroons permanently in the frontier colony of Sierra Leone. Their former habits and prejudices had not left them. They sought to "gratify their delight in predatory war, sensuality and variety, which this country does not afford." Without supervision, the Maroons would betray British interests for their own irrepressible desires. Just as the French clandestinely sent blacks from Saint-Domingue to instigate rebellion in the United States, British enemies could employ Maroon men to shatter the Sierra Leone settlement. The opportunistic Maroons, Wentworth warned, might hatch dangerous plans. Far from expanding the antislavery experiment in West Africa, they had hopes of conquering Africans and either selling them as slaves or owning them. Nor had they lost their yearning for Jamaica; some viewed Sierra Leone, as they had Nova Scotia, only as a stopgap measure.[30]

Wentworth's paternalism disappeared after the Maroons showed resistance. In May he dismissed their concerns over the cold climate as a "trumpery story." The "bombast declaration"—that they preferred death to living in Nova Scotia—was pure humbug. He shrewdly observed that the Maroons happily consumed what was available in a cold climate. They did not "refuse food altho' without cayenne pepper, yams, and pineapple." Moreover, Maroon men, some dressed in the "highest priced white silk stockings with a hat and a feather," went in the coldest days of the winter to find opportunities for gaming they "brot with them from Jamaica"—cards and cockfighting. But when asked to adopt a routine of labor, they complained of the cold. Wentworth related one incident colorfully: a Maroon man came "bounding like a Caribou deer, his black skin shining with profane perspiration," and disingenuously complained "oh massur—dissa country too cold." Nova Scotia had done far too much for these ungrateful, lazy refugees; the colony should henceforth assist only those who showed need or demonstrated loyalty, namely, infants, elderly, childbearing women, the infirm, and school-attending boys. The Maroons grumbled not because they suffered unbearably or died catastrophically but because they sought to hold on to their way of life and to do better. They were cunning, opportunistic, and unmanageable. In his distaste for the entire cause, Wentworth clumped all the Maroons together, neglecting to mention the Maroon families settled in Boydville as a small example of success.[31]

Wentworth, however, remained ambitious and optimistic. To incorporate the Maroons into Nova Scotian society, he had to deal with tensions felt by the Maroons that he neither understood nor could mend. Arising as a compromise, Palmer's Boydville set an unexpected example of Maroons' potential. In 1798 Wentworth boasted of the achievements of the Boydville Maroons in order to mask his failure with the majority of Trelawney Town Maroons in Preston. His perseverance had resulted in the "most happy, benevolent and desirable effect." They progressed in cultivating their lands and requested a chaplain to administer public worship. Thirteen Maroon children were baptized. Within a year the Boydville Maroons' gardens, producing Indian corn, potatoes, and beans, looked as "forward as any one's about them." Their example led eleven additional Maroon families to join them a year later. Together with a hundred white families, the Boydville group, comprised of sixty people, attended Christian service in a barn.[32]

The Boydville contingent seemed to have fulfilled Wentworth's vision of a black peasantry in Nova Scotia. On May 5, 1799, these families distanced themselves from the Preston resistance and announced their ideological separation from "our brethren at Preston." They requested seed, grain, and one or two cows from Wentworth. They asked for schools to be located closer to them, as Preston lay too far away for their children.[33]

Wentworth worried about the Boydville group's reintegration with the Preston Maroons. In October 1799 he faithfully, but foolhardily, conveyed to Portland their wish to settle fifteen miles from their Preston brethren when they reached Sierra Leone. The duke lost all patience. The "fear and dislike" some Maroons had for others did not concern him. Maroons would carry no weapons on board and hence posed no serious danger to other Maroons. Portland was impatient with Wentworth's coddling of a small community of black Christians.[34]

The Maroons' fate was sealed in October 1799, when Portland wrote to Wentworth informing him that the agent for the Sierra Leone Company, an irascible Scottish clerk by the name of George Ross, had sailed for Halifax to proceed with them as their agent to Sierra Leone. Ross would assist in managing the Maroons, especially with "a view of preparing their minds for entering upon that mode and those habits of life which it is necessary that they should adopt on their arrival at that settlement." Portland pointedly informed Wentworth that every one of the Maroons should be embarked on the ships.[35]

Neither Portland nor Wentworth could fully control who left Nova Scotia. At least four Maroons deserted, choosing Nova Scotia over Sierra Leone. A man by the name of David Millar, not identified as a Maroon, accompanied the Maroons to Sierra Leone. He may have been a black Loyalist who hoped to reunite with his family in Sierra Leone or perhaps was a man born of a mixed-race union between a black Loyalist and a Mi'kmaq woman. He was definitely not a Maroon.[36]

In August 1800, almost a year after plans for their relocation had been finalized, the majority of Maroon families from both the Preston and Boydville settlements embarked from Halifax. As had happened in Jamaica and in Nova Scotia, some British officers, showing an affinity for fellow military men, protected the Maroons' interests during their voyage to Sierra Leone. When Lieutenant Lionel Smith of His Majesty's 24th Regiment noticed that the ship's lieutenant, John Sheriff, was hoarding their provisions and diluting their rum, he spoke in defense of the Maroons. Smith declared that "he was the King's Officer and he would not see the provisions squandered away—and as a man he dared to support the cause of humanity—and he would not see the Maroons in future treated as they had been without bringing him to a severe account for it."[37] Lieutenant Smith would continue to watch over the Maroons during his stay in Sierra Leone.

The Maroons verbally agreed to the terms Ross promised for their stay in Sierra Leone. Maroon men over the age of twenty-one would receive three acres of land; they would receive two acres each for a wife and one acre for a child. The Maroons would receive some land within three months of arrival and the remainder in the first three years. Starting the first day of January after they received their land grant, they would pay a yearly rent of twenty cents per acre. Each Maroon would commit to clearing land and building a house. If a Maroon left the land for three years, the land would be forfeited. The Maroons could not sell or transfer land without the consent of the company. Full provisions would be provided for three months and then diminished. Each Maroon must contribute ten days of annual labor for public works. No Maroon could be involved in the slave trade. Married Maroons could not procure additional wives in Sierra Leone. All Maroons must obey British laws. Finally, each Maroon must be ready to repel a foreign attack or suppress an internal disturbance. No one could have known that this last stipulation—the expectation of Maroons' willingness to take up arms to defend British interests—would launch Maroons' integration into British Sierra Leone.[38]

Within hours of reaching Freetown the Maroons demonstrated that Wentworth had been terribly wrong about them. He had misinterpreted their unwillingness to toil full-time in rocky soil and to accede to a life of permanent dependency as an indication of indolence and indiscipline. The Maroons, in fact, demonstrated exactly the opposite behavior: they employed vigor and practiced absolute discipline in seizing their chance to gain military honor and recognition in Sierra Leone. No less than Lieutenant Governor Balcarres, they would do everything to protect the name of the British king and his colonies. But one of Wentworth's suspicions would have rung true to Sierra Leone's leaders: the deported Trelawney Town Maroons yearned to find their way home to Jamaica.[39]

SIERRA LEONE

(Overleaf): *"A View of the New Settlement in the River at Sierra Leone" (c. 1790). This romanticized view shows the early settlement of Sierra Leone. The slave ship in the bay suggests an antislavery perspective.* (*© The British Library Board [Maps.K.Top.117.(100)].*)

7
Crisis

On September 30, 1800, sometime between 9 and 10 a.m., the two-decker transport *Asia,* carrying 551 Maroons, anchored near Freetown, Sierra Leone. On the ship was Martin Sewell, the Maroon who had voluntarily sailed to Nova Scotia to join the deported group. It also carried the Maroon superintendent, George Ross, and 45 invalid soldiers commanded by Lieutenant Lionel Smith. The Maroons received a surprisingly warm welcome from Governor Thomas Ludlam and the Sierra Leone Council. The current inhabitants of Sierra Leone, black Loyalists from Nova Scotia, had launched an insurrection just days before the Maroons' arrival, and the administrators needed help to crush the rebellion and restore order in the colony. The Maroons arrived just in time.[1]

The Nova Scotians' hostility toward the government made Sierra Leone's situation more precarious in 1800 than it had been in 1796, when the directors first considered settling the Maroons. The colony was still dependent on native African allies. The British administration and existing black settlers claimed less than twenty square miles of the peninsula, and they occupied a peculiar position in relation to the African states around it. Thinly and unreliably provisioned from Britain, the colony depended on local African support for sustenance and could hardly afford to overplay its tenuous hold in the region. The lack of a regularly occurring market in or near Freetown is further evidence of the ad hoc nature of exchange in the neighborhood of the colony.[2]

The Sierra Leone settlers' survival depended on having nonantagonistic relations with native groups. Without native collaborators, the settlement could not survive. In contrast to Jamaica, which had a powerful and independent colonial legislature, Sierra Leone had a weak government. Unlike Lord Balcarres in Jamaica, Governor Ludlam in Sierra Leone could not depend on assemblymen, trusted middlemen, or British officers to protect the colony's interests. Between 1796 and 1802 no more than twenty-eight European administrators would serve the colony at any given time, some as members of the council, others in the roles of apothecary, surgeon, storekeeper, school instructor, or minister. The governor, assisted by two councilmen, did everything: preached sermons, conducted correspondence with the directors in London, visited neighboring African leaders, and embarked on diplomatic missions into interior regions. Far from presiding magisterially over the region, the governor backed and rewarded some African rulers over others and, when possible, seized the chance to manipulate local politics.

Although Britain possessed much greater real military power than any African power in their neighborhood, complete with a mobile artillery fleet that could strike along the coast, Sierra Leone did not benefit from this potential. In the midst of war with France, the British navy was otherwise engaged. The colony, hence, was militarily weaker than any other African state in the region; its best option was to maintain strict neutrality with the native chiefs. Presents in the form of clothing, sugar, and such exotic items as showy eardrops, walking canes, swords, and silk umbrellas continued to smooth relations between the British and nearby African groups.[3]

Governor Ludlam understood that some African groups opposed British settlement and expressed ill will and envy toward the colony.

The Temne ruler, King Tom, believed that his people had signed a lease with British visitors in 1788. In King Tom's accounting, the Temne had not given away their land forever to foreigners who kept them at a distance. In May 1799 Ludlam blamed the native hostility on irrational jealousy: "The moment it [the soil] is useful to another it becomes valuable to themselves; they are too deep in indolence and the slave trade to let slip any opportunity of making profit without labor and too selfish to let another person possess an advantage merely because they cannot enjoy it themselves." Ludlam disregarded the Africans' claim to lands he considered could be put to better use by the British-led projects in West Africa.[4]

From its founding years, Sierra Leone's leaders worked hard to avert the hostility of neighboring African leaders. Freetown was surrounded by decentralized African polities, for example, the Temne and the Bullom, that appreciated British trade goods but opposed the company's expansion into the interior and begrudged its interference with slavery. The natives objected more to the British settlement than to the British slave factories in Bunce Island. The latter confined themselves to commerce without any "agricultural views" and sought a trade relationship with the natives involving slaves as well as provisions, while the company wanted to gain "full possession of their country" and interfered with the slave trade by offering a potential haven for runaways. As was the case with European slave traders, the company's agitation against slavery did not equate to a full-blown assault against African slave traders in their neighborhood. Protecting some slave runaways conveniently gave symbolic weight to the company. But the governing men avoided antagonizing headmen by offering refuge to their runaways.[5]

Notwithstanding the company's utopian aims, the terms of the colony's founding necessitated that its administrators also associate with white slave traders. The Sierra Leone Company did not gain exclusive trading rights in the region; British slave traders plied their trade legally and in close proximity to the settlement. Between 1791 and 1795 eighty-three slave ships visited Sierra Leone, embarking with over nineteen thousand slaves. Just as important, the vulnerable colony could not afford to have European enemies. The British Parliament had not abolished the slave trade in 1792, as had been anticipated. The following year, with the onset of Britain's global war against France, antislavery debates became interlocked with the slave rebellion in Saint-Domingue, and it seemed abolition was unlikely to be enacted in the near future. Antagonizing neighboring slave traders would have created great risks for the colony: hostile neighbors would provide no provisions to the settlement in times of acute crisis and no warning in case of a French attack.[6]

The colony's greatest asset, the black Nova Scotians, who were specifically imported to realize the founders' goals of establishing a plantation society without slavery, had consistently refused to cooperate. In light of their unquenched expectations of gaining civil and political equality with whites, the Nova Scotians had long defied their subordinate position in Sierra Leone's governance. But until 1800 their attacks on the company had been limited to verbal abuse. In the third week of September the rebels declared their own independence: they proposed a settler constitution that established terms for political autonomy, set maximum prices for provisions, and conceded only commercial authority to the company's government. Fifty active and armed rebels awaited the company's decision. Some Nova Scotian hardliners plundered the farms of those who supported the company. The rebels waited, anticipating that the company would agree to their demands to avoid the destruction of the settlement. Never before had the company employed force against the Nova Scotians.[7]

The issue at the core of the Nova Scotians' resistance involved land. For over five years, the rebels maintained, the government had practiced gross deceit, providing them with less than a fifth of the land promised to them in Nova Scotia. They additionally insisted that the mandatory annual rent payments—five or six times the amount considered customary in the American colonies—would leave them with no security. As Governor Ludlam remarked a year after the insurrection, the Nova Scotians equated the quitrent with insecure title and believed that a "single unavoidable failure of payment would forfeit their lands." He emphasized further that "it was the great, the constant, the successful argument by which people were persuaded they were abused, oppressed & enslaved." Moreover, not having pledged to pay this rent upon their departure from Nova Scotia, they were not morally bound to submit to this demand. The deep Christian faith of the Nova Scotians shaped their political outrage, and by 1800 their armed resistance forced the issue.[8]

A week before the Maroons landed in Sierra Leone, the council noted worrisome indications of insurrection, especially "meetings of a most seditious and dangerous nature held by the factious party." It advised the company's servants, Europeans, and the "well-affected" to form a strong guard to maintain civil order. It distributed arms to some loyal settlers. The government had given up reclaiming the "misguided part of these men to a sense of their duty." But it did little else, hoping that the rebels' demands would fade instead of taking on the "character of public importance." Attempts to persuade the Nova Scotians only seemed to "harden their hearts rather than to raise in them a corresponding desire for peace." Having fewer than fifteen white administrators in Sierra Leone in 1800, the government had little recourse against direct attack.[9]

The arrival of the Maroons provided the settlement with an extraordinary opportunity: the colony could, once and for all, reduce the rebels to "unconditional submission." Previously ambivalent about accepting troublesome blacks, the council regarded the Maroons as their chance to stabilize the settlement in West Africa. It awaited confirmation of the Maroons' loyalty, and George Ross happily provided it. The Scot had spent almost a year with the Maroons in Nova Scotia before embarking with them to Sierra Leone. Most recently, on the voyage across the Atlantic he had witnessed the Maroons' active involvement in the capture of *El Angel,* a Spanish ship. He had also seen firsthand that the Maroons could be trusted to quell a mutiny by the crew on board. He never doubted that the Maroons would ally with the British official administration and not with rebels, white or black. Ross's confidence in the Maroons echoed George Walpole's faith in them in Jamaica: both men accepted black soldiers as natural allies against enemies of British authority.[10]

In the intimate quarters of the ship Ross's paternalism was apparent. He held prayers each day and taught Maroon children—he called them scholars—the tenets of Christianity. He distributed mangoes, guavas, bananas, and coconuts to the families. He made note of two births on ship: Sam Stone's wife delivered a daughter and Elsy Jarrett gave birth to a son. Jarrett's son was fathered by Captain Charles Shaw, a Maroon who John Wentworth believed was particularly irredeemable. Shaw claimed not to be related to "Elsee Jarrett" or his son. She would, fifteen years later, petition as a single mother to live in her own lot.[11]

Ross's familiarity with the Maroon officers and with at least one Maroon woman was apparent. Ross confided select memories about Sierra Leone to both Captain Andrew Smith of the Preston Maroons and Captain John Palmer of the Boydville group. As he did with Walpole and Wentworth, Smith emerged as the favorite. Like whites in Jamaica and in Nova Scotia, Ross referred to the Maroons by their last name or their full name and did not use merely their first name, as slaves were addressed. Further, he referred to the men by their habits or temperament: "drunken Bailey," "old stupid grumbling dog Davy Bonard," "noisy and troublesome" Jarrett, and the "good old man" whom Ross esteemed greatly, Montague James. Much less authoritarian than Wentworth, Ross nonetheless shared the roving tendencies of Nova Scotian administrators: Ross too had relations with a Maroon woman—Bailey's daughter, Rozey.[12]

The Maroons' military experience offered Ross, an enterprising Scot, an opportunity to advance his own position. He had served as a clerk for the Sierra Leone Company for at least two years and, while on sick leave in London, had committed to superintending the Maroons during the journey from Nova Scotia to Sierra Leone. He understood that the small number of whites and the vulnerability of the settlement offered him an unprecedented possibility. Upon his return to Sierra Leone in 1800 he believed he witnessed improvement: "The Settlement is certainly improving fast in point of health—I wish my Face [?] may say the same three years after this." By offering the Maroons as an auxiliary military force, he would align himself with British interests and secure a tenured position. Like Alexander Ochterloney in Nova Scotia, Ross envisioned himself as a liaison between the Maroons and the empire. Ross came on shore the first night and assured the council that the Maroons had arrived healthy and that their conduct throughout had been "orderly and submissive in a degree unusually seen even among the most uncivilized people." Despite his compassion for the Maroons, Ross was a man of his time and could not imagine the Maroons as being culturally equivalent to whites. The following day Ross introduced six men who comprised the military leadership of the Trelawney community—Preston's influential military leaders, Montague James and Andrew Smith, as well as Boydville's head, John Palmer, were among them. The tensions that had divided the Trelawney Town Maroons in Jamaica and in Nova Scotia seemed to have temporarily ended when they landed in Freetown, and they presented a united front.

The Maroons' reputation for courage and toughness had preceded them.[13] According to Ross, the councilors expressed "admiration at this specimen of Maroons—far exceeding their beliefs." Governor Ludlam's initial attitude toward the Maroons, however, took Ross by surprise. When Ludlam gave a speech instructing the Maroons on the situation that confronted the settlement, he refused to make eye contact with them. Ross observed that Ludlam "kept looking at the ground and never looked any of them in the face all the while." The Maroons, Ross knew, admired everything that is "open and has a Manly presence." Ross could not read Ludlam's motivation. Perhaps the twenty-three-year-old Ludlam, who had arrived in Sierra Leone in 1798 and had experience only as a printer's apprentice, was overwhelmed by the awesome Maroons.[14]

A high proportion of young men had comprised the tiny Sierra Leone elite since its founding. But the first leaders had more experience in colony building than Ludlam. Zachary Macaulay, who had served as governor from 1793 to 1799, was thirty years old when he began his tenure, but he had already served as an overseer in a Jamaica plantation for five years. William Dawes, who served in the council with Macaulay, had been part of the initial British settlement of white convicts in Botany Bay and knew the issues around colonizing a frontier region. But the frequency of illness and death in the colony, its peripheral stature in imperial eyes, and its supposed frontier context in relation to the British American colonies led to high turnover. To whites, Sierra Leone represented a distressful exile from what was familiar and dear. As Macaulay wrote to his sister in February 1795, "I am already so metamorphosed that you would scarce know me were you to see me." The colony attracted whites who had no administrative experience or returnees with few alternatives. Ludlam may indeed have been nonplussed as he confronted an old cadre of Maroon leaders. It is impossible to know the exact ages of the Maroon officers, but repeatedly Ross referred to their leaders as an elderly lot: "Old Jarrett," "Old Montague," "Old Palmer," "Old rebel," "Old Tom Bucknor," "Old Hutchins Stone," and "Old Stone."[15]

Prior to the Maroons' arrival, Sierra Leone's founders had imagined multiple scenarios in regard to the Maroons' relationship with the Nova Scotians. In London the directors had unavoidably overheard some of the heated conversations concerning the Trelawney Town Maroons as they considered their realities. In 1799 they weighed the risks of admitting an exiled community of war veterans against the advantages of adding settlers to their establishment. On the one hand, over five hundred settlers, managed properly, would stiffen the settlement's backbone as well as promote the colony's humanitarian mission. Henry Thornton declared that the Sierra Leone Company's assumptions about colonization by the Maroons followed their earlier acceptance of the Nova Scotian blacks: "I mean the wish of contributing to the Civilization of Africa and to lessen the evils of the slave trade." New arrivals could act as intermediaries, securing and extending antislavery in the region.[16]

But the company's directors also worried about the Maroons' political temperament. The black Loyalists who arrived in Sierra Leone from Nova Scotia in 1792, just eight years earlier, had not conducted themselves in the manner of grateful and loyal settlers. Neither had an earlier group of economically distressed blacks from London who had reached Sierra Leone in 1787; many of these settlers had fled to join the English slave factory in nearby Bunce Island, just eighteen miles upriver from Freetown. Neither group had advanced the interests of the company. And the Maroons were an unknown people. Approximately 150 Maroon men could be a tremendous military boon to the colony—or cause its undoing. A potentially beneficial force, the Maroons might just as easily buttress the strength of the Nova Scotians, many of them rebellious and suspicious of white authority; the two black groups could form an alliance and topple the weak colonial regime.

The company also feared the Maroon refugees might become incendiary aliens. Some councilors even asked if the Maroons were accustomed to "animal vs. vegetable food." The Maroon families were polygamous, mostly non-Christian, and had more experience on battlefields than in agricultural labor. Most worrisome, the Maroons had recently proven themselves to be dangerous enemies of British authority in Jamaica. The council asked for details about the "abilities, dispositions, and past habits and conduct" of the Maroons, fearing the immigrants "will require to be ruled with some degree of strictness." Governor Ludlam worried that the "fierce and independent" Maroons would "indulge their wandering spirits" and cause trouble by trespassing on lands not claimed by the Sierra Leone Company. A people accused of practicing a "wild and lawless freedom" hardly warranted trust.[17]

From the first, the Sierra Leone Company advocated separating the Maroons from the Nova Scotians; they feared the latter's influence over the former would create volatility that the colony was ill-equipped to handle. As the council noted, the "turbulent disposition of our present settlers [the Nova Scotians]" could contaminate the newcomers; the Maroons would become of a "similar cast" by mixing with the Nova Scotians and create expense and disorder for the settlement. The Nova Scotians' desire for representative institutions, landownership, and civil equality was regarded as evidence of their litigiousness and insubordination; they could not be allowed to taint the Maroons. The council conveyed its determination to isolate the Maroons: "We shew no inclination at all to admit the Maroons into our colony—you will perceive this."[18]

But the Maroons could not be settled too far from British oversight. If placed too distant from Freetown, the Maroons could alienate African chiefs, who would retaliate by attacking Sierra Leone. Sierra Leone's leaders knew better than to let the Maroons disturb the precarious balance the colony had established after some dozen years.

The colony's directors made plans for the Maroons' settlement that would leave nothing to chance. The Maroons, the company decided, would need proper tools for horticulture and husbandry to promote cultivation in the colony. When the Duke of Portland ordered that the Maroons embark from Nova Scotia, he instructed that they take "their implements of agriculture" with them. Although the Maroons had expressed no desire to cultivate in Preston, the principle of transforming free blacks into a population of self-sustaining farmers persisted. As the duke described the Maroons, "They were accustomed in Jamaica to raise their own provisions, to build their own huts, and in short, to depend upon themselves for every necessary of life." Perhaps Sierra Leone's ideal settlers were not ex-slave Christian families influenced by republican principles, that is, the Loyalists, but a free community like the Maroons, long acculturated to living in tough conditions.[19]

Both Portland and the company directors proposed incentives to encourage the Maroons to construct the farming settlement they envisioned for them. Black settlers should get premiums for cultivating land, raising fences, keeping a specified acreage under cultivation, and rearing cows. Temporary huts could store their provisions and provide accommodations. Buildings would include mud houses for the Maroons, a government house for the superintendent, a storehouse, a church, a schoolhouse, a surgeon's house, and a kitchen. As it was expected that the Maroons would arrive in the dry season, Sierra Leone's government assumed that they "will have nothing to do but erect huts for themselves." The company rejected the possibility of constructing homes for their arrival; ingeniously they noted that the Maroons should erect their own homes because "our taste in buildings might not accord with theirs."[20]

The company had originally decided that the Maroons should settle eight miles from Freetown on the Bullom Shore, the north side of the Sierra Leone River, where the company had paid an annual rent since 1793. There would be no connection with the Nova Scotians, and the Maroons would remain "very much under our [government] Eye." The Maroon establishment would formally bring the region under British jurisdiction; as Ludlam wrote, "Our right will thus be preserved." Otherwise, if no labor was bestowed upon it, "it will inevitably revert to the natives the moment our farm is given up." But the Nova Scotians' rebellion transformed the company's priorities. Despite the investment the company had already made in the Bullom Shore, by the time the Maroons actually arrived in Sierra Leone Governor Ludlam, with strong encouragement from Ross, thought it better to keep them closer to Freetown.[21]

The newly arrived Maroons quickly grasped the opportunity presented by the upheaval in the settlement. Upon meeting the governor, Montague James proffered the Maroons' allegiance in no uncertain terms. They had left Nova Scotia because it had been too cold for them. They liked "King George and white man well—if them settler don't like King George nor this Government—only let Maroon see them." As reported by Ross, Captain Andrew Smith repeated Montague Smith's words in a kind of "explanatory repetition." Smith's higher fluency in English benefited him in his relations with Walpole in Jamaica and Wentworth in Nova Scotia and remained valuable vis-à-vis Ludlam in Sierra Leone. In the same way they had preserved British security in Jamaica by catching runaway slaves, the Maroons would protect British interests in Sierra Leone by suppressing the Nova Scotian rebels. As the council recorded, the Maroons "with one heart and one voice" expressed their "cheerful consent." The Maroons' loyalty remained on the side of the monarch; it encompassed protecting the slavery establishment of Jamaica as well as the antislavery settlement of Sierra Leone. The Maroons reproduced royalism in Sierra Leone.[22]

The Maroons' royalism stood distinct from the allegiance Nova Scotians expressed toward King George. The black Loyalists too vowed loyalty and declared gratitude to their king. Members of the Sierra Leone Council had noticed that the "mere name of the king will have an influence upon them [Nova Scotian settlers] which it would be vain to expect from the highest obligations of gratitude" to the company. From this experience, the local administrators had advised Sierra Leone's directors that the "name of king be used as much and that of the Company as little as possible" in their interactions with the Maroons. But the Nova Scotians' sense of loyalty differed from that of the Maroons in important ways. Recent refugees of the American Revolution, the ex-slaves regarded whites suspiciously and vigilantly guarded their political and religious autonomy. They maintained their own Methodist, Baptist, and Huntingdonian churches in Sierra Leone, separate from those established officially by the government. The Maroons, on the other hand, had shared an intimate, even affectionate, relationship with some Jamaican whites before the rebellion of 1795. In Sierra Leone, the Trelawney Town Maroons sought to reestablish relations with the white administration, to replicate their protected position in a new context. Their royalism embraced local white leaders as well as a distant king.[23]

Ready to fight to defend order for Governor Ludlam and King George, the Maroons had not, however, forgotten their betrayal by the Jamaican legislature. The memories of their own deportation compelled them to question taking a possible role in suppressing the Nova Scotians. As the council reported, "It was recommended by Maroons themselves (a circumstance worthy to be recorded as it does honor to their character) to try once more the effects of another of mercy and accommodation." The Maroons urged the council to come to terms with the rebels, and Ludlam used the presence of the Maroons as a negotiating tactic. He sent a declaration to the rebels: "Governor and Council have now a considerable military force under a king's officer. It is plain that further resistance can only shed blood without use." Ludlam guaranteed that those who surrendered would not suffer death. Likewise, Captain Lionel Smith issued a military ultimatum to the rebels in which he warned that the Maroons would "allow no quarter."[24]

Only a few Nova Scotians surrendered. As the council noted, they continued to treat with "contempt all subsequent offers of accommodation and money." Having no direct experience with an autonomous community of black veterans in the "old thirteen" colonies or in Nova Scotia, the black Loyalists could not have imagined the Maroons' cohesiveness or military effectiveness.[25]

On October 2, under the supervision of Lieutenant Lionel Smith, George Ross, and some invalid soldiers, the company planned a three-pronged attack against approximately fifty black Nova Scotian Loyalists. About forty to fifty natives, men employed in navigating the company's boats, sided with the British government in repressing the rebellion. Another thirty Nova Scotians remained loyal to the government, of whom six served as guides for the Maroons. The sudden appearance of a tornado compromised the British military efforts, so that only one unit finally moved to attack the rebels. It proved sufficient. The rebels dispersed almost immediately. The culmination of years of discontent, the uprising ended in hours. Ross praised the Maroons as a "set of the finest fellows and the best Bushmen ever was."[26]

Sierra Leone's administrators moved immediately to restore order to the colony. On October 3 Ludlam warned neutral Nova Scotians to stay in their homes, for Maroons would "fire on a flying enemy." Simultaneously, the company promised a one-hundred-pound reward for anyone who could produce rebels hiding in the mountains. One of the chiefs of the Temne nation promptly brought in three rebels. In the end, thirty-five rebels were captured. Two leaders were executed; their conspirators were compelled to work in the public works. Another twenty-five rebels, including one man who called himself British Freedom, were sent to Bullom Shore, the very destination earlier imagined as ideal for the Maroons. By October 15 a new charter abolishing representative institutions for black settlers arrived from Britain.[27]

The Maroons' skill in guerrilla warfare and their bravery under conditions of duress proved to be a mixed benefit to the Sierra Leone Company. On the one hand, they demonstrated the value of black veterans in West Africa. But on the other, their experience could not compensate for their unfamiliarity with the local context, which was only superficially similar to that in Jamaica. On October 3 the Maroons mistook African native laborers loyal to the British administration for Nova Scotian rebels and shot them. In Jamaica inexperienced British troops confused trusted slaves with rebellious Maroons, with the result that they killed British allies; in Sierra Leone the Maroons misidentified neutral natives as rebellious Nova Scotians and did the same. One native died immediately, and the second had to have his hand amputated. The council lamented the mistake, but the members' low estimation of African life precluded any serious concern about the tragedy. To them, the shootings were simply further evidence of the Maroons' vigor.[28]

The Maroons' military leverage compelled white concessions. In the aftermath of the rebellion, the Maroons refused to commit to a written agreement with the Sierra Leone government. They grounded their decision on the betrayal they had sustained in Jamaica, where Lieutenant Governor Balcarres had breached a treaty they had signed voluntarily. As Montague James explained, "They had determined never to put their hands to any public paper in the future, though they regarded their verbal assent as equally binding with their signature." In Nova Scotia they had refused to sign any paperwork that stipulated how they were to behave in Sierra Leone. The council casually dismissed the import of the Maroons' refusal. It was more "formal than essential" and, if insisted upon, would only "sour their minds" and "indispose them to render those services which were so much wanted." In an age of written constitutions, the council effectively acceded to the Maroons' veto. Verbally, the Maroons agreed to obey the existing government, make no attempt to take land beyond company territory, bear arms in the company's defense, and leave all matters of the natives and slave traders to the government without "murmurings."[29]

Everyone left in the colony, it seemed, benefited from the suppression of the Nova Scotians' insurrection. The council no longer bothered about the refractory conduct of the Nova Scotians that had degraded the government in the eyes of some natives. Eight Maroon leaders received fifty pounds each for their service in the rebellion. As he had hoped, Ross received favors in kind from the council. A month after the suppression of the Nova Scotians, it recommended him as superintendent of the Maroons, with rent-free housing and an annual salary of two hundred pounds.[30]

Before the Maroons' arrival, the company had imagined two alarming scenarios: a dangerous alliance between Maroons and Nova Scotians or explosive hostility between the Maroons and the natives. The Nova Scotians' rebellion transformed the Maroons' fate. Months of deliberations about keeping them isolated came to naught. Ross, as the new superintendent, recommended that they should be "settling [in] the back of the present settlers on this side of the water." Granville Town, just two miles from Freetown and on the same side of the river, became the Maroons' first home in Africa. Maroons would serve as standby militia and showcase an example of British strength. Both dependent and dependable, they appeared ideal imperial allies.[31]

The Maroons' residence in Granville Town, moreover, precluded confrontation with natives outside of the company's supervision and limited the chance of a Maroon-provoked native assault against the colony. A year after the rebellion the council marked the year of peace by celebrating the anniversary of the "late unnatural rebellion" as a day of "public thanksgiving to the Almighty God." The Maroons had strengthened the company's foothold in West Africa.[32]

But then the unimaginable happened. The presence of the Maroons as well as their military display of strength disrupted the balance the company had long maintained with its neighbors along the West African coast. More than in earlier years the settlement took on the appearance of a garrison rather than a weak trading base, triggering a political alliance between the ostracized Nova Scotians and some native groups. The last native attack against the colony had occurred in 1789, when the Temne entirely destroyed the Sierra Leone establishment in retaliation for the burning down of their village by an English captain. Since that time the colony had largely avoided any large-scale opposition by offering presents and forming shrewd alliances with heterogeneous native groups who feared losing their influence. Since 1795 it had also hosted fifty representatives from the Foulah, the powerful Islamic community to the north. Unknown to the company, however, rebel Nova Scotians and local African groups had joined to weaken the power of the white establishment.[33]

Warning signs appeared in October 1801, when nearby chiefs told a few hundred native laborers, referred to as Grumetta, to return home. The Grumetta worked as domestic servants and laborers but did not make their permanent homes in Sierra Leone. As long as Sierra Leone provided attractive trade goods these laborers found value in selling their labor. But the company had long known that the pool of workers was unreliable: a dispute with a nearby chief could occasion a sudden departure of all workers.[34]

On November 18 the Temnes, allied with the ousted Nova Scotian rebels, attacked the colony. At daybreak the Temnes, under their leader King Tom, forced their way into the unfinished fort in Freetown, Fort Thornton, and a desperate fight took place for two hours. The Maroons again displayed their military value to the British administration. Within minutes at least five British soldiers were killed and some company officials, including Ludlam's replacement, Governor William Dawes, were wounded severely. The first mayor of the colony, Thomas Cox, died immediately. After that, however, Maroons and loyal Nova Scotians took the brunt of the fight. Of the fifty-four settlers killed or wounded that morning, most were members of black families. By evening the combined British, Maroon, and Nova Scotian force had compelled the natives to retreat and occupied the towns they had left abandoned. But the natives did not disappear.

For nearly a month they maintained a "threatening formation" to the west of the colony, until they were finally dislodged on December 14. An ensuing treaty, signed on March 31, 1802, ceded the Temne land to the west of Freetown to the Sierra Leone Company but did not ensure peace.[35]

As it had in Jamaica, British authority in Sierra Leone depended on the visible presence of British troops. Just as the Maroon war in 1795 had followed the departure of regiments from the island, the monthlong winter war was followed by a second attack in April 1802 as soon as the British ship *Wasp* had left the Freetown harbor. This attack consisted of four hundred men of the Temne, some Nova Scotians, and some Susus from the eastern side of the colony. This time, however, the settlers were prepared. In less than thirty minutes King Tom's army was routed. The colony lost only a fifth as many men as the rebels, who suffered devastating losses, at least one hundred being killed or wounded. The Sierra Leone Council attributed both attacks to the natives' fear of the "growing power of the Sierra Leone settlement." The Maroons' arrival had signaled the expansionist aims of the colony, and an alliance of native groups sought to preserve their position.[36]

The Maroons lessened the company's dependence on natives. They allowed the colony to forego the risks of allying with African chiefs whose expectations of rewards remained unclear. Blessed with numbers and military force, the colony could afford to reject hiring the native soldiers offered by friendly African kings. In 1802 the Maroons provided a convenient substitute for native soldiers, whose allegiance lay with African patrons, not the British government. As the council observed, there was no reason to trust "allies of this description [natives] unless there should be a strong necessity for it." The colony also saved on the expense of maintaining native soldiers.[37]

With or without the Maroons, rumors about native advances kept the British administrators nervous during most of the first decade of the nineteenth century. In October 1802, less than six months after Henry Thornton praised the Maroons for their loyalty to the colony, he received disturbing news that some Nova Scotian rebels were buying powder kegs being sold by slave traders in Bunce Island. One clerk observed that it was "shameful [for slave traders] to supply them with powder to fight the white people." The opportunism of nearby slave traders raised the risk of another attack by armed rebels allied with natives.[38]

Since 1792 Sierra Leone's founders had committed to the colony, even in the context of the retrenchment in the antislavery campaigns, internal insurrections, and Anglo–French wars. Just a decade later, however, an official mocked the limited achievements of the company. Late eighteenth- and early nineteenth-century representations of the West African colony show virtually no views of the West African interior because British influence did not extend far. Insurmountable obstacles prevented the company's officials from building a thriving settlement with commercial connections to the interior. Whites feared the climate, and penetration into the hinterlands was opposed by African middlemen. Long-distance trade with native empires involved expertise beyond the scope of the company: establishing trusted African intermediaries, providing expensive gifts, and identifying loyal white and black settlers with familiarity in African customs. Disputes over land, trade goods, and the slave trade kept the administrators on edge.[39]

In 1802, as Sierra Leone's leaders confronted the reality of warfare, they understood only too well the demographic limits of their colony. Native Africans outnumbered settlers and soldiers in Freetown. Of the 551 Maroons who had reached Sierra Leone in October 1800, 515 remained in the colony two years later, 247 males and 268 females. Almost 40 percent were children. The Maroons represented 30 percent of the population of British Sierra Leone; most of the remaining 70 percent were Nova Scotians, still regarded as untrustworthy. Between the two groups of black settlers, fewer than 250 men could serve in the military defense. Because of the Maroons' earlier experience in warfare, more Maroon men than Nova Scotian men qualified for the militia. Fewer than 100 healthy British soldiers were stationed in Freetown. The colony's future depended not on its white or black settlers but on its formation of a deep alliance with African nations.[40]

8
Accommodation

In 1802 the Sierra Leone Company lost the will to continue its experiment in West Africa. Following the second attack by African natives allied with Nova Scotian rebels in April, the directors asked to relinquish the colony to the Crown. After fifteen years the dream of creating a model farming settlement based on the labor of free blacks had gone unrealized, as had the related vision of establishing a profitable trade with the interior in which exportable African produce was exchanged for British manufactures. Members of Parliament took five years to grant the company's request, embroiled as they were in the global war with France. The Treaty of Amiens, signed in March 1802, conceded a stalemate between the French and British Empires, but both sides remained wary, suspecting the deadlock was only a temporary truce. As Sierra Leone's future hung in the balance, the Maroons confronted disease and starvation in an underfunded and vulnerable establishment of minor importance in imperial eyes.[1]

At its simplest, the company's plan for Sierra Leone had entailed three processes: black settlers would create thriving farming settlements; their example would inspire Africans to set up plantations in the interior; and, finally, British traders would establish factories to exchange these "laboured products of the soil" for finished goods. Indeed, blacks, not white convicts, were desired for Sierra Leone because of the strong association made between plantation work and black bodies. The inextricable linkage of cultivation and trade and of both to the British economy was unmistakable. Years later Sierra Leone's ex-governor Zachary Macaulay summed up the "close connection there is between the regular and uninterrupted progress of agriculture within the [Sierra Leone] colony and its extension in the neighboring districts of Africa; and between these effects and enlargement of our trade with that country."[2]

The force of geography and local exigencies, more than ideology, militated against the establishment of a farming society. In 1800 the plan to shape the Maroons into farmers had been abandoned because of their more immediate utility as soldiers, but the prospect of farming in Sierra Leone had long been limited by the lack of arable land in the few square miles of coast controlled by the British company. The lush coastal vegetation that had impressed the botanist Henry Smeathman when he had proposed Sierra Leone as a settlement site in 1787 proved to be deceptive. Europeans assumed that the vegetation along the coastal area indicated the presence of fertile land in the hinterlands as well. But over the centuries, the tides of the sea had washed away the nutrients of the soil and left arid sands in its place. And the soil on the steep, wooded mountain slopes around Freetown had little depth, which made the land there also unsuitable for farming.[3]

British policy in Sierra Leone only grudgingly acknowledged the unsuitability of the coastal land for farming. The eighteenth-century conviction of an improving world was premised on a necessary connection between agriculture and commerce: British colonies would produce while the British economy, based on the metropole, would control the produce. The reality of the acidic and saline soil around Freetown did little to dispel this ideal.[4]

The founders of the Sierra Leone colony held farming to be important not only for what it could produce but also for how it would transform the bodies and minds of the colonists, presumed to be free blacks. The era of antislavery was also the age of agricultural utopianism. Thomas Clarkson expressed the assumptions so typical of evangelical reformers: without continuous work, immigrants would "retire into the woods and lead a savage life." Their removal from the fields would not only leave Britain without exportable produce but also deprive the empire of communities of respectable and dependable subjects. More than on treaties and gifts, British occupation of the region relied on the permanent presence of loyal settlers.[5]

The colony faced a more immediate crisis in the form of disease. But contemporaries knew that whites died quickly upon entering the tropics. This in fact prevented Parliament in 1787 from sending convicts to Sierra Leone. Although the colony was sufficiently remote to preclude the convicts' easy return to England, MPs argued that the British government could not send white convicts, some of whom were sentenced for minor infractions, to die there. Since the 1780s British visionaries intent on establishing settlements in West Africa had minimized the disease environment. Smeathman, for example, covered up the real causes of white fatalities in the region, blaming the deaths on "unwholesome" and "rancid" provisions, "intemperate lives," and "ardent spirits."[6]

Sierra Leone proved to be a burying ground for black settlers from Europe and North America also. In 1788 the evangelical founder of Sierra Leone, Granville Sharp, could not ignore the casualties suffered by the first group of 439 black and white settlers from London. They landed in Sierra Leone in May 1787—the malaria season. Only two-thirds of those who originally embarked were still alive after seven months. Sharp attributed the deaths to avoidable conditions: insufficient provisions, inadequate housing, and torrential rains. At least 34 people, he wrote, died in crowded ships before they reached the African coast, "so the climate of Sierra Leone is not to be blamed." Others died within the first four months because they "continued intemperate," lacked fresh provisions, and did not have time to build huts before the rainy season. Some remained unaccounted for not through sickness or death but from emigration; they had fled the settlement to live with the natives. Heavily invested in the success of Sierra Leone, Sharp dismissed climate as a detriment to colonization.[7]

But the evidence was unmistakable: American-born blacks did not survive the diseases in West Africa any better than whites. The pattern of death repeated itself when the Nova Scotia Loyalists arrived in 1792. In May of that year the Swedish botanist Adam Afzelius struggled to explain the sickness: "I found then a great confusion and want, particularly of houses and fresh provisions. . . . The evils have since that time daily increased . . . about 500 persons, over half the colony, is now sick and about 200 are already dead, and we have no Medical or Chirugical assistance, but from a very young surgeon who is ill himself." The British surgeon's notebook from 1793 captures the prevalence of sickness among black Nova Scotians. The notes were divided into columns listing the names of sick people along with their age, complexion, and disease; the last column was labeled "Recovered or Died." Although they had lived in desperate circumstances in Nova Scotia, black Loyalists had not suffered the same rate of fatalities in a colder climate. But the leaders of Sierra Leone continued to resist concluding what had become starkly apparent: transplanted settlers, white and black alike, died in large numbers in West Africa.[8]

Remarkably, in 1799, when the imperial government planned the Maroons' relocation from Nova Scotia to Sierra Leone, no one seriously raised concerns about the disease environment. The preoccupation with Nova Scotia's winters invited comparisons only with the less severe winters in West Africa, whose climate somewhat resembled

Jamaica's. The malarial summers in Sierra Leone never came up in discussions of the Maroons' fate. And yet the Maroons proved no more resistant to malaria and fevers than previous waves of settlers. In addition to his own sickness, George Ross recorded fatalities of Maroons within weeks of their arrival. Infants and the elderly were least able to survive the onslaught of the new environment. On October 22 John Ellis's child died; two more of his children would die in the next months. Two days later Bob Brown's daughter died. The next day, "Old Phibi Stone." On October 28 "Old Palmer gave up the ghost," as did a daughter of Thomas Harding. The next day the child of Sam Stone "gave up breathing." By November 7, barely a month since their arrival, 84 Maroons appeared on the sick list; a week later, 132. Two weeks later Ross remarked that the Maroon houses in Granville Town were "scenes of misery and sickness." Shaken, he recognized that the colony had a limited number of medical specialists: "Dear dear when will there be an end? I think I must commence surgery or apothecary or something." On November 22, when Captain Andrew Smith's youngest son died, Ross believed the baby had chosen wisely: the two-month-old infant saw trouble in the "smoky house" that was his world, decided "the sooner I'm out the better," and took his leave. By December 6, 22 Maroons had died and 155 were sick. Within three months the Maroon community lay devastated. Lacking adequate medical treatment, hospitalization, and shelter, the Maroons—"poor vagabonds," as Ross called them—struggled for survival. Ross recorded each death together with the name of the father or the husband. Major Bailey's daughter Venus gave up breathing on December 1. Another of Bailey's daughters, Nanny, died within the same week. John Ellis's daughter, Ann, died on December 24. Two weeks later Captain G. Lawrence's son and Captain Palmer's wife died. The names of the wives and mothers remain largely hidden.[9]

The deaths surprised the directors of the Sierra Leone Company in London. It "may have been reasonably expected," they wrote, "that persons inured to a hot climate would not have suffered in any material degree by their migration to Sierra Leone." The surgeon in Sierra Leone, Dr. Chadwick, tried to explain the reasons for the sicknesses. He pointed to the deficiency of food and the weakness of the very old and the very young upon their arrival in Freetown. In his journal entry for October 13 Ross noted that the Maroons sometimes received nothing to eat till late in the afternoon; he lamented that the "poor creatures have been truly starved since they came into port." Five days later he noted that bread and flour had "come to an end."[10]

According to Chadwick, the Maroons' ailments also came from the "strong bodily exertions" which were required of the most healthy of them on their arrival. He had in mind the Maroons' role not only in repressing the rebellion of the black Nova Scotian Loyalists but also in constructing homes in Granville Town in an environment thick with "heavy rains, night air and the intense heat of the sun in the daytime." Overwhelmed by the extent of disease, Chadwick criticized the Maroons for their suspicion of the medicinal cinchona bark. This "perverseness," he wrote in his letter to the governor, "retards their recovery." In much the same way that Wentworth had attributed the Maroons' frustration with Nova Scotia to their indolence, Chadwick blamed the Maroons' sickness on their pigheadedness.[11]

Cinchona indeed held the key to recovery, but even had the Maroons been willing to use it, there was not much of it available. Long before the Maroons' arrival, a shortage of the bark needed to combat malaria accounted for the high rates of death among white as well as black settlers. The British war with the French interrupted shipping; it created a shortage of food as well as of bark. Some of the bark that reached Sierra Leone was of such poor quality that it contained no alkaloids at all and did nothing to combat malaria. When whites such as Governor Zachary Macaulay became ill, they rested, ate regularly, and took the bark "plentifully." Some hid their illness to avoid showing any weakness to the natives and Nova Scotians. White administrators in high positions who trusted the curative capacities of the bark monopolized it; others who could not tolerate so precarious an existence found a ship back to England. Tropical medicine started to reduce the horrifying death rate only after the isolation of quinine from cinchona bark in 1820 made effective prophylactic treatment of malaria possible.[12]

Even in the face of all this infirmity, by late January 1801 the colony had assumed a modicum of normality. The onset of the dry season created healthier conditions for the Maroons. The surgeon reported that the sickness among the Maroons had almost subsided. Instead of worrying about Nova Scotian insurgents or the Maroons' health, officials began to focus on the Maroons' morals and their future establishment in the colony. They determined to draw a sharp line between polygamy and monogamy and to impart only to the monogamous "solemnity and dignity." Monogamy they associated with order and good character; polygamy, with the worst excesses of an un-Christian people. They also established a police force to maintain peace and good order in the settlement. Ross appointed trusted Maroons as constables. The newcomers would display orderly conduct, follow the company's rules, and become a model minority in Sierra Leone.[13]

But, as in the case of the Nova Scotians, the company's demands for quitrent from the Maroons sparked anger and unrest. Their resistance caught the company by surprise. One Maroon, Major Jarrett, refused to pay twenty cents per acre of land in an "inflammatory" manner. Other Maroons joined him, including Colonel Montague James, Major John Jarrett, Major Samuel Bailey, Colonel Thomas

Johnstone, and Captains John Parkinson and Nash Hamilton. Governor William Dawes, the more experienced returning governor who replaced Ludlam in January 1801, was convinced that the Maroons' refusal came from the "artful insinuation & misrepresentations of some disaffected Nova Scotian settlers." Keeping the new settlers in their place required a "watchful eye." Having learned his lesson from the Nova Scotians' rebellion just months before, Dawes made no allowances: "I told them not a man of them should have one foot of land in this colony without a positive agreement to pay the quit rent for it." Ludlam, aware of the colony's need of Maroon fighters, cautioned against Dawes's hard-line stance: he worried that opposition to the quitrent would unite the Maroons and the Nova Scotians against the interests of the Europeans.[14]

The Maroons' resistance to quitrent suggested that their allegiance to Sierra Leone's leaders went only so far. As the Maroons worked to construct homes in Granville Town, the governor remarked on their "industrial spirit." But his next comments revealed that the Maroons were far from subservient and their loyalty was far from blind. Dawes continued, "They are apt to be precipitate in adopting & engaging in any measures which coincide with the present temper of their minds, of course they are easily led astray." Already, the government was expressing concerns about providing rations for "absentee Maroons" who explored unknown opportunities outside of the company's oversight. Despite the Maroons' proven usefulness, the government perceived them as being too independent and hence potentially unreliable. The British administrators measured black settlers' loyalty by a single dimension: their willingness to subordinate their aspirations to meet the company's objectives in Africa.[15]

Even those Maroons inclined to make a home in West Africa found the local conditions challenging. The Nova Scotians' rebellion, along with the Maroons' sickness, had delayed the allocation of Maroon lots to the worst possible time: the beginning of the rainy season. The Maroons were not assigned plots until March 1801, far too late in the season to clear the land. They nevertheless planted small gardens and sought any kind of paid work to sustain their families. A few served as constables, and others were involved in public works. Some earned enough to purchase doors and windows for their homes. The Temne war in November 1801 devastated what little progress they had made. Fearful of catastrophe, the company, just two days after the assault, ordered the Maroons to evacuate Granville Town; a concentrated settlement in Freetown offered better defense to the colony. The relocation was catastrophic for the Maroons, as it meant abandoning their crops and depending on the company for scarce provisions. After the first year, the company came under no obligation to support the Maroons; anything additional was an act of charity.[16]

The Maroons' wretched circumstances swayed them again toward Jamaica. In May 1802 the directors' report to the House of Commons conveyed their disappointment. The Maroons, they observed, "universally harbor a desire of going back at some period of their lives to Jamaica and therefore may with more difficulty be induced by prospects of future benefit to labour for the improvement of their habitations or plantation." As they had in Nova Scotia, the Maroons resisted improving land they hoped to abandon. They were more interested in laboring for hire, and, indeed, some had become expert workmen already. As Henry Thornton summarized, the longing to return home rendered the Maroons "not easy to be governed and to be brought into that state of society which would best promote the civilization of Africa." A proud and independent people who saw Sierra Leone as only a temporary stop did not make for ideal colony builders.[17]

Disappointment impelled them. As they had in Nova Scotia, the Trelawney Town Maroons attached themselves to British sympathizers. They could no longer turn to Ross because he had left Sierra Leone in frustration eighteen months earlier, in July 1801, when the Sierra Leone Council refused to give him sufficient authority over the Maroons. He resented "fagging away for them [Maroons] in cold and heat." Ross too had become sick in the months he had spent in Sierra Leone. Just six months earlier, on January 16, he expected to die: "I thought I must have given up the Ghost." Professionally, Ross achieved nothing like the status accorded to Lieutenant Lionel Smith, who was knighted and, as Sir Lionel Smith, eventually served as governor of Barbados and then governor of Jamaica. Personally, Ross gave up his relationship with the Maroon woman Rozey. Just one month before leaving, he asked about her intentions of continuing with him and, as he recorded, "She said yes." But we know nothing more about his attachment to her or her regard for him.[18]

Ross's leaving appears to have left the Maroons without representation. His replacement, Lieutenant Henry Adlum, who had arrived in Sierra Leone with Dawes, served until September 1802, after which the Maroons were under the immediate authority of the governor and the council. Like Walpole, Wentworth, and Ross before him, Adlum depended on Captain Andrew Smith; Smith ensured that the Maroons punctually repaired roads and took part in other public service projects in Freetown. In 1803 the Maroons shared with Commodore Benjamin Hallowell their concerns about their new home—and their desire to leave it. As Hallowell conveyed to the House of Commons, "Nothing on earth would have given them more pleasure than such an event [evacuation] taking place when I was there." But this time they avoided submitting formal petitions for a second relocation for fear they should be thought "troublesome." Intuitively, the refugees understood the double-edged nature of the support of antislavery advocates: the same paternalistic well-wishers who opposed slavery as sinful and evil worried about the radical consequences of black equality. Blacks' appeals rather than blacks' confidence are what merited paternalism. The Maroons' obsequiousness won regard from Hallowell as it had earlier drawn praise from Wentworth and Ross: the Maroons appeared to be of "peaceable demeanor" and "cheerful acquiescence," exercised "spirited exertions against common enemy," and displayed respect for "due administration of justice." Their best chances of survival lay in showcasing their gratitude for and loyalty to all things British.[19]

Hallowell communicated the Maroons' disappointments to Parliament. Nothing had prepared them for such total dependence. Neither the climate nor the soil in Sierra Leone was anything like that of the mountains in Jamaica. They had received no rations since the Temne war in November 1801 had destroyed much of the town. They had no means of raising sufficient provisions to support their families, some of which numbered fifteen members. The land allotted to them in Granville Town had been rocky and largely nonarable. As the Maroon leaders told Hallowell, the land "did not yield them Indian corn enough for six months consumption of their different families." In Freetown, the "bug-a-bug" (ants) destroyed their yam and corn; they could grow only cassava. They begged for rice or flour. No vegetables could be found in the colony.[20]

The Maroons' very survival lay at stake. Some had already suffered deep wounds during the wars, while others continued to suffer sicknesses and die from diseases during the rainy season. In January 1803 Charles Spenser, the surgeon in the colony, noted that illness was higher among the Maroons than among the Nova Scotians. He attributed their rheumatism to moist floors, mud halls, and tiny dwellings. Those, he reported, whose houses were larger and who slept at a proper height above the floor were less affected. Thirteen Maroons, eleven men and two women, had died in the past five months alone. Reed Barnet had received a wound in his leg from the April 1802 attack that kept him permanently in bed. His three brothers had "sore legs of the worst kind," and his mother was in a "bad state of health." Having no rations, they were in "absolute want of food."[21]

As much as sickness and starvation, self-preservation haunted the Maroons. Lacking provisions, the Maroons hoped to cultivate the land taken from the Temne after their defeat in 1802. But they feared that the natives would not allow them to "remain in quiet possession of it." Hallowell noted that they "*cannot* and *dare* not venture out on account of the hostile disposition of the natives." He sympathized. One black settler was murdered on January 5, 1802, seven weeks after the first rupture with the natives. When the Maroons went to their farms to procure cassava, they went as an armed group of fifteen to twenty men "to prevent being surprized by the natives on their way there." They remained apprehensive about the safety of their families. As Governor Ludlam observed years later, unlike those in Europe, wars in Africa affected men, women, and children, as well as the armed and unarmed.[22]

In 1803 the Maroons' future appeared bleak. Hallowell noted that anxieties about native attacks and concerns over evacuation had created a terrible impasse: "No cultivation of any sort took place last year." And the colony, unfortunately, had lost some of the most valuable Nova Scotian cultivators after the rebellion in 1800—men who had been executed or banished. The war in the Sherbro region fifty miles to the south disrupted rice supplies. All the cattle had been killed for food after the first attack in November 1801. The governor and council purportedly borrowed rations allocated for Maroons, beef, pork, and flour, to meet the wants of the handful of undersupplied Europeans in the colony. The newly arrived governor William Day, a half-pay naval officer born in the West Indies, who reached Freetown in February 1803, acknowledged that he was obliged to "curtail allowance to Maroons." The company feared famine and waited urgently for provisions to arrive from Britain.[23]

Hallowell lost faith in Sierra Leone as the future home of the Maroons. He believed an allotment of cultivable land in the Banana Islands, thirty-six miles south of Freetown and at the mouth of the Sherbro River, was their best option. In fact, in 1799 this had been one of the locations that Sierra Leone's directors had considered for the Maroons. The Bananas, Sierra Leone's governor and council wrote, would be the "fittest place in the neighborhood" because of their "insular" location. The islands were also a convenient distance from Freetown, small enough to purchase, and large enough to sustain the next generations of Maroon families. Only about twenty "old people" lived in the island and, "upon approach of any person, they fly into the woods." Only two square miles of the Bananas were deemed adequate for the Maroons' needs.[24]

But negotiations for settling the Maroons in the Banana Islands had fallen apart in 1799, and in 1803 the Sierra Leone Council had no desire to repeat the experience. They had already spent time and energy on the Maroons' settlement in the Bullom Shore, Granville Town, Freetown, and, twice, the land ceded by the Temne nation. The council saw only two options: abandon the colony or transfer it to the Crown. Transferal was the only means of receiving compensation from Parliament for the land acquired and the buildings constructed in Sierra Leone. Moreover, if the colony was abandoned, the company's founders would garner no credit as initiators of British colonization in Africa. Instead, the company would appear as a harebrained scheme doomed to failure.[25]

To guard their reputation and to receive funds from the House of Commons, the company's agents created an extraordinary justification for transforming Sierra Leone into a Crown colony. The Maroons, they alleged, necessitated British supervision. In May 1802 they reminded the House that the original goal of the evangelical reformers was to promote antislavery campaigns in Africa and to Christianize Africans. In 1799 the company had worried that the Nova Scotians would taint the Maroon newcomers with their unruly political spirit; somewhat surprisingly, given the colony's purported function, the influence of the Nova Scotians' devout Christian faith on the non-Christian Maroons did not merit remark. Four years later the status of the majority of the Maroons as unbaptized heathens rose to paramount significance. Company officials suggested that, left unchecked, the Maroons' values, so antithetical to those of Britain, might spread to the natives in West Africa. If left without British missionaries in Sierra Leone, their "savage and warlike spirit" would turn against the natives.[26]

Moreover, the company represented the Maroons' military experience—their impressive service on behalf of British interests—as a terrible liability. Officials warned Parliament that the Maroons, in the absence of British governmental oversight, would contaminate Africa. If "unawed" by British might, they would think themselves superior to both Nova Scotians and Europeans and get involved in an "offensive war against the natives." Even worse, they would capture natives and become involved in the slave trade. Britain would have unwittingly imported slave traders to the shores of Africa! Good Africans—potential Christians—needed British intervention to ward off the irredeemable Maroons and their war-mongering potential.[27]

Cannily, the company diverted Parliament's attention from the difficulties that plagued British conversion efforts in Africa. For over ten years the company's attempts at converting Africans despite not having a deep knowledge of the languages and customs of African nations had met with disappointment. The administration faced ancillary expenses for printing books in native languages, travels into the interior, and maintaining schoolmasters and missionaries in native towns. Most damaging were the high fatalities of whites that discouraged white missionaries from settling in Sierra Leone. Decades later Thomas Clarkson remarked that two missionaries should learn an African language in case one died. Goals imagined in London did not match the realities of life in Africa.[28]

Hallowell's report placed the Sierra Leone Company on the defensive. In 1805 the directors cast doubt on his observations. They alleged that his pessimism stemmed from an unfortunately mistaken understanding of the local context. Hallowell, they said, had entered the colony during "a complete interruption of cultivation" and only a short time after the war with the natives. The colony, they insisted, had since improved and was rendered secure. They also deflected parliamentary attention away from the local context of war, hunger, and sickness to the global problem of slavery and left historians to do the same. At ex-governor Macaulay's behest, the company recommended that the Crown take the colony back and use it as a base to oppose the slave trade. The abolition of the slave trade would make Sierra Leone the "most important station on the coast of Africa." Its deep natural harbor provided the British a perfect naval base from which to interrupt the slave trade as well as an opportunity to expand its claims in the interior regions. Sierra Leone would remain in British hands, unlike other regions in West Africa like Goree Island, which could revert to the French under the terms of a peace treaty. Because Sierra Leone had never been a French colony, the British would never have to forego it. In fifteen years Sierra Leone shifted dramatically from

Granville Sharp's "Province of Freedom," imagined as a flourishing settlement of free blacks, to a naval base. Its prominence would come from its strategic location rather than its agricultural exports or its black colony builders.[29]

The antislavery vision of a free black colony in West Africa had been captured in the company's coinage, minted by the Soho Mint at Birmingham in the late 1780s. One side of the coin featured a lion couchant circled by the words "Sierra Leone Company." Underneath the lion was the word "Africa." The reverse side of the Sierra Leone coin depicts, in low relief, two hands, one of them, delicately etched to represent that of a black person, clasped in the other, which is white. This side also had the denomination of the coin and the date of issue. Twenty years later the symbolism seemed impossibly far-fetched. Still, Thornton did not find his colony deficient. "You and I," he wrote in 1807 to Ludlam in Sierra Leone, "shall not repent at the close of our lives, of the sacrifices which we have respectively made with a view to the interests of the Black part of our species." Thornton claimed founders' pride.[30]

As discussions between the company's directors and the MPs continued in England, the Maroons appeared to have adjusted to the inevitability of their situation. By 1805, despite the distress caused by lack of medicine and food, they had become reconciled to their new life in Sierra Leone. Their situation improved as the company fortified the settlement, mounting twelve cannon and building a wall two feet thick and eleven feet high. As anxieties about attacks from neighboring natives gradually subsided, the Maroon families received land allocations, granted free of quitrent.[31]

The Maroons also became part of the standby military force of the colony. In December 1799 the company had taken a chance on them, hoping to convert the "fierce lawless vagabonds" into "dependent allies." The Maroons had proven themselves many times over. By July 1803 a militia composed of 270 black men, of whom at least 140 were Maroons, served as the colony's defense force. Like slave-soldiers who served in British regiments and protected British territories in the West Indies, the ex-slave communities of Maroons and Nova Scotians protected British imperial interests in Africa. Aware of its new vulnerability after the two attacks, the company also employed friendly natives on an annual salary to counteract the designs of enemy natives.[32]

An extraordinary letter sent by the Trelawney captains, Andrew Smith and Charles Shaw, indicates that the Maroons increasingly saw life in Sierra Leone as a plausible alternative to returning home. The captains addressed the letter to William Dawes Quarrell, the Jamaican superintendent who had traveled with them to Nova Scotia and stayed with them in Halifax until 1798. They clearly held him in their affection. In a last effort to bring together their divided community, the two Maroons implored Quarrell to reunite them with their kin still in Jamaica. But instead of asking to go home, they implored Quarrell to transport their remaining families *from* Jamaica *to* Sierra Leone.[33]

Writing as representatives of the entire community, Smith and Shaw emphasized the Maroons' military service, their orderly living, and their allegiance to the British establishment. They highlighted their roles as leaders, as captains in a military corps of one hundred men comprised of Maroons and Nova Scotians. In 1804 a military officer in London had remarked on the benefits of extending military privileges to blacks in the West Indies, as it excited a "feeling of attachment, of fidelity and loyalty to the country." The Maroons' letter proved him right in yet another context. Smith and Shaw praised the stability of their settlement and lamented that, had they arrived in Sierra Leone in 1796 rather than 1800, they might have "been instrumental in preventing the natives from making war on this place, or even thinking of such a thing." They went on to say they lived well, in "good framed houses." They esteemed both the king and George Walpole, whom they continued to remember fondly. If Smith had christened his son George Walpole, the Maroons named a road in Freetown Walpole Street. They vowed loyalty to the monarch and hoped they would "prove true to our King and country, and never forget to celebrate his Birthday (the 4th of June) with heartfelt gratitude."[34]

The arrival of Sierra Leone's new governor, Captain William Day, in February 1803 marked a shift in the Maroons' demeanor. Day's praise of the Maroons in 1805 hints at the magnitude of their accommodation to Sierra Leone, or what he called an improvement in the Maroons' character. Day observed that the Maroons had relaxed their overall militancy: "The practice of going armed on all occasions and of firing their muskets in town are left off." The Maroons adapted to the task of making an impregnable establishment. They constructed fortifications and labored in public works projects in Freetown, asking for high wages. They worked as carpenters, sawyers, and masons and encouraged their children to take up apprentice positions to learn mechanical skills. Captain Smith's oldest son, John Smith, was a carpenter by 1820.[35]

Other Maroons adjusted to new kinds of work. In 1815 Captain Shaw was listed as running a one-room licensed public drinking house in Freetown. He was not alone. Another Maroon, Sally Harding, was also on that list. One of her relatives, Thomas Harding, would become a shopkeeper. One of the Maroons who had received Christian schooling in Nova Scotia, John Thorpe, became assistant to the schoolmaster in 1803. Applying their experience in metalsmithing, the Maroons became some of the first silversmiths in Freetown. As a group, the Maroon men resolutely turned away from fieldwork. The Maroon James Sacville, who cultivated twelve acres of cassava, rice, corn, yam, cocoa, and sugar west of Freetown, was an exception.[36]

The Maroon community followed the law, acted as jurors, served proudly as constables, and respected British authority. In 1808 at least three Maroons, one of whom was Captain Shaw, served as police. One Maroon woman's keen remark captures the Maroons' confident self-appraisal. She shrewdly observed that the titles of native chiefs and the title of white administrator did not mean much, next to the military experience of the Maroon constables: "In this country every where King, every where Governor; *not one so good as half a constable.*" She echoed Montague James who, when he wanted to put someone in his place, challenged, "Who are you? You're Nobody." A military pride kept the Maroons distinct and aloof from natives.[37]

By 1808 some Maroon children showed a new acceptance of Christianity and monogamy. Day welcomed the Maroons' absorption of the religious and cultural mores of the black Nova Scotians. He exulted in this development: "Without any *direct* influence being used by their superiors to induce them to follow European cultures several of the younger Maroons married and baptized their children." The Maroons' initial encounter with Nova Scotians in the context of rebellion did not lead to permanent hostility. Just three weeks after the insurrection, when the rebels were banished to the Bullom Shore, Colonel Montague James appealed to the governor on their behalf, for "the Maroons did not wish any people should be drove away from their places for them." The Trelawney Town Maroons remembered too well the injustice of their own deportation.[38]

From the very beginning the Nova Scotians exerted a formative impact on the Maroons, including their growing receptivity to the

Christian faith. John Ellis, one of the Maroon settlers, succeeded the Nova Scotian Loyalist Cato Perkins as pastor in 1805. The Maroons had encountered Christianity during their four-year stay in Nova Scotia through Wentworth's proselytizing. The Boydville Maroons entered Sierra Leone as a Christian community. Although the older Maroons stayed away from the church and Christian teachings, as they had in Nova Scotia, the group as a whole waged no sustained opposition to conversion. Indeed, less than three weeks after reaching Sierra Leone, George Ross eavesdropped on two Maroons who were arguing inside a church. A week later some Maroons requested that Ross read prayers over the grave of a loved one. And in July 1802, less than two years after the Maroons had landed in Sierra Leone, the first instance of a marriage between a Maroon man and a Nova Scotian woman was recorded. Between the first and third decades of the nineteenth century the Trelawney Town Maroons constructed their own church in Freetown. But, despite their contact with Nova Scotian Loyalists and their growing interdependence, the Maroons' sense of having a separate identity from other black settlers persisted: the church they called Maroon Chapel survives to this day.[39]

Colonel Montague James's sway carried beyond Jamaica and Nova Scotia. Starting on April 21, 1801, he received a weekly pension of one dollar. In 1807 he received two hundred dollars annually. The Maroons' pre-Christian rites traveled with him. In October 1800, when a Maroon woman named Fanny was stabbed in the breast by a Maroon man with the name of Barnet, Colonel Montague James sang a "Kormantyn song" that "electrified" all who heard it. The Englishmen in the colony believed that the Maroon song expressed loss and sadness. But Ross noted that the lyrics expressed outrage toward the man who had tried to kill Fanny: "Blood has been shed. . . . Shaw Barnet has done the deed—he has fled—let him be pursued and taken that justice—vengeance may seize him." The Maroons called on their ancestors to pursue and punish Barnet. Perhaps they succeeded. Barnet, after trying to kill the daughter of Fanny Williams, shot himself. It is likely that this was the same Barnet who had "thumped" Elsy Jarrett in Nova Scotia.[40]

Death rituals persisted in Sierra Leone. Funerals occasioned drumming and drinking by all the Maroons. Ross found it "strange that Maroons should be sure to get drunk on the death of their nearest relatives." Each Maroon death meant a gift of rum from the council to the Maroon families; higher personages in the Maroon order demanded a higher apportionment. Ross gave half a gallon of rum for the death of an infant, and as many as six gallons for the death of a Maroon captain. The succession of Maroons' deaths mandated expenditures new to the British administration in Sierra Leone. The Nova Scotians, for all their litigiousness, did not "frolic" or demand rum after each death.[41]

Cultural practices aside, the Maroons in Sierra Leone sought to integrate into the British class. Having been born in a country that was part of the British Empire, they felt that put them in a position superior to that of native Africans. Absorbing Christian teachings from the Nova Scotian Loyalists and taking advantage of their own knowledge of English laws and customs, the Maroons came much closer to joining the British world than the natives did. By one estimate at least half the white personnel sent to Sierra Leone died of disease. The high number of whites' deaths favored free blacks: Maroons as well as Nova Scotians came to occupy the lower civil service positions in the government simply because they were alive.[42]

The Crown's takeover of Sierra Leone followed the British abolition of the slave trade in 1807. Like Jamaica and Nova Scotia, Sierra Leone became an official colony. As British naval vessels stationed in

Sierra Leone harbor captured slave ships and freed the enslaved, local administrators once again imagined transforming liberated slaves into active peasants. Cultivation kept people "more at home with their families," allowed for close supervision, and promoted conversion to Christianity. In 1808 Sierra Leone's newest governor thanked Providence for bringing natives who were "tractable, docile, and intelligent" and who should make up for the "defects" of the black settlers and "promote the interests of Great Britain in Africa." Of the more than 100,000 African slaves liberated from European slave ships, over half made their home in Sierra Leone and thus afforded British reformers another chance at atonement. The rescued slaves occupied the lowest rung in the social hierarchy of British Sierra Leone, and the Trelawney Town Maroons, who numbered 807 members by 1811, moved up the ladder to become essential to the administration in the colony. They joined the Nova Scotian blacks in becoming English instructors, Christian preachers, and conveyors of "civilized conduct." As the Maroons had known for generations, freedom lay in associating not with others of African ancestry but with the British.[43]

Sierra Leone's need for trusted employees blurred racial boundaries but did not eliminate them. Ludlam, the governor again in 1808, noted the difficulties in retaining Europeans in clerkship positions because of the low salaries: "A good clerk becomes fit for a higher situation: a bad one does more harm than good: the greater part of our European clerks have given us so much trouble, that we find it much better to employ Maroons or natives." In 1808, of the forty officers required for carrying out the duties of civil service in Sierra Leone, twelve were free blacks, both Nova Scotians and Maroons. But the separation between white and black was nevertheless explicit. Former governor Macaulay echoed the views of many abolitionists who believed that slaves needed a long preparation for freedom when he observed that all but subordinate positions in administration "must for some time to come be filled with able and intelligent Europeans." Again, in 1810, the need to fill official positions stood apparent, but black candidates were kept at a distance. As the council recorded, "However desirable it may be to bring forward black and color'd young men of merit, yet it would be extremely injudicious to advance them to the higher situations in the colony." British order depended on a three-tiered hierarchy, with whites on top, free blacks in the middle position, and natives at the bottom.[44]

Epilogue

In September 1841 a Jamaican agent drew notice of new arrivals to Jamaica: "The ship *Hector* and Brig *Commissioner Barclay* from Sierra Leone brought Africans and Maroons." Remarkably, four decades after being deported in 1796, some Trelawney Town Maroon families made their way back to Kingston. Their homecoming marked the intersection of two plantation labor systems, the first based on coerced and permanent unfree labor, the second on dependent and temporarily unfree labor. The Trelawney Town Maroons' deportation to Nova Scotia and their settlement in Sierra Leone belong within the history of slavery in the British Empire. The return of Maroon families to Jamaica indicates the beginning of a new era, one transformed by the abolition of slavery and dominated by the transport of overseas contract migrants. Worldwide events had touched the Trelawney Town Maroons in unthinkable ways: they left Jamaica as a free community and returned in the guise of indentured laborers.[1]

The Maroons who returned in 1841 can be identified both by their ages and by the persistence of last names adopted in Jamaica. In April 1799 Governor John Wentworth had singled out "Harding" and four other Maroons as incendiaries who should be separated from the other Maroons and sent off to some remote place. In 1841 a William Harding Sr., aged fifty-four, with three children, two of whom were twin boys, embarked for Jamaica. The typical African emigrants on these ships were between the ages of seventeen and twenty-five. Yet the passenger lists include some who were much older, men and women in their fifties who may have remembered Trelawney Town and the Maroon war or who were raised hearing stories about their birthplace. In addition to William Harding Sr. and his family, these passengers included Sarah Haney, fifty years old; Sally Stone, fifty-three; Mary Kidd, sixty; Diana Grey, fifty-two; George Barett, fifty-two; Peter Campbell, sixty-three; and William Lawson, at sixty-eight years of age the oldest emigrant. Others who returned were Rosey Johnston, fifty-five years old, along with five members of her family ranging in age from eighteen to twenty-five; Sophie Rickets, fifty-eight years old, along with twenty-five-year-old Nancy; and Ana Williams, aged fifty years, with her two daughters, Sophia and Rachel. Rickets and Williams had been widowed at least twenty years earlier. The high number of women-led Maroon families seeking to return to Jamaica is striking; it may indicate that Maroon men with property in their name and with military experience and artisan skills advanced faster in Freetown than widows or single women. A paternalistic empire upheld the patriarchal authority of Maroon households.[2]

William Wilberforce had imagined that a relocation to Africa would unlock an entirely new identity for displaced blacks. Like white Americans who reached back to England or Scotland for their ancestry, blacks would naturally turn toward Africa. In 1792 he had suggested substituting "Africans" for "blacks" and "Negroes" because it was a "more respectable way of speaking of them, and a means of removing the odium which every other name seems to carry with it." Contrary to Wilberforce's vision, the Maroons rejected the connection between complexion and home and shunned a future as Africans. Some, having "no mean opinion of their own importance," boldly suggested that a Jamaica-bound ship should be sent "purposely for them!" Decades after their arrival in Sierra Leone, whites too had no difficulty distinguishing between Maroons and liberated Africans.[3]

The Maroons' identity as a group survived two Atlantic relocations. A visible manifestation of the Maroons' family structure comes to us by way of lists kept by Maroon superintendents in each colony: the names of Maroon men, with their military ranks, were listed in long columns on the left, and across each row were the numbers of wives, sons, daughters, and other kin. By the early 1810s the Maroons had established a separate neighborhood to the west of Freetown. In 1813 Betsy Shaw, "[the] daughter of one of the Maroon settlers," petitioned to live "among her connections." In 1813 and again in 1816 the Maroon widow Nancy Jarrett noted that the Maroons quitted the east and moved as a body to the west of the town; she petitioned to move west to live among her "nation." The Maroons John Gray and John Libert, settlers of Freetown for sixteen years, wanted a town lot to the "westward of the town." Mary Brown, John Libert's sister, took over the lot when he died in 1819. In 1820 Daniel Parkinson, with his wife and two male children, requested land on the west end of Freetown. That both family men and widows sought to live in this neighborhood indicates the vitality and support derived from Maroon kinship.[4]

In 1821 the *Royal Gazette and Sierra Leone Advertiser* published a story about a former slave who returned from Spanish-ruled Havana to his home in Goree, near Senegal, in West Africa. Motivated by his desire "to finish his days on the land of his fathers and to bring his descendants with him," he brought his children and grandchildren, all free, to Goree. But the sons, who knew no other home but Havana and who were Spaniards in "language, habits, and modes of living," were "disinclined" to the voyage and "refused absolutely to pass from the Goree to the interior." They worried about the "envy, jealousy, and malignity" of Africans who would strip them of their wealth and sell them as slaves. Perhaps some of these same sentiments drove the Trelawney Town Maroons back to Jamaica.[5]

Only a resilient, creolized community would have dared to return to Jamaica. War, dispersal, disease, and death had not permanently destroyed the fabric of the Trelawney Town Maroons. Enduring the trauma of multiple relocations and vast uncertainties in remote regions far from Trelawney Town, the Maroons embarked again to confront yet another unknown. Their reasons for leaving Sierra Leone are fuzzy. Perhaps the liberated Africans, more knowledgeable about West African diplomacy, more familiar with African languages and terrain, and more useful to the British government, eclipsed the Maroons. They too, like the Maroons, adopted British names. Or perhaps the principle of legal equality offered to all blacks in Sierra Leone did not compensate for the privileged status the Maroons had held in Jamaica. In 1866 a British naval captain heard some Maroons boast about their descent from King Cudjoe. In the end the Maroons were neither Africans nor British but a precipitate of the Old World's encounter with the Americas—and its enslavement of Africans.[6]

We can hardly begin to imagine the Maroons' emotions as they searched for kin and assessed their place in a postslavery Jamaica. We cannot be sure that the Maroons welcomed the abolition of slavery, an institution they had protected to safeguard their own place. Without slavery, the Maroons' stature became terribly precarious. If abolition brought slaves freedom, it brought Maroons, an already free people, new competition for white patronage. But a people used to accommodation would adjust to another novel situation and again seek benefactors like George Walpole and George Ross. The Maroons knew from long personal experience that loyalty eased the burden of descent from a servile caste.[7]

The Trelawney Town Maroons seized on a short window of opportunity to return, an opening tied to the dynamics of slavery and emancipation and to the labor needs of postemancipation Jamaica. The end of slavery came gradually to the British Empire. The Abolition Act of 1833 came with a series of compromises and signified a victory of the conservative vision of abolition. The most ardent reformers feared that immediate emancipation would lead to social disorder: slaves would run away to establish jungle societies, and the plantations would face ruin. The Abolition Act therefore implemented a rite of passage, termed an apprenticeship, to deal with this potential problem: the legal state of slavery would be replaced by an intermediate period of semifree status in which ex-slaves would serve under white owners before they received full freedom. Under apprenticeship, ex-slaves worked fewer hours under supposedly less severe conditions but remained rooted in the same power dynamic with their former masters. Only in 1838, after the apprenticeship period drew to a premature end, did ex-slaves of white masters have the full legal right to establish independent households.[8]

A different set of rules applied to slaves held by Maroons. Under a special provision, those slaves received unconditional freedom in May 1835, three years before slaves owned by white masters.[9] Bereft of their slaves and forbidden apprentices, the island's Maroon communities turned to policing apprentices in much the same way they formerly policed slaves. A "Proclamation by the Governor addressed To the Negro Population Throughout the Island of Jamaica" (1835) addressed to ex-slave apprentices captures the paternalism of white planters, the alliance between planters and Maroons, and the social distance between Maroons and apprentices:

> My Friends: Our Good King, who was himself in Jamaica a long time ago, still thinks and talks a good deal of this island. He has sent me out here to take care of you and to protect your rights; but he has also ordered me to see justice done to your owners, and to punish those who do wrong. Take my advice, for I am your friend—be sober, honest, and work well when you become apprentices, for should you behave ill and refuse to work because you are no longer slaves, you will assuredly render yourself liable to punishment.
>
> It will therefore depend entirely upon your own conduct whether your apprenticeship be short or long, for should you run away you will be brought back by the *Maroons* and the police, and have to remain in apprenticeship longer than those who behave well.
>
> Bear in mind that everyone is obliged to work—some work with their hands, others with their heads, but no one can live and be considered respectable without some employment.
>
> Your lot is to work with your hands.
>
> I trust you will all be obedient and diligent subjects to our good King so that he may never have cause to be sorry for all the good he has done to you.

The balance of inclusion and differentiation among blacks remained key to white stability in the island.[10]

The end of the apprenticeship period in 1838 led British planter societies to a global search for new laborers. As thousands of ex-slaves cultivated holdings in small, detached plots of land, unwilling to abide the backbreaking work and disciplinary mechanisms of the slavery era, planters looked for alternatives. Without dependable laborers they could not compete with slave-grown sugar in Spanish Cuba and Portuguese Brazil, where slavery continued to flourish. Attempts to enlist plantation workers from Europe and the United States stalled, then failed. Next, they turned to Chinese and Indian workers, colored workers whose constitutions, the planters believed, prepared them to work in tropical fields and to save British sugar plantations from ruin. But before they turned to any of these workers, planters experimented with a region closer to home, from which they had acquired laborers for almost two centuries: West Africa.[11]

From the perspective of white Jamaican planters, liberated Africans in Sierra Leone were the ideal indentured laborers. The population primarily consisted of West and Central African families who had been rescued from slavery in Sierra Leone by the British navy after the abolition of the slave trade in 1807. By the 1840s more than fifty thousand freed slaves had joined the descendants of black Loyalists and Jamaican Maroons in Sierra Leone. The planters fervently hoped this scheme would save Jamaica; as one put it, there was "no doubt that Africans are the most suitable laborers for field cultivation in this climate." As the West Indian planters saw it, the Africans would benefit in obvious ways from an indentured servitude in Jamaica. To them, it was obvious that Jamaica was an improvement over the supposedly heathen conditions in Africa. Moreover, once in Jamaica, the West Africans would never be seized as slaves by African chiefs—if British ships had saved them from slavery the first time, Jamaican planters would rescue them from slavery a second and final time.[12]

Determined to avoid allegations of a covert resumption of the slave trade, British agents wooed liberated Africans to emigrate to Jamaica, promising fertile soil, liberal wages, and free institutions. In 1840 and 1841, 1,417 people left Sierra Leone in British ships, bound for the British colonies of Trinidad, Jamaica, and British Guyana. Remarkably, the passenger lists included Trelawney Town Maroons.[13]

The planters' blueprint to sustain their economy by importing African natives proved an utter failure. By 1843 Jamaican elites were baffled. As they saw it, natives of Africa were entering a favorable climate in which they obtained agricultural employment at high wages and benefited from the security of free institutions. Indeed, Jamaica was destined to become a highway for trade among nations around the globe. What had gone wrong with this scheme?[14]

The Africans refused to come. Familiar with the long history of trickery on which the slave trade relied, they refused to cross the ocean without hearing testimony from emigrants who had reached Jamaica. The labor agents knew that Africans' trust depended on regular and quick communication between Jamaica and Sierra Leone; for that reason they had ensured that the *Commissioner Barclay*, on its return trip to Sierra Leone, carried some Africans. The ship, however, was lost at sea. Having heard nothing about the conditions in Jamaica, the Africans in Sierra Leone imagined the worst.

The emigration scheme, already hampered by its association with slavery, never quite recovered from this early loss. Emigration agents in Jamaica had originally planned on four voyages between August and December 1841 that would carry thousands back to Jamaica; these preparations came to nothing. Women especially dreaded entering the "salt water." Emigration resumed in spring 1842 but never in the numbers expected.[15]

In the spring of 1844 only 139 adults of both sexes agreed to leave for Jamaica. The agents gave up. They concluded, "We have been hitherto unable, either through the instrumentality of their own countrymen, or the active exertions of our agent, aided by the influence of the colonial government of Sierra Leone, to make any sensible impression in favor of a removal to the West Indies upon the village population of that colony, or upon the neighboring tribes." By 1846 only 2,110 people from Sierra Leone had reached Jamaica. The representations of a Caribbean paradise could not erase the legacy of the slave trade, which precluded further immigration from West Africa. To most Africans—and undoubtedly for black Nova Scotians—Jamaica signified a foreign, terrifying place, one forever linked with enslavement and death. But for William Harding and other Maroon returnees, the island beckoned. Slavery, after all, had provided them a means of keeping alive.[16]

The Trelawney Town Maroons comprised a tiny percentage of the black population in Jamaica. They should not disguise the reality of Caribbean slavery founded on backbreaking work, terrible punishments, and heartbreaking mortality. Most runaway slaves did not become Maroons: they were captured and punished severely, banished, or killed. The survival of the Trelawney Town Maroons shows us the few and painful possibilities open to those seeking to escape enslavement. Freedom, to the Maroons, did not translate into a once-and-for-all movement into legal security, civil freedoms, and economic opportunities. It was a transitional state, bringing benefits unknown to slaves but nothing comparable to the place accorded to and titles reserved for whites. The Maroons, because they were creolized and had become increasingly cosmopolitan through their serial migrations, understood and resisted, time and again, this fundamental inequality. Loyalty could trump their African ancestry but only under special circumstances.

By examining the serial migrations of the Trelawney Town Maroons we capture something which otherwise would remain lost: the Maroons' repeatedly successful efforts at achieving self-emancipation.

After the 1738–39 treaties, the Maroons escaped the primary colonial punishment dealt to Maroons, that is, their communities were not destroyed and their people were not reenslaved. These treaties appear to be a terrible compromise if we imagine that families hiding, estranged from kin, individuals living in fear without readily available goods, are somehow more free than a community who lived by treaty with a colonial government. The treaties provided the Maroons a means to survive, by living a dependent existence, based on their connections with the plantations and their owners and on their indirect links to Atlantic trade networks.[17] As slaves in African societies found protection in conjugal unions with masters or through conversion to Islam, the Maroons in Jamaica escaped enslavement by accepting legal protection from the colonial government. In a slave society in which whites were vastly outnumbered by slaves, the Maroons' strategy—of resistance through accommodation—proved successful from the 1740s to the 1790s. They were not black Robin Hoods.[18]

We can best make sense of the Maroons' choices if we see them as enacting mini-emancipations, well before the era of British antislavery and well after the legal abolition of slavery.[19] Although legally free after the 1738–39 treaties, the Trelawney Town Maroons remained a marginalized community. As much as slaves who resisted violently and free blacks who launched legal struggles, the Maroons did everything possible to find a place in white society that protected their families from hunger, brutality, and banishment and guaranteed their children a future free of enslavement. The Maroons held on to African-derived beliefs about the meaning of the dead in the memories of the living, but they rejected an idealized past. Seen in this light, the Maroons' return to Jamaica in the early 1840s—another migration—represents another decision aimed at becoming more emancipated.[20]

The Maroons' choices in Nova Scotia and Sierra Leone reflect their ongoing struggle to preserve a privileged status in empire. During this "age of democratic revolutions," the Maroons did not win the 1795–96 war and were removed from the island.[21] But the Trelawney Town Maroons' decisions indicate that they viewed their deportation as a singular event, one without precedent or pattern—and potentially reversible. They did not lose faith in the empire or even in colonial governments. If anything, bereft of everything familiar to them, their loyalty intensified. In a moment of Atlantic upheaval, their steadfastness secured favors. The same antislavery momentum that had fueled the fears of white Jamaicans and led to their exile permitted the Maroons, in Nova Scotia, to turn the humanitarian tide in their favor to return to a tropical environment where they could survive without dependence. The same wars between Britain and France that had temporarily made their race more salient than their loyalty and led to their extirpation presented the Maroons with a critical intermediary role in Sierra Leone. In Freetown they offered their military service to the colonial government in return for preferential treatment over other subordinate groups. In each British colony they steered clear of the agricultural work associated with slaves, black Loyalists, and African laborers. In the political and ideological tumult that swept through the British Atlantic, they learned that loyalty ensured survival, mobility, even advancement. Most of all, attachment to the empire ensured their survival as a community.[22]

The time-space of the Trelawney Town Maroon serial migrations occurs within the framework of slavery and emancipation, on the one hand, and British expansionism and consolidation, on the other. The collisions and overlap between these two forces created a space for particular pressure groups and enabled the Maroons to keep alive the possibility of going home. In the midst of a costly war from without and antislavery agitation from within, the empire did, despite its contempt for people of African ancestry, use dependent black men as military allies and black families as colony builders in regions with insufficient white soldiers or settlers. In a period dominated by foreign threat and driven by strategic necessities, the empire made suitable accommodations: racial attitudes, which ranged from liberal paternalism to blatant racism, did not require racial exclusion. The Maroons' marginality made them unthreatening, their longing for the respect and freedom whites enjoyed made them exploitable, and their intense loyalty made them trustworthy. The Maroons had long served the imperial cause by protecting sugar and slavery in Jamaica. After 1795 the Trelawney Town Maroons became valuable to a larger British constituency: they served as a moral cause for evangelical abolitionists and an auxiliary military force to the Sierra Leone establishment; decades later, some entered Jamaica's ex-slave society as voluntary laborers. Their longing for home made them a useful people.[23]

Abbreviations

BC	John J. Burns Library, Boston College
BL	British Library, London, United Kingdom
CL	Clements Library, University of Michigan, Ann Arbor, Michigan
CO	Colonial Office Records
FBC	Fourah Bay College Archives, Freetown, Sierra Leone
JARD	Jamaican Archives and Records Department, Spanish Town, Jamaica
JCB	John Carter Brown Library, Brown University, Providence, Rhode Island
LAC	Library and Archives Canada, Ottawa, Ontario
MHS	Massachusetts Historical Society
NLJ	National Library of Jamaica, Kingston, Jamaica
NSA	Nova Scotia Archives, Halifax, Nova Scotia
RG	The Royal Gazette and Sierra Leone Advertiser
THL	The Huntington Library
TNA	The National Archives, Kew, United Kingdom

Notes

Introduction

1. The slaves outnumbered whites 13:1 in the island and 20:1 or 30:1 in the interior sugar estates. See David Beck Ryden, *West Indian Slavery and British Abolition, 1783–1807* (New York: Cambridge University Press, 2009), 134.

2. A large proportion of any given Maroon community was probably African-born. Note that Jamaican-born slaves had the additional possibility of escaping into urban areas because they blended in more easily with free blacks. Orlando Patterson underlines the connection between slavery and marronage: "All sustained slave revolts must acquire a Maroon dimension since the only way in which a slave population can compensate for the inevitably superior military might of their masters is to resort to guerilla warfare with all its implications of flight, strategic retreat to secret hideouts and ambush." Orlando Patterson, "Slavery and Slave Revolts: A Socio-Historical Analysis of the First Maroon War in Jamaica, 1655–1740," *Social and Economic Studies* 19, no. 3 (1970): 317. Scholars have intensively studied the Maroons in the Caribbean colonies and in North America. For some of the foundational work on Maroons in the Americas, see Richard Price, ed., *Maroon Societies: Rebel Slave Communities in the Americas* (Garden City, N.Y.: Anchor Books, 1973). For more recent work on Maroons in North America, see Timothy Lockley, *Maroon Communities in South Carolina* (Charleston: University of South Carolina Press, 2009); Nathaniel Millett, *The Maroons of Prospect Bluff and Their Quest for Freedom in the Atlantic World* (Gainesville: University Press of Florida, 2013); and Sylviane Diouf, *Slavery's Exiles: The Story of the American Maroons* (New York: New York University Press, 2014). Note that the Trelawney Town Maroons of Jamaica, subjects of the British Empire, may have negotiated from a stronger position than Maroons in what became the United States. Their odyssey ended not with separatism but with integration into the larger British

establishment; Herbert S. Klein defines the preconditions for marronage: see *African Slavery in Latin America and the Caribbean* (New York: Oxford University Press, 1986), 197.

3. Archaeological evidence indicates that Maroon bands in some islands were descendants of Arawak Indians. See E. Kofi Agorsah, "Scars of Brutality: Archaeology of the Maroons in the Caribbean," in *Archaeology of Atlantic Africa and the African Diaspora,* ed. Akinwumi Ogundiran and Toyin Falola (Bloomington: Indiana University Press, 2007), 344. One historian refers to the Maroons as half-castes, implying that the Maroon descendants of the eighteenth century originated in the era of Spanish rule in Jamaica. See Holden Furber, *Henry Dundas, First Viscount Melville, 1742–1811* (London: Oxford University Press, 1931), 101; Maroon communities also emerged in colonies such as Brazil, Colombia, Cuba, Ecuador, Española, Mexico, and Suriname. Some Maroons, who may have had experience in warfare in Africa, extended their military experience to a new context. Philip D. Curtin, *Why People Move: Migration in African History, the Sixteenth Charles Edmondson Historical Lectures* (Waco, Tex.: Markham Press Fund, 1994), 20; Supplement to *Royal Gazette,* April 30, 1796, to May 7, 1796, NLJ; Samuel Vaughan to Lewis Cuthbert, July 28, 1795, Votes of Assembly of Jamaica, JARD; David Geggus, "The Enigma of Jamaica in the 1790s: New Light on the Causes of Slave Rebellions," *William and Mary Quarterly* 44, no. 2 (1987): 275, 284; Gad J. Heuman, *Between Black and White: Race, Politics and the Free Coloreds in Jamaica, 1792–1865* (Westport, Conn.: Greenwood Press, 1981), 10–15. On their journey from Nova Scotia to Sierra Leone the Maroons carried not only aprons, shoes, kettles, and blankets but also petticoats and gowns, coats and vests, handkerchiefs and stockings; the ranking structure is apparent upon the Maroons' arrival in Sierra Leone. Approximately 140 Maroon men fought against African natives in 1801 in Sierra Leone. Of these, there were 18 captains, 2 majors, 1 colonel, and 1 general. See April 1, 1802, WO 1/ 152.

4. Work on Maroon communities in the Americas has been extensive and continues to grow. Scholars interested in the Maroons cover an incredibly broad range: they study Atlantic and Caribbean histories, European colonization and expansion, comparative African diasporas, geographical formations of Maroon-created homelands, military technologies of the early modern era, the evolution of Maroon (hybrid) identities, relations between Maroons and indigenous societies, coercion and patron–client relationships in slave societies, kinship networks, historical memory, African and Atlantic slaveries, slave resistance and survival, black citizenship, and abstractions such as creolization, democratic revolutions, and utopias. Mavis C.

Campbell has written extensively and impressively on the Trelawney Town Maroons inside and outside of Jamaica, and I have remained inspired by her efforts. Campbell's *The Maroons of Jamaica, 1655–1796: A History of Resistance, Collaboration, and Betrayal* (Granby, Conn.: Bergin and Garvey, 1988) provides a comprehensive history of the Maroons in British Jamaica until the time of the Trelawney deportation. Her second work on the Trelawney Town Maroons, an edited volume, *Nova Scotia and the Fighting Maroons: A Documentary History* (Williamsburg, Va.: College of William and Mary Press, Studies in Third World Societies, 1990), includes correspondence related to the Maroons' stay in Nova Scotia. Her third work, *Back to Africa: George Ross and the Maroons from Nova Scotia to Sierra Leone* (Trenton, N.J.: Africa World Press, 1993), is an annotated diary of George Ross, who accompanied the Maroons to Sierra Leone in 1800 and served as their superintendent for a short period. My work takes up her challenge to put the Trelawney Town Maroons' migrations within a single framework. In *Maroons of Jamaica,* Campbell writes, "The work was originally conceived of as a transatlantic history, under one cover, tracing the Maroons to Nova Scotia and from there to Sierra Leone. But the monumental proportion of the primary sources precluded this scheme as a one-volume proposition" (11); on the Jamaican Maroons, also see Carey Robinson, *The Fighting Maroons of Jamaica* (Kingston: William Collins and Sangster, 1969); Barbara K. Kopytoff, "Colonial Treaty as Sacred Charter of the Jamaican Maroons," *Ethnohistory* 26, no. 1 (Winter 1979); Sylvia W. de Groot, "A Comparison Between the History of Maroon Communities in Surinam and Jamaica," in *Out of the House of Bondage: Runaways, Resistance and Marronage in Africa and the New World,* ed. Gad Heuman (London: Frank Cass, 1986); Richard B. Sheridan, "The Maroons of Jamaica, 1730–1830: Livelihood, Demography and Health," in *Out of the House of Bondage;* and Bev Carey, *The Maroon Story: The Authentic and Original History of the Maroons in the History of Jamaica, 1490–1880* (New York: Agouti Press, 1997); for an anthropological study of Jamaican Maroons, see Kenneth M. Bilby, *True-Born Maroons* (Kingston: Ian Randle, 2006). On Jamaican Maroons in Nova Scotia, see John N. Grant, *The Maroons in Nova Scotia* (Halifax: Formac, 2002). I am not aware of any studies that explore the Maroons' settlement in Sierra Leone. For a thoughtful essay on Trelawney Town Maroons' serial migrations, see Jeffrey A. Fortrin, "Blackened Beyond Our Native Hue: Removal, Identity and the Trelawney Maroons on the Margins of the Atlantic World, 1796–1800," *Citizenship Studies* 10, no. 1 (February 2006). For an important comparative perspective, see Sylvia W. de Groot, Catherine A. Christen, and Franklin W. Knight, "Maroon Communities in the Circum-Caribbean," in *General History of the Caribbean: The Slave*

Societies of the Caribbean, ed. Pieter C. Emmer (London: UNESCO/Macmillan, 1997). For more works related to the Maroons, see the bibliography.

5. Scholars such as Kenneth Bilby have sensitively noted the polarized reaction to Maroons, regarded either as revolutionaries or as "mimic men" who negated their own cultural values. See Bilby, *True-Born Maroons,* 429; on works related to marginalized blacks who accommodated to slavery in some manner, see Gerald W. Mullin's important discussion of the "assimilateds" in *Flight and Rebellion: Slave Resistance in Eighteenth-Century Virginia* (New York: Oxford University Press, 1972); and, more recently, Jeff Forret, *Slave Against Slave: Plantation Violence in the Old South* (Baton Rouge: Louisiana State University Press, 2015). For a discussion refuting the binary between consent and coercion, it is also valuable to consider works on sexual relations between white masters and slaves and between Europeans and Africans in West Africa. For example, see Clarence Walker, *Mongrel Nation: The America Begotten by Thomas Jefferson and Sally Hemings* (Charlottesville: University of Virginia Press, 2009), and Carina E. Ray, *Crossing the Color Line: Race, Sex, and the Contested Politics of Colonialism in Ghana* (Athens: Ohio University Press, 2015). We do not have the evidence to determine if the Maroons' mindset echoed those of the colonized described by the subaltern scholars Ranajit Guha and Gayatri Spivak or by Frantz Fanon in *Black Skins, White Masks* (New York: Grove Press, 2008). The Maroons never created an autonomous *society* with its own economic base. They remained dependent on the plantations for food, guns, and women; by 1803 no superintendent managed their community.

6. Michael Craton, "Jamaican Slavery," in *Race and Slavery in the Western Hemisphere: Quantitative Studies,* ed. Stanley L. Engerman and Eugene D. Genovese (Stanford: Advanced Study in the Behavioral Sciences, 1975). Also see J. R. Ward, *British West Indian Slavery, 1750–1834* (Oxford: Clarendon Press, 1988), 191. Ward notes the following about the composition of the Jamaican slaves in the eighteenth century: 67.8 percent field slaves, 6.6 percent crafts, 6.1 percent watch, 5.5 percent domestic, 6 percent invalid or aged, 8 percent children not working. Slaves owned by Maroons received formal emancipation on May 23, 1835. See July 27, 1835, CO 137/198, TNA.

7. Winthrop D. Jordan, "Planter and Slave Identity Formation: Some Problems in the Comparative Approach," in *Comparative Perspectives on Slavery in New World Plantation Societies,* ed. Vera Rubin and Arthur Tuden (New York: New York Academy of Sciences, 1977), 37–39. Jordan notes the importance of acquiring a "moving picture" of slavery and of thinking about "the New World experience as part of the process of migration."

8. Stanley L. Engerman, "Some Implications of the Abolition of the Slave Trade," in *The Abolition of the Atlantic Slave Trade: Origins and Effects in Europe, Africa, and the Americas,* ed. David Eltis and James Walvin (Madison: University of Wisconsin Press, 1981), 6.

9. David Patrick Geggus, "British Opinion and the Emergence of Haiti, 1791–1805," in *Slavery and British Society, 1776–1846* (Baton Rouge: Louisiana State University Press, 1982); David Patrick Geggus, "Slavery, War and the Revolution in the Greater Caribbean, 1789–1815," in *A Turbulent Time: The French Revolution and the Greater Caribbean,* ed. David Barry Gaspar and David Patrick Geggus (Bloomington: Indiana University Press, 1997); Geggus, "The Enigma of Jamaica in the 1790s"; Michael Duffy, "The French Revolution and the British Attitudes to the West Indian Colonies," in *A Turbulent Time;* David Northrup notes, "It is likely that more people of African descent resided in Britain in the latter part of the eighteenth century than in all the rest of Europe combined." This may be one reason the Maroons made the British news. See David Northrup, *Africa's Discovery of Europe, 1450–1850* (Oxford: Oxford University Press, 2002), 128. An increase in violent resistance and the spread of news through print were essential to the spread of abolitionist sentiments. See Laurent Dubois, "Emancipations," and Steve Pincus, "Empires," in Joseph C. Miller, ed., *The Princeton Companion to Atlantic History* (Princeton: Princeton University Press, 2015).

10. For the debate on the primary drivers of antislavery, the lines have been long set by Eric Williams in *Capitalism and Slavery* (Chapel Hill: University of North Carolina Press, 1944), who argued that abolition was primarily an economic, not a humanitarian, imperative. Others have conceded that the decline of mercantilism made antislavery action more plausible. The Maroons' migrations demonstrate that the economic imperative was ever present but also that the Maroons made use of the humanitarian face of abolition. Those who argue that economic motives drove the end of slavery cannot adequately explain why—given the mature stage of industrial capitalism—indentured laborers, not free wage laborers, replaced slaves. See O. Nigel Bolland, "Colonization and Slavery in Central America," in *Unfree Labour in the Development of the Atlantic World,* ed. Paul E. Lovejoy and Nicholas Rogers (London: Frank Cass, 1994). For the extensive literature on the causes of abolitionism, see the bibliographic essay below. For recent works on antislavery moral imperatives, see Christopher Leslie Brown, *Moral Capital: Foundations of British Abolitionism* (Chapel Hill: University of North Carolina Press, 2006); David Brion Davis, *Inhuman Bondage: The Rise and Fall of Slavery in the New World* (New York: Oxford University Press, 2006).

11. Despite the fact that two-thirds of the Maroons who were exiled were women and children, most of the sources available for the Maroons largely concern the behavior of Maroon men. Richard Sheridan compares the better lot of Maroon women over that of slave women, noting that the former "probably had diet richer in animal protein, a lighter work load which did not include night work and the digging of cane holes and a disease environment that was less enervating and more hygienic." See Sheridan, "The Maroons of Jamaica, 1730–1830," 170. He notes that the slave population was not self-sustaining because of high mortality among infants, unstable sexual unions, difficulty of acclimation of newly imported slaves, malnutrition, hard labor, brutal punishment, and epidemic diseases (287). On humanitarianism in Nova Scotia, see Robin Winks, "A Sacred Animosity: Abolition in Canada," in *The Antislavery Vanguard: New Essays on the Abolitionists,* ed. Martin Duberman (Princeton: Princeton University Press, 1965); and Judith Fingard, "English Humanitarianism and the Colonial Mind: Walter Bromley in Nova Scotia, 1813–1825," *Canadian Historical Review* 54 (1973). John G. Reid addresses the limits of humanitarianism for indigenous groups in "Pax Britannica or Pax Indigena? Planter Nova Scotia (1760–1782) and Competing Strategies of Pacification," *Canadian Historical Review* 85, no. 4 (2004): 669–92. Harvey A. Whitfield's *North to Bondage: Loyalist Slavery in the Maritimes* (Vancouver: University of British Columbia Press, 2016) shows the limitations of humanitarianism for ex-slaves.

12. Manuscript Orders for the Directors of the Sierra Leone Company, 1792, FBC; for romantic understandings of antislavery, see Deirdre Coleman, *Romantic Colonization and British Anti-Slavery* (Cambridge: Cambridge University Press, 2005). Also see John Peterson, *Province of Freedom: A History of Sierra Leone, 1787–1870* (Evanston: Northwestern University Press, 1969) and Bronwen Everill, *Abolition and Empire in Sierra Leone and Liberia* (London: Palgrave Macmillan, 2013). For more on the three groups of black exiles, see my forthcoming essay " 'Wayward Humours' and 'Perverse Disputings': Exiled Blacks and the Foundation of Sierra Leone, 1787–1800," in *Africans in Exile: Mobility, Law, and Identity, Past and Present,* ed. B. N. Lawrance and Nate Carpenter (Bloomington: Indiana University Press, forthcoming).

13. Between 25 and 50 percent of children died before they were five. See Kenneth Morgan, "The Struggle for Survival: Slave Infant Mortality in the British Caribbean in the Late Eighteenth and Nineteenth Centuries," in *Children in Slavery through the Ages,* ed. Suzanne Miers, Gwyn Campbell, and Joseph C. Miller (Athens: Ohio University Press, 2009), 187. Richard B. Sheridan notes that slaves were more "susceptible to diseases associated with malnutrition, fatigue from hard labor, punishment, and

unhygienic conditions, while the Maroons were more prone to suffer physical accidents, infection, smallpox, and accidental poisoning from unfamiliar leaves and herbs." In contrast to slave women, Maroon women had a diet richer in animal protein, a lighter workload, and a more hygienic environment. See Sheridan, "The Maroons of Jamaica, 1730–1830," 170; and Richard Sheridan, "Mortality and Medical Treatment of Slaves in the British West Indies," in *Race and Slavery in the Western Hemisphere: Quantitative Studies,* ed. Stanley L. Engerman and Eugene D. Genovese (Stanford: Center for Advanced Study in the Behavioral Sciences, 1975), 196. Sheridan, citing B. W. Higman, notes that the most common age of death of Jamaican slaves in the 1830s, on the eve of emancipation, was between thirty and forty years. Also see Stanley L. Engerman and B. W. Higman, "The Demographic Structure of the Caribbean Slave Societies in the Eighteenth and Nineteenth Centuries," in *General History of the Caribbean: The Slave Societies of the Caribbean,* ed. Pieter C. Macmillan (London: UNESCO/Macmillan, 1997), 89; and by the beginning of the nineteenth century the Maroon population had achieved a crude birthrate of 47 per 1000 whereas the slave population had a rate of only 27; John G. Reid emphasizes the problems the British confronted, before 1815, in defending isolated colonial settlements, especially in the face of outside invasion. See John G. Reid, "Response—Historical Analysis and Indigenous Dispossession," in *Shaping an Agenda for Atlantic Canada,* ed. John G. Reid and Donald J. Savoid (Halifax: Fernwood, 2011), 60; Maya Jasanoff writes, "Tracing the loyalist diaspora is like drawing a map of the expanding British empire, featuring every major site of imperial involvement after 1780." See "Revolutionary Exiles: The American Loyalist and French Émigré Diasporas," in *The Age of Revolutions in Global Context, c. 1760–1840,* ed. David Armitage and Sanjay Subrahmanyam (London: Palgrave Macmillan, 2010), 47.

14. Consider the number of books devoted to slave rebellion and slave resistance in various parts of the Americas. In the case of the Maroons, it is important to paraphrase the words of James Baldwin: nonviolent resistance was not the same as nonresistance. In his discussion of a Maroon community in Florida, Nathaniel Millett emphasizes that a community of independent ex-slaves would have been the "envy of most people of color in the revolutionary Atlantic world." See Millett, *The Maroons of Prospect Bluff,* 9. I. E. Thompson, in 1937, noted that the Maroons used the phrase "white-a-middle" for children who had a Maroon father and a slave mother. Maroon blood hence bestowed "whiteness" on the children. See "The Maroons of Mooretown," in the Williams Collection, MS 5070, Box 19, BC. (I have not found this reference, so the phrase may have appeared in the latter part of the nineteenth century.)

15. I hope to show the complexity of the slave experience and not in any way chronicle "black foibles and criminality," as Jeff Forret also emphasizes in *Slave Against Slave,* 8. Forret continues, "Scholars ought not to permit the expectation of political correctness to become burdensome by obstructing scholarly inquiry." The inhuman conditions of slavery itself bred violence; they also generated internal, complicated, and long-lasting hierarchies within the black community. Eric Williams speaks of the Caribbean mentality, "conceived in slavery, cradled in indenture and nurtured in colonialism," cited in Juanita de Barros, Audra Diptee, and David V. Trotman, "Introduction," in *Beyond Fragmentation: Perspectives on Caribbean History,* ed. Audra Diptee, Juanita de Barros, and David V. Trotman (Princeton: Markus Wiener, 2006), xviii. Edward Long presents one example of whites' thinking about blacks in Jamaica in 1774. Long wrote that the natives of Africa are "a brutish, ignorant, idle, crafty, treacherous, bloody, thievish, mistrustful, and superstitious people." In Jamaica, we "find them marked with the same bestial manners, stupidity, and vices which debase their brethren on the continent." See Howard Johnson, "Introduction: Edward Long, Historian of Jamaica," in Edward Long, *The History of Jamaica: Reflections on Its Situation, Settlements, Inhabitants, Climate, Products, Commerce, Laws, and Government* (Montreal: McGill-Queen's University Press, 2002), ix.

16. The reality of Caribbean slavery made decolonization in nineteenth-century Jamaica very different from the postcolonial movements of the twentieth century. For ex-slaves there was no recovery of ancestral lands in Jamaica. Notably, only Haiti re-established a connection with a symbolic indigenous history. See de Barros, Diptee, and Trotman, "Introduction," xix.

17. On "creolization," see the entry by Richard Price in *Princeton Companion to Atlantic History.* Fortrin emphasizes how current exiles draw our attention to the way dispersed people occupy "multidimensional social, economic, cultural and political spaces" and "experience a continual process of redefinition" (*Slave Against Slave,* 25). On humans' shared values about death across cultures, see Thomas W. Lacquer's recent work, *The World of the Dead: A Cultural History of Mortal Remains* (Princeton: Princeton University Press, 2015); Verene A. Shepherd, "Questioning Creole: Domestic Producers in Jamaica's Plantation Economy," in *Questioning Creole: Creolisation Discourses in the Caribbean Culture, in Honour of Kamau Brathwaite,* ed. Verene A. Shepherd and Glen L. Richards (Kingston: Ian Randle, 2002).

18. The Maroons immortalized colonial administrators, British statesmen, and royalty. Halifax has a street named after one of the Maroon superintendents (Ochterloney Street), and some black Nova Scotians believe Preston still bears the impression

of the Maroons. Freetown has a Maroon chapel and a Walpole Street, named after the British general who supported the Maroons, George Walpole. In Mona, the University of West Indies offers courses that celebrate the legacy of the Maroons.

19. In Jamaica, the leader of the Windward Maroons, Nanny, continues to inspire deep admiration. In 1866 Commander Beford Pim of the Royal Navy observed that the Maroons continued to "boast of being directly descended or having been concerned in the Jamaica rebellion at the end of the eighteenth century, as partisans of King Cudjoe, their leader." See Pim, "The Negro and Jamaica," read before the Anthropological Society of London, February 1, 1866, at St. James Hall, London (Special Number of *Popular Magazine of Anthropology*), in MHS, 65.

20. Multiple spaces and times can coexist over a "colonial period." On rethinking political imaginaries outside our given frames of religion, nation, state, and empire, see Nira Wickramasinghe, *Metallic Modern: Everyday Machines in Colonial Sri Lanka* (New York: Berghahn, 2014). Bogumil Jewsiewicki cautions us to note the uneven memory of slavery, reminding us that in Africa "the memory of being colonized is more pervasive than the slave trade." See "In the Empire of Forgetting: Collective Memory of the Slave Trade and Slavery," in *Crossing Memories: Slavery and African Diaspora,* ed. Mariana C. Candido, Ana Lucia Araujo, and Paul E. Lovejoy (Trenton, N.J.: Africa World Press, 2011), 7.

21. Campbell, *Back to Africa,* 60. Like enslaved Africans, the Maroons were prisoners of war. But, unlike slaves, their forced migration from Jamaica met the needs of the sending society, not the receiving one.

Chapter 1. War

1. Philip Thicknesse, *Memoirs and Anecdotes of Philip Thicknesse, Late Lieutenant Governor of Land Guard Fort and Unfortunately Father to George Touchet, Baron Audley* (Dublin: Graisberry and Campbell, 1790), 56; Frank Cundall, *The Governors of Jamaica in the First Half of the Eighteenth Century* (London: West India Committee, 1937), 163.

2. Carla G. Pestana, in private correspondence, pointed out that the English tried unsuccessfully to get rid of the Maroons. They had no option but to tolerate them. See her work on the founding of Jamaica, *The English Conquest of Jamaica: Oliver Cromwell's Bid for Empire* (Cambridge: Harvard University Press, 2017).

3. R. C. Dallas, *The History of the Maroons, from Their Origin to the Establishment of Their Chief Tribe at Sierra Leone, Including the Expedition to Cuba for the Purpose of Procuring Spanish Chasseurs and the State of the Island of Jamaica for the Last*

Ten Years with a Succinct History of the Island Previous to That Period (London: Frank Cass, 1968), 1:35.

4. "A New and Exact Account of Jamaica," Rare Books, THL, 362; Dallas, *History of the Maroons,* 1:27; at this time, there were eighty thousand blacks in the island and eight thousand whites. See W. J. A. Gardner, *A History of Jamaica from Its Discovery by Christopher Columbus to the Year 1872: Including an Account of Its Trade and Agriculture; Sketches of the Manners, Habits, and Customs of All Classes of Its Inhabitants; and a Narrative of the Progress of Religion and Education in the Island* (London: Frank Cass, 1971), 117.

5. Thicknesse, *Memoirs,* 56, 70; Clinton V. Black, *The Story of Jamaica, from Prehistory to the Present* (London: Collins, 1965), 76.

6. Almost 50 percent of Jamaica's slaves were in units of more than 150, so labor tasks were specialized. See B. W. Higman, "African and Creole Slave Family Patterns in Trinidad," in *Africa and the Caribbean: The Legacies of a Link,* ed. Margaret E. Crahan and Franklin W. Knight (Baltimore: Johns Hopkins University Press, 1979), 42; J. Lewis, December 20, 1743, "Papers Relating to Jamaica, presented by C. E. Long," BL. It is difficult to say whether some Maroons brought blacksmithing skills with them from Africa; see Candice L. Gouchera, "African Metallurgy in the Atlantic World," in *Archaeology of Atlantic Africa and the African Diaspora,* ed. Akinwumi Ogundiran and Toyin Falola (Bloomington: Indiana University Press, 2007), 283–84. Gouchera writes, "Even as individual craftsmen, the transplanted African blacksmiths negotiated positions of leadership in the plantation hierarchy and were presumably instrumental in the exercise of ritual continuities."

7. For the full text of the treaties, see Mavis C. Campbell, *The Maroons of Jamaica, 1655–1796: A History of Resistance, Collaboration, and Betrayal* (Granby, Conn.: Bergin and Garvey, 1988), chapter 5. Also see Sir William Young, *Historical Survey of the Island of Saint Domingo together with an account of the Maroon negroes in the island of Jamaica; and a history of the war in the West Indies, in 1793 and 1794; also a tour through the several islands of Barbados, St. Vincent, Antigua, Tobago, and Grenada in the Years 1791 and 1792* (London, 1801), 317–18. Young notes that he took his account of the Maroons from Edward Long, *History of Jamaica,* written in 1774. "The Importance of Great Britain Considered in a Letter to a Gentleman, 1740," Rare Books, THL. According to Bryan Edwards, "If peace had not been made in 1738, the Maroons would soon have been forced to surrender unconditionally." Also see Long, *History of Jamaica,* 2:344; Dallas, *History of the Maroons,* 1:97–98, 96; John Guthrie and Francis Saddler (?), And the mark of Captain Cudjoe (circle with

two lines—vertically and horizontally), March 10, 1738/39, Agreement with Captain Cudjoe, BL.

8. Richard Price, "Jamaica," in *Maroon Societies: Rebel Slave Communities in the Americas* (Garden City, N.Y.: Anchor Books, 1973), 228. According to Price, the treaty granted existing Maroon chiefs lifetime tenure so that older men, who would have been replaced in the pretreaty era, became an obstruction for aspiring leaders. On important differences between U.S. and Caribbean slaveries, see Henry Hoetink, *Slavery and Race Relations in the Americas: Comparative Notes on Their Nature and Nexus* (New York: Harper and Row, 1973).

9. On Cudjoe, see Michael A. Gomez, *Reversing Sail: A History of the African Diaspora* (Cambridge: Cambridge University Press, 2005), 115; Maureen Warner-Lewis, "The Character of African-Jamaican Culture," in *Jamaica in Slavery and Freedom: History, Heritage and Culture,* ed. Kathleen E. A. Monteith and Glen Richards (Kingston: University of West Indies Press, 2002), 91; Sylvia W. de Groot, Catherine A. Christen, and Franklin W. Knight, "Maroon Communities in the Circum-Caribbean," in *General History of the Caribbean: The Slave Societies of the Caribbean,* ed. Pieter C. Emmer (London: UNESCO/Macmillan, 1997), 3:181; George Metcalf, *Royal Government and Political Conflict in Jamaica, 1729–1783* (London: Royal Commonwealth Society, 1965), 62–63; John Guthrie to the Hon. John Gregory, February 21, 1738/39, Papers Relating to Jamaica, Add Ms 12431, BL; Supplement to *Royal Gazette,* November 28 to December 5, 1795, NLJ; Campbell, *Maroons of Jamaica,* 3. Carla G. Pestana, in private correspondence, points out that the requirement to speak English was earlier imposed by the English on the Maroons.

10. Blood, taken from a cut in the hand, was mixed with water and clay, added to rum, and drunk by both parties from a calabash. See Sylvia W. de Groot, "A Comparison Between the History of Maroon Communities in Surinam and Jamaica," in *Out of the House of Bondage: Runaways, Resistance and Marronage in Africa and the New World,* ed. Gad Heuman (London: Frank Cass, 1986), 180.

11. Kenneth Bilby, "Swearing by the Past, Swearing to the Future: Sacred Oaths, Alliances, and Treaties among the Guianese and Jamaican Maroons," in *Origins of the Black Atlantic,* ed. Laurent Dubois and Julius S. Scott (New York: Routledge, 2010), 237.

12. The blood oath was not unique to Maroons; slaves too continued this practice. See de Groot, "A Comparison Between the History of Maroon Communities in Surinam and Jamaica." Viewed from one perspective, a military establishment—with its rules and hierarchies—comes as close as any human organization can be to the

ideal type for rational and secular enterprise. Yet from another point of view, the great stress placed on explicit standards for *individual* behavior in the military—in the daily business of remaining sober as much as in killing or in dying—makes the military a sacred community. The Maroons' loyalty extended to their captains and from them to a blind faith in an all-powerful king who would not fail them. The religious nature of the secret blood oath may have allowed the Maroons and their descendants to sustain this faith. See Lucian W. Pye, "Armies in the Process of Political Modernization," in *The Role of the Military in Underdeveloped Countries,* ed. John J. Johnson (Westport, Conn.: Greenwood Press, 1962).

13. The Maroons foreshadowed the loyalty of the black West Indian regiments that would be established officially by the end of the eighteenth century. Like the Maroons, the fighting slaves were in a position superior to that of farming slaves; the freedom offered to some allowed the more effective exploitation of others. See Roger Norman Buckley, *Slaves in Red Coats: The British West India Regiments, 1795–1815* (New Haven: Yale University Press, 1979); Martin Klein and Paul E. Lovejoy, "Slavery in West Africa," in *The Uncommon Market: Essays in the Economic History of the Atlantic Slave Trade,* ed. Henry A. Gemery and Jan S. Hogendorn (New York: Academic Press, 1979); and Christopher Leslie Brown and Philip D. Morgan, eds., *Arming Slaves: From Classical Times to the Modern Age* (New Haven: Yale University Press, 2006).

14. By 1782 the militia numbered between three thousand and four thousand men. "Letterbook of Stephen Fuller," vol. 2, April 2, 1782, and December 23, 1778, Burns Library, Williams Collection, BC. See ad from Postscript to *The Royal Gazette,* Saturday, July 4, 1795, to Saturday, July 11, 1795, NLJ. The ad reads, "Half a Joe Reward: Supposed to be inveighled away, a Sambo Girl, about 30 to 35 years of age, named Gracey, and *that by a mulatto man named Dick, who is in the militia* (emphasis added)." See David Geggus, "The Enigma of Jamaica in the 1790s: New Light on the Causes of Slave Rebellions," *William and Mary Quarterly* 44, no. 2 (1987): 275, 278; Buckley, *Slaves in Red Coats,* 97; Robert Sewell to Duke of Portland, November 9, 1795, Committee of Correspondence Out-Letter Book, JARD. Guerrilla warfare resulted in greater casualties in the Maroon war; Thicknesse, *Memoirs,* 46.

15. Gardner, *A History of Jamaica,* 119; Cundall, *Governors of Jamaica,* 183. In 1740s the assembly granted the following: "Two cows should be presented to colonel Cudjoe, and two for Captain Accompong, and one for Captain Johnny, one for Captain Cuffie, one for Quaco, one for Bumbager and one for Captain Quao, with two bulls; one for Trelawney-Town and one for Accompong Town; as also a cow for each

of the captains in Accompong's Town"; John Guthrie and Francis Saddler (?), And the mark of Captain Cudjoe, March 10, 1738/39, Agreement with Captain Cudjoe, BL.

16. Christopher L. Brown, "The Politics of Slavery," in *The British Atlantic World, 1500–1800,* ed. David Armitage and Michael J. Braddick (New York: Palgrave Macmillan, 2002), and Buckley, *Slaves and Redcoats;* William Beckford, Spanish-Town, August 19, 1741, Papers Relating to Jamaica, presented by C. E. Long, BL; John Guthrie and Francis Saddler (?), And the mark of Captain Cudjoe, March 10, 1738/39, Agreement with Captain Cudjoe, BL.

17. Trevor Burnard, "Not a Place for Whites? Demographic Failure and Settlement in Comparative Context: Jamaica, 1655–1780," in *Jamaica in Slavery and Freedom,* 77–78; B. W. Higman, *Plantation Jamaica, 1750–1850: Capital and Control in a Colonial Economy* (Kingston: University of West Indies Press, 2005), 227. Higman notes that the "quieting" of the region led to sugar plantations; when the treaty was signed in 1739 St. James Parish, which had 8 sugar estates, produced 660 hogsheads of sugar with the labor of 2,588 slaves. By 1790 it had 139 sugar estates and produced 23,000 hogsheads of sugar with 43,864 slaves. See "Sugar Plantations in Jamaica with the Quantity of Sugars made generally for some years past on them, Christmas, 1739," presented by C. E. Long, BL; also see Colonization of Jamaica, 1792, Laws (Record, RB.23.a.9830), BL; Richard B. Sheridan, "The Maroons of Jamaica, 1730–1830: Livelihood, Demography and Health," in *Out of the House of Bondage,* 170; de Groot, Christen, and Knight, "Maroon Communities," 184.

18. Dallas, *History of the Maroons,* 1:134; Mr. Vaughan to Mr. Cuthbert, July 28, 1796, Council Minute Book, 1B/5/3/20, JARD. The Maroons appealed to the obligations of paternalism to claim better treatment. We must distinguish between the paternalism of slaveholders and the paternalism of British abolitionists. See, for example, Elsa V. Goveia, *A Study on the Historiography of the British West Indies to the End of the Nineteenth Century* (Washington, D.C.: Howard University Press, 1980), 89; and Michael Barnett, *Empire of Humanity: A History of Humanitarianism* (Ithaca: Cornell University Press, 2011), 60; Dallas, *History of the Maroons,* 1:84; Philip D. Morgan, *Black Experience and the Empire* (Oxford: Oxford University Press, 2004), 90.

19. J. L. Winn, July 26, 1795, in Council Minute Book, 1B/5/3/20, JARD. According to Gardner, Winn was a Quaker. See Gardner, *A History of Jamaica,* 227; petition of G. Love, December 9, 1795, in Votes of Assembly of Jamaica, JARD; J. L. Winn, July 26, 1795, in Council Minute Book, 1B/5/3/20, JARD.

20. John Tharp to Samuel Vaughan, July 13, 1795, in Votes of Assembly of Jamaica, JARD; Mr. Vaughan to Mr. Cuthbert, July 28, 1796, in Council Minute

Book, 1B/5/3/20, JARD; Jan Vasina notes, "Age as a quality of leadership was ubiquitous and became a striking feature of African diasporic communities." See Vasina, "Foreword," in *Central Africans and Cultural Transformations in the African Diaspora,* ed. Linda M. Heywood (New York: Cambridge University Press, 2002), xiii. Also see I. H. Konter, "Rulership in the Traditional and Modern African Society: Some Striking Differences between Rural Traditional and Modern Elites," *Journal of the Historical Society of Sierra Leone* 1, no. 2 (June 1977): 43–56.

21. Dallas, *History of the Maroons,* 1:100, 102; Mr. Vaughan to Mr. Cuthbert, July 28, 1796, in Council Minute Book, 1B/5/3/20, JARD; Vincent Brown, *The Reaper's Garden: Death and Power in the World of Atlantic Slavery* (Cambridge: Harvard University Press, 2008), 148. But some Maroons' loyalty may have wavered as well. As Bryan Edwards noted, "The ears [brought by the Maroons] came from dead negroes which had lain unburied," not from slaves they had killed. Bryan Edwards, *Historical Survey of the Island of Saint Domingo Together with an Account of the Maroon Negroes in the Island of Jamaica and a History of the War in the West Indies in 1793 and 1794* (Salt Lake City: Filmed by the Genealogical Society of Utah, 1995), 3:326; Mr. Vaughan to Mr. Cuthbert, July 28, 1796, in Council Minute Book, 1B/5/3/20, JARD.

22. George Wilson Bridges, *Annals of Jamaica by the Reverend George Wilson Bridges, A.M.* (London: John Murray, 1828), 1:30; Supplement to *The Royal Gazette,* Saturday, April 30, 1796, to Saturday, May 7, 1796, NLJ.

23. This attachment could equally be called royalism. See especially Marcela Escheverri, *Indian and Slave Royalists in the Age of Revolution: Reform, Revolution, and Royalism in the Northern Andes, 1780–1825* (Cambridge: Cambridge University Press, 2016); the Queen of Montego Bay had clear precedents. In Tacky's revolt of 1760, Abena presided as the "Akan queen-mother in Jamaica." See Gomez, *Reversing Sail,* 132.

24. Gad J. Heuman, *Between Black and White: Race, Politics and the Free Coloreds in Jamaica, 1792–1865* (Westport, Conn.: Greenwood Press, 1981), 7; Earl of Balcarres to Duke of Portland, December 31, 1795, in Anne Barnard, *Lives of the Lindsays, or a Memoir of the Houses of Crawford and Balcarres by Lord Lindsay, of Which Are Added Extracts from the Official Correspondence of Alexander Sixth Earl of Balcarres, During the Maroon War; Together with Personal Narratives by His Brothers, the Hon. Robert Colin, James, John, and Hugh Lindsay; and by His Sister, Lady Anne Barnard* (London: John Murray, 1849), 3:103; John Tharp to Lieutenant Governor, July 25, 1795, *Journals of the Assembly of Jamaica,* 9:371, JCB; Higman, *Plantation Jamaica,* 290. John Tharp returned to Jamaica in 1802.

25. Earl of Balcarres to Duke of Portland, October 27, 1795, in Barnard, *Lives of the Lindsays,* 85; Earl of Balcarres to Duke of Portland, August 25, 1796, in Barnard, *Lives of the Lindsays,* 60.

26. Council of War, August 2, 1795, in Council Minute Book, 1B/5/3/20, JARD; Supplement to *The Royal Gazette,* Saturday, August 15, 1795, to Saturday, August 22, 1795, NLJ; the handful of Maroons who surrendered were immediately imprisoned, deterring others from doing the same.

27. Geggus, "The Enigma of Jamaica in the 1790s," 274.

28. Balcarres to Dundas, September 21, 1795, WO 1/92, TNA; Dallas, *History of the Maroons,* 1:120; Supplement to *The Royal Gazette,* Saturday, September 19, 1795, to Saturday, September 26, 1795, NLJ; Balcarres had worried about this in May: see Balcarres, May 3, 1795, MS 606, NLJ; Kenneth Bilby, citing David Geggus, notes that the Maroons inspired Toussaint L'Ouverture during the struggle for Haitian liberation. Mentioned in Kenneth M. Bilby, *True-Born Maroons* (Kingston: Ian Randle, 2006), 433, 53n.

29. As these French slaves spoke no English, it is not clear how much communication they had with Jamaican slaves; Geggus, "The Enigma of Jamaica in the 1790s," 278; Gardner, *A History of Jamaica,* 223–224.

30. Balcarres to President of Council, October 18, 1795, in Barnard, *Lives of the Lindsays,* 83; Balcarres to Dundas, August 29, 1795, WO 1/92, TNA; Balcarres to Walpole, October 1, 1795, in Barnard, *Lives of the Lindsays,* 75; Balcarres to Dundas, August 29, 1795, WO 1/92, TNA.

31. Thomas Munro to Mr. Brodie, August 16, 1796, Hardwicke Papers, Add MS 35916, BL; Balcarres to Duke of Portland, October 27, 1795, in Barnard, *Lives of the Lindsays,* 85; Alexander Balcarres, September 27, 1795, Box 19, MS 5035, Private, Nicholas M. Williams, Ethnological Collection, BC; Committee of Correspondence Out-Letter Book, September 26, 1795, JARD; John Wentworth to John King, May 23, 1799, CO 217/37, TNA; Mavis C. Campbell, in *Maroons of Jamaica,* observes that from their inception Maroon communities included women warriors (4); Balcarres to Duke of Portland, October 1, 1796, Hardwicke Papers, vol. 568, Add MS 35916, BL. It is unclear if the Maroons were united in this oath. Dallas, in his account of the Maroons, reported that a "few drunken Maroons" had made this threat when their leader, Old Montague, was "sick and absent." Dallas, *History of the Maroons,* 1:147.

32. Balcarres to Duke of Portland, October 7, 1795, in Barnard, *Lives of the Lindsays,* 79. Balcarres wrote, They would "not be so soon squashed"; Balcarres to

Dundas, August 24, 1795, WO 1/92, TNA; Balcarres to Duke of Portland, October 24, 1795, in Barnard, *Lives of the Lindsays,* 80. Two Maroon rebels, Leonard Parkinson and James Palmer, were the most sought after. The announcements in the *Royal Gazette* on September 12, 1795, offered twice the reward money for the capture of Maroon men. But Maroon women were also seen as threatening. Ten pounds were offered for the capture of a "Maroon woman, or young child"; Robert Sewell to Duke of Portland, November 9, 1795, Committee of Correspondence Out-Letter Book, JARD; Sewell reported that 233 men were sick. See Votes of the Assembly of Jamaica, November 28, 1795, JARD; Balcarres to Duke of Portland, October 7, 1795, in Barnard, *Lives of the Lindsays,* 79.

33. James Vaughan to his brother, William, September 27, 1795, WO 1/92, TNA. In September Samuel Vaughan reflected on measures to keep the Maroons in check after the war. He maintained that military support was necessary "if there is a single Trelawney Maroon left in the country." His familiarity with the Maroons led him to concede that some "straggling ones" would never be captured.

34. Geggus, "The Enigma of Jamaica in the 1790s," 275; Kingston received more slaves than any other port in the Americas; slave imports averaged 5,662 per year between 1785 and 1787; through the 1790s they averaged close to 12,000 per year.

35. Dallas, *History of the Maroons,* 1:125, 97–98.

36. Examination of William from Spring Garden Estate, August 14, 1795, in Council Minute Book, 1B/5/3/20, JARD; this blood oath was not unique to Maroons. As Vincent Brown notes, Tacky's revolt in 1760 had also involved blood oaths. See Brown, *Reaper's Garden,* 149.

37. Supplement to *The Royal Gazette,* Saturday, October 31, to Saturday, November 7, 1795, NLJ. The practice of displaying decapitated heads on poles did not begin with the Maroon war.

38. Votes of the Assembly of Jamaica, August 1795, JARD.

39. Supplement to *The Royal Gazette,* Saturday, November 21, to Saturday, November 28, 1795, NLJ; Robert reported that Cudjoe returned with him to Mr. Winn but suspects that he is a spy; Supplement to *The Royal Gazette,* Saturday, October 17, to Saturday, October 24, 1795, NLJ; Supplement to *The Royal Gazette,* Saturday, November 28, to Saturday, December 5, 1795, and Saturday, November 21, to Saturday, November 28, 1795, NLJ. They also captured Zell, an "Eboe man slave," the property of Isaac Lascelles Winn, to carry salted provisions and yams when they had taken him from Amity Hall; Supplement to *The Royal Gazette,* Saturday, November 28, to Saturday, December 5, 1795, NLJ. It is impossible to know Jamaica's motivations.

Maroons' role as catchers of runaways had alienated slaves. Other slaves found more freedom in establishing their own Maroon communities.

40. Examination of William from Spring Garden Estate, Council Minute Book, August 14, 1795, 1B/5/3/20, JARD; Supplement to *The Royal Gazette,* Saturday, November 21, to Saturday, November 28, 1795, NLJ. General Walpole found two hundred to three hundred huts, capable of containing eight hundred people, which appeared to have been recently inhabited; ibid.

41. Henry Hoetink, "The Cultural Links," in *Africa and the Caribbean: The Legacies of a Link,* ed. Margaret E. Crahan and Franklin W. Knight (Baltimore: Johns Hopkins University Press, 1979), 26–30. Hoetink discusses how certain cultural transfers do not require big groups and can happen in smaller mother–child units. In another context, Hoetink notes, "Patron–client relationships, extended kinship, and ritual kinship have proved to be sufficiently elastic to function under drastically changed economic and ecological conditions." See Hoetink, *Slavery and Race Relations in the Americas.* Other historians have explored the use of "bro" and "uncle" among slaves. See, for example, Richard Price and Sidney W. Mintz, *An Anthropological Approach to the Afro-American Past: A Caribbean Perspective* (Philadelphia: Publication of the Institute for the Study of Human Issues, 1976), 5; S. C. Ukpabi discusses how "pure" mercenaries valued comradeship more than kinship. See Ukpabi, "The Military in Traditional African Societies," *African Spectrum* 9, no. 2 (1974): 200–217. Edward Shills discusses the role of kinship in relation to the role of citizenship. See Shills, "The Military in the Political Development of the New States," in *The Role of the Military in Underdeveloped Countries,* ed. J. Johnson. (Westport, Conn.: Greenwood Press, 1962).

42. Balcarres to Duke of Portland, August 29, 1795, in Barnard, *Lives of the Lindsays,* 62; Nicholas M. Williams, September 27, 1795, in Williams Collection, Box 19, MS 5035, BC; Supplement to *The Royal Gazette,* Saturday, October 31, to Saturday, November 7, 1795, NLJ; Supplement to *The Royal Gazette,* Saturday, January 2, 1796, to Saturday, January 9, 1796, NLJ; Zell had reported seeing three slaves who had guns and cutlasses, in Supplement to *The Royal Gazette,* Saturday, November 21, to Saturday, November 28, 1795, NLJ; Neptune, the property of J. Graham, was armed with a gun, a cutlass, and ammunition when recaptured, in Supplement to *The Royal Gazette,* Saturday, November 28, to Saturday, December 5, 1795, NLJ.

43. Balcarres to Duke of Portland, August 24, 1795, in Barnard, *Lives of the Lindsays,* 56; Sidney W. Mintz and Douglas Hall, "The Origins of the Jamaican Internal Marketing System," in *Papers in Caribbean Anthropology* 57, ed. Sidney W. Mintz (New Haven: Yale University Press, 1960), 5.

44. Supplement to *The Royal Gazette,* Saturday, November 21, to Saturday, November 28, 1795, NLJ; Supplement to *The Royal Gazette,* Saturday, November 28, to Saturday, December 5, 1795, NLJ.

45. Examination of William from Spring Garden Estate, August 14, 1795, in Council Minute Book, 1B/5/3/20, JARD; Balcarres to Forster Barham, May 23, 1796, Add MS 35916, BL.

46. Alexander Balcarres, September 27, 1795, Private, Nicholas M. Williams, Ethnological Collection, Box 19, MS 5035, BC; in a private letter to Secretary of War Henry Dundas, Balcarres expressed his anxiety: "[The] danger to the island is not less than it was"; Balcarres to my Lady Hardwick, September 27, 1795, Hardwicke Papers, vol. 568, Add MS 35916, BL; Votes of the Assembly of Jamaica, August 12, 1795, JARD; Nicholas M. Williams, September 27, 1795, Williams Collection, Box 19, MS 5035, BC; Postscript to *The Royal Gazette,* Saturday, September 26, to Saturday, October 3, 1795, JARD; Earl of Balcarres to Captain Douglas, superintendent of Moore Town, September 30, 1795, in Barnard, *Lives of the Lindsays,* 75.

47. Balcarres to Captain Douglas, superintendent of Moore Town, September 30, 1795, in Barnard, *Lives of the Lindsays,* 75.

48. Samuel Vaughan Jr., Esq., to Lewis Cuthbert, Esq., July 28, 1795, Votes of Assembly of Jamaica, JARD. In this letter Vaughan anticipated that the Accompongs would align with the Trelawney Town Maroons; some Accompong women were linked to men from Trelawney Town; it is hard to determine if the ties were voluntary. Walpole to Balcarres, January 24, 1796, Proceedings of the Governor and Assembly of Jamaica, JCB. When captured, two women of Accompong Town asked to return to their town. They told Walpole they were brought to Trelawney Town "against their own consent"; George Walpole to Earl of Balcarres, April 29, 1796, undated, Hardwicke Papers, vol. 568, Add MS 35916, BL; Jonny, captured during the war, was born of an Accompong man and a Maroon woman; the Accompong community had 160 Maroon members. See Edgar Corrie, November 1, 1795, WO 1/92, TNA. The Accompong Maroons would help the whites again in the 1831 Baptist War. See David Brion Davis, *Inhuman Bondage: The Rise and Fall of Slavery in the New World* (New York: Oxford University Press, 2006), 220; Postscript to *The Royal Gazette,* Saturday, August 23, 1795, to Saturday, August 29, 1795, NLJ; Supplement to *The Royal Gazette,* November 21 to November 28, 1795, and October 31 to November 7, 1795; evidence of Accompong service continues through February 1796. See Walpole to Balcarres, February 18, 1796, Proceedings of the Governor and Assembly of Jamaica, November 1796, 72, JCB; Colonel Reid of the Accompong

Maroons died during the war; Votes of the Assembly of Jamaica, December 17, 1795, JARD.

49. Meeting of Council and Assembly, December 24, 1795, in Barnard, *Lives of the Lindsays,* 101; Balcarres to President of the Council, October 18, 1795, in Barnard, *Lives of the Lindsays,* 83; Meeting of Council and Assembly, December 24, 1795, in Barnard, *Lives of the Lindsays,* 100.

Chapter 2. Bloodhounds

1. Elsa V. Goveia, *Slave Society in the British Leeward Islands at the End of the Eighteenth Century* (New Haven: Yale University Press, 1965), 27. Also see Wylie Sypher, *Guinea's Captive Kings: British Anti-Slavery Literature of the Eighteenth Century* (New York: Octagon Press, 1969); Stiv Jakobsson, *Am I Not a Man and a Brother? British Missionaries and the Abolition of the Slave Trade and Slavery in West Africa and the West Indies, 1786–1838* (Lund: Gleerup, 1972); Ronald Kent Richardson, *Moral Imperium: Afro-Caribbeans and the Transformation of British Rule,* Contributions in Comparative Colonial Studies 22 (New York: Greenwood Press, 1987); Deirdre Coleman, *Romantic Colonization and British Anti-Slavery* (Cambridge: Cambridge University Press, 2005); Christopher Leslie Brown, *Moral Capital: Foundations of British Abolitionism* (Chapel Hill: University of North Carolina Press, 2006); David Beck Ryden, *West Indian Slavery and British Abolition, 1783–1807* (New York: Cambridge University Press, 2009); Gad Heuman, "Slavery, the Slave Trade, and the Abolition," in *The Oxford History of the British Empire: Historiography,* ed. Robin W. Winks (New York: Oxford University Press, 1999); David Patrick Geggus, "Slavery, War and the Revolution in the Greater Caribbean, 1789–1815," in *A Turbulent Time: The French Revolution and the Greater Caribbean,* ed. David Barry Gaspar and David Patrick Geggus (Bloomington: Indiana University Press, 1997); Tim Barringer examines how Jamaican land was depicted as a place of leisure, not slave labor. See "Picturesque Prospects and the Labor of the Enslaved," in *Art and Emancipation in Jamaica: Isaac Mendes Belisario and His Worlds,* ed. Gillian Forrester, Tim Barringer, and Barbaro Martínez-Ruiz (New Haven: Yale University Press, 2007).

2. Brown, *Moral Capital;* Eric Williams, *Capitalism and Slavery* (Chapel Hill: University of North Carolina Press, 1944); Eric Robert Taylor, *If We Must Die: Shipboard Insurrections in the Era of the Atlantic Slave Trade* (Baton Rouge: Louisiana State University Press, 2006), 169; Fiona Spiers, "William Wilberforce: 150 Years On," in *Out of Slavery: Abolition and After,* ed. Jack Hayward (London: Frank Cass, 1985), 49; Robin Hallett, *The Penetration of Africa: European Exploration in North and West*

Africa to 1815 (New York: Praeger, 1965), 181; John Oldfield, "Abolition and Emancipation," in *Representing Slavery: Art, Artefacts, and Archives in the Collections of the National Maritime Museum,* ed. Douglas Hamilton and Robert J. Blyth (Aldershot, England: Lund Humphries, 2007), 66; Jakobsson, *Am I Not a Man?,* 32; James Walvin, "The Propaganda of Anti-Slavery," in *Slavery and British Society, 1776–1846* (Baton Rouge: Louisiana State University Press, 1982), 52.

3. David Geggus, "The Enigma of Jamaica in the 1790s: New Light on the Causes of Slave Rebellions," *William and Mary Quarterly* 44, no. 2 (1987): 275.

4. Roderick A. McDonald, *The Economy and Material Culture of Slaves: Goods and Chattels on the Sugar Plantations of Jamaica and Louisiana* (Baton Rouge: Louisiana State University Press, 1993), 45.

5. Letter from I. L. Winn to Lewis Cuthbert, July 26, 1795, in Votes of Assembly of Jamaica, JARD; Earl of Balcarres to President of the Council, October 18, 1795, in Anne Barnard, *Lives of the Lindsays, or a Memoir of the Houses of Crawford and Balcarres by Lord Lindsay, of Which Are Added Extracts from the Official Correspondence of Alexander Sixth Earl of Balcarres, During the Maroon War; Together with Personal Narratives by His Brothers, the Hon. Robert Colin, James, John, and Hugh Lindsay; and by His Sister, Lady Anne Barnard* (London: John Murray, 1849), 83; Votes of Assembly of Jamaica, November 28, 1795, JARD. The seasons also affected when ships entered Jamaica's ports. See B. W. Higman, *Plantation Jamaica, 1750–1850: Capital and Control in a Colonial Economy* (Kingston: University of West Indies Press, 2005), 130.

6. Extract of a letter from a Gentleman in Jamaica to Lord Melville, September 27, 1795, Francis Hart Collection, Box 1, Folder 32, MHS.

7. Extract of a letter from a Gentleman in Jamaica to Lord Melville, September 27, 1795, Francis Hart Collection, Box 1, Folder 32, MHS; An Account of Jamaica and Its Inhabitants by a gentleman, long resident in the West Indies, 1808 (Record 10470.e.5), 290, BL. Also see Paul Youngquist, "The Cujo Effect," in *Gorgeous Beasts: Animal Bodies in Historical Perspective,* ed. Paula Young Lee, Joan B. Landes, and Paul Youngquist (University Park: Pennsylvania State University Press, 2012); Richard Sheridan mentions that dogs had also been used in the 1730s to suppress various communities of Jamaican Maroons. See Richard B. Sheridan, "The Maroons of Jamaica, 1730–1830: Livelihood, Demography and Health," in *Out of the House of Bondage: Runaways, Resistance and Marronage in Africa and the New World,* ed. Gad Heuman (London: Frank Cass, 1986), 155; Geggus, "Slavery, War and Revolution," 21; W. J. A. Gardner, *A History of Jamaica from Its Discovery by Christopher Columbus to the Year 1872: Including an Account of Its Trade and Agriculture; Sketches of the Manners, Habits,*

and Customs of All Classes of Its Inhabitants; and a Narrative of the Progress of Religion and Education in the Island (London: Frank Cass, 1971), 232–36.

8. *Journals of the Assembly of Jamaica,* November 4, 1796, JCB; *Journals of the Assembly of Jamaica,* November 2, 1796, JCB; Letter from David Hood to James Stothert, December 24, 1795, CL.

9. *Journals of the Assembly of Jamaica,* February 11, 1796, JCB; Journal Assembly Records, March 5, 1796, 444, NLJ.

10. *Journals of the Assembly of Jamaica,* February 11, 1796, 9:449, JCB.

11. R. C. Dallas, *The History of the Maroons, from Their Origin to the Establishment of Their Chief Tribe at Sierra Leone, Including the Expedition to Cuba for the Purpose of Procuring Spanish Chasseurs and the State of the Island of Jamaica for the Last Ten Years with a Succinct History of the Island Previous to That Period* (London: Frank Cass, 1968), 2:56–61.

12. Ibid., 2:119–20. Also see Sara E. Johnson, "You Should Give Them Blacks to Eat: Waging Inter-American Wars of Torture and Terror," *American Quarterly* 61, no. 1 (2009): 65–92; and Sara E. Johnson, *The Fear of French Negroes: Transcolonial Collaboration in the Revolutionary Americas* (Berkeley: University of California Press, 2012); Dallas, *History of the Maroons,* 2:129, ibid., 2:62; An Account of Jamaica and Its Inhabitants by a Gentleman, long resident in the West Indies (1808), 292, BL.

13. Terrorizing a population by staging animal violence had been a European tactic since Cortés's conquest of Mexico in 1519–21. See Inga Clendinnen, "Fierce and Unnatural Cruelty: Cortés and the Conquest of Mexico," *Representations* 33 (Winter 1991): 65–100. Claims of the Jamaica Maroon settlers at Sierra Leone (to be asked to be sent to Jamaica) on questions raised by General Walpole (précis by Mr. Taylor—undated but after 1835), CO 142/33, TNA.

14. See Marcus Rainsford, "Appendix," in *An Historical Account of the Black Empire of Hayti (1805),* ed. Paul Youngquist and Gregory Pierrot (Durham: Duke University Press, 2013); Supplement to *The Royal Gazette,* April 30, 1796, to May 7, 1796, NLJ; Adams George Archibald, "Story of Deportation of Negroes from Nova Scotia to Sierra Leone, Read by Ex-Governor Archibald," March 12, 1885, *Collections of NS Historical Society for the years 1889–1891,* 7:150.

15. Proceedings of the Governor and Assembly of Jamaica, December 22, 1795, and March 2, 1796, JCB; *Journals of the Assembly of Jamaica,* December 24, 1795, 441, JCB; Walpole to Balcarres, December 25, 1795 (private), *Journals of the Assembly of Jamaica,* 437, JCB; Supplement to *The Royal Gazette,* January 2, 1796, to January 9, 1796, NLJ.

16. Proceedings of the Governor and Assembly of Jamaica, January 5, 1796, 20; December 24, 1795; January 5, 1796, 22; December 29, 1795, 17; and January 14, 1796, 28, all JCB.

17. Proceedings of the Governor and Assembly of Jamaica, January 8, 1796, 22; January 12, 1796, 26; January 14, 1796, 27; January 20, 1796, 38; February 12, 1796, 67, all JCB. A particular concern for and focus on women and children remained connected to British humanitarianism during the Maroons' migrations. The sources repeatedly point to the Maroons' complete devotion to the people within their households. For a discussion on families in a slave society, see B. W. Higman, "Methodological Problems in the Study of the Slave Family," in *Comparative Perspectives on Slavery in New World Plantation Societies,* ed. Vera Rubin and Arthur Tuden (New York: New York Academy of Sciences, 1977); Proceedings of the Governor and Assembly of Jamaica, December 30, 1795, 18; Walpole to Balcarres, *Journals of the Assembly of Jamaica,* January 1, 1796, JCB. "Only Smith, Dunbar, Williams and two boys are here. I shall send them to Falmouth tomorrow," JCB.

18. Proceedings of the Governor and Assembly of Jamaica, January 8, 1796, 23, JCB; *Journals of the Assembly of Jamaica,* January 13, 1796, JCB; *Journals of the Assembly of Jamaica,* January 17, 1796, 9:457, JCB.

19. Proceedings of the Governor and Assembly of Jamaica, January 12, 1796, JCB; *Journals of the Assembly of Jamaica,* January 15, 1796, JCB.

20. *Journals of the Assembly of Jamaica,* January 16, 1796, JCB; *Journals of the Assembly of Jamaica,* January 23, 1796, JCB.

21. In Nova Scotia, the Maroons complained about their lack of access to rum; *Journals of the Assembly of Jamaica,* January 29, 1796, JCB; Journal Assembly Records, March 23, 1796, NLJ, 457; Journal Assembly Records, March 23, 1796, 457, NLJ. Also see Michael Barnett, *Empire of Humanity: A History of Humanitarianism* (Ithaca: Cornell University Press, 2011); Christer Petley, *Slaveholders in Jamaica: Colonial Society and Culture During the Era of Abolition* (London: Pickering and Chatto, 2009). On the paternalism of Sierra Leone's government in the 1790s, see Suzanne Schwarz, "Zachary Macaulay and the Development of the Sierra Leone Company, 1793–94" (Part 2: Journal, October–December 1793), in *University of Leipzig Papers on Africa, History and Cultural Series,* No. 9, 2002, xxiv; Neil Ramsey, *The Military Memoir and Romantic Literary Culture, 1780–1835* (Burlington, Vt.: Ashgate, 2011); Proceedings of the Governor and Assembly of Jamaica, February 12, 1796, JCB. It is hard to determine if his persuasion relied on diplomacy or violence.

22. George Walpole to Lord Balcarres, January 31, 1796, Proceedings of the Governor and Assembly of Jamaica, JCB; Undated, CO 142/33, TNA.

23. *Journals of the Assembly of Jamaica,* January 29, 1796, JCB; Proceedings of the Governor and Assembly of Jamaica, December 24, 1795; Proceedings of the Governor and Assembly of Jamaica, February 1, 1796, 57.

24. *True Briton* (London), Tuesday, March 22, 1796. Mr. Courtenay related this incident.

25. Debate on General Macleod's Motion respecting the Employment of Bloodhounds in the War against the Maroons, March 21, 1796, Hansard, 32:925, 927.

26. *Times* (London), October 22, 1796, Issue 3721.

27. Debate on General Macleod's Motion respecting the Employment of Bloodhounds in the War against the Maroons, March 21, 1796, Hansard, 32:928–29. On noble savages, see Coleman, *Romantic Colonization,* Richardson, *Moral Imperium,* and Brown, *Moral Capital.* Also see Roxanne Wheeler, "Colonial Exchanges: Visualizing Racial Ideology and Labour in Britain and the West Indies," in *An Economy of Colour: Visual Culture and the Atlantic World, 1660–1830,* ed. Geoff Quilley and Kay Dian Kriz (Manchester: Manchester University Press, 2003). Wheeler writes, "Britons frequently confused Africans and Indians because of the noble savage tradition that embraced North Americans, Pacific Islanders and Africans," 43.

28. Debate on General Macleod's Motion respecting the Employment of Bloodhounds in the War against the Maroons, March 21, 1796, Hansard, 32:923. "The Parliamentary History of England from the Earliest Period to the Year 1803, from Which Last-Mentioned, vol. 32, from May 27, 1795, to March 2, 1797" (London: Hansard, 1818).

29. Debate on General Macleod's Motion respecting the Employment of Bloodhounds in the War against the Maroons, March 21, 1796, Hansard, 32:926; *St. James's Chronicle or the British Evening Post* (London), October 20, 1796–October 22, 1796; *Times* (London), October 22, 1796.

30. Extract of a letter from a Gentleman in Jamaica to Lord Melville, September 27, 1795, Francis Hart Collection, Box 1, Folder 32, MHS; Debate on General Macleod's Motion respecting the Employment of Bloodhounds in the War against the Maroons, March 21, 1796, Hansard, 32:925.

31. Quoted in Vincent Brown, *The Reaper's Garden: Death and Power in the World of Atlantic Slavery* (Cambridge: Harvard University Press, 2008), 180. The amelioration laws began in 1781. See Elsa V. Goveia, *West Indian Laws of the Eighteenth Century* (Barbados: Caribbean University Press, 1970), 35; in the 1788 and 1792

Consolidated Slave Acts, Jamaicans decreed that planters provide basic necessities for their slave laborers; slaves should also have time to provide for their own maintenance and avoid starvation. See McDonald, *Economy and Material Culture of Slaves*, 25; every master should, "once in every year, provide and give to each slave they shall be possessed of, proper and sufficient clothing." See McDonald, *Economy and Material Culture of Slaves*, 111. On sex ratios, also see Stanley L. Engerman and B. W. Higman, "The Demographic Structure of the Caribbean Slave Societies in the Eighteenth and Nineteenth Centuries," in *General History of the Caribbean: The Slave Societies of the Caribbean*, ed. Pieter C. Emmer (London: UNESCO/Macmillan, 1997), 80; and B. W. Higman, "Slavery and Development of Demographic Theory in the Age of Industrial Revolution," in *Slavery and British Society, 1776–1846*, ed. James Walvin (Baton Rouge: Louisiana State University, 1982), 183.

32. Supplement to *The Royal Gazette*, April 30 to May 7, 1796, NLJ.

33. Sir William Young, *Historical Survey of the Island of Saint Domingo together with an account of the Maroon negroes in the island of Jamaica; and a history of the war in the West Indies, in 1793 and 1794; also a tour through the several islands of Barbados, St. Vincent, Antigua, Tobago, and Grenada in the Years 1791 and 1792* (London, 1801), 1:562, 563.

34. Record 10470.e.5. (bound book)—An Account of Jamaica and Its Inhabitants by a Gentleman, Long Resident in the West Indies (1808), 289, 290–91, BL.

35. Supplement to *The Royal Gazette*, April 30 to May 7, 1796, NLJ.

36. Like Balcarres, Lieutenant Governor John Wentworth of Nova Scotia would view the Maroons as being akin to the Mi'kmaq. This association became both a condition for their deportation from Jamaica and a reason for their rescue in Nova Scotia. In Jamaica they were wild savages; in Nova Scotia, noble savages. B. W. Higman quotes David Brion Davis when he writes that the universal stereotype of slaves framed them "as loyal and faithful as good dogs, but also lazy, irresponsible, cunning, rebellious, untrustworthy and sexually promiscuous." See Higman, "Methodological Problems in the Study of the Slave Family," 369; Supplement to *The Royal Gazette*, April 30 to May 7, 1796, NLJ.

Chapter 3. Deportation

1. The legislature met on March 1. Balcarres to Walpole, February 3, 1796, *Journals of the Assembly of Jamaica*, JCB; Saturday, April 23, 1797, Proceedings of the Governor and Assembly of Jamaica, November 1796, JCB. The meeting was postponed to Wednesday, April 27, 1796; Postscript to *The Royal Gazette*, August 8, 1795,

to August 15, 1795, NLJ. A forty-year-old slave, Trophane, had returned to Jamaica to find his mother and sister after being "sold for transportation" fifteen years earlier; David Patrick Geggus, "Slavery, War and the Revolution in the Greater Caribbean, 1789–1815," in *A Turbulent Time: The French Revolution and the Greater Caribbean,* ed. David Barry Gaspar and David Patrick Geggus (Bloomington: Indiana University Press, 1997), 7.

2. Numbers of Maroons in remaining towns: Charles-Town: 289 (79 men, 74 women, 44 boys, 53 girls, 36 children, 3 invalids [no slaves]); Moore-Town: 245 (55 men, 69 women, 19 boys, 14 girls, 88 children [23 slaves]); Accompong-Town: 159 (33 men, 52 women, 48 boys, 26 girls [no slaves]); Scot's Hall: 45 (12 men, 12 women, 9 boys, 12 girls [3 slaves]). *Journals of the Assembly of Jamaica,* October 31, 1797, JCB; Committee of Correspondence Out-Letter Book, May 15, 1797, JARD; An Account of Jamaica and Its Inhabitants by a gentleman, long resident in the West Indies, 1808 (Record 10470.e.5), 9, 292, 295. On the Jamaican terrain that tempted Maroons to escape and the livelihood possible, see B. W. Higman, *Jamaica Surveyed: Plantation Maps and Plans of the Eighteenth and Nineteenth Centuries* (Kingston: Institute of Jamaica Publications Limited, 1988). On terrain and marronage in general, see Leslie F. Manigat, "The Relationship between Marronage and Slave Revolts and Revolution in St. Domingue-Haiti," in *Comparative Perspectives on Slavery in New World Plantation Societies,* ed. Vera Rubin and Arthur Tuden (New York: New York Academy of Sciences, 1977). On the proliferation of ports in small, elongated islands with "centrifugal coastlines," see B. W. Higman, "Jamaican Port Towns in the Early Nineteenth Century," in *Atlantic Port Cities: Economy, Culture, and Society in the Atlantic World: 1650–1850,* ed. Franklin W. Knight and Peggy K. Liss (Knoxville: University of Tennessee Press, 1991), 117.

3. Bryan Edwards, *The History Civil and Commercial of the British Colonies in the West Indies,* 1801. Rare Books, CL 1:570; An Account of Jamaica and Its Inhabitants by a gentleman, long resident in the West Indies (1808), 250.

4. Proceedings of the Governor and Assembly of Jamaica, January 4, 1796, JCB; *Journals of the Assembly of Jamaica,* June 5, 1798, 10:113, JCB; this actually happened in 1798, as reported by Captain Lauchlan McLaine, JCB; Votes of Assembly of Jamaica, April 20, 1796—letter read from Duke of Portland, JARD; Earl of Balcarres to Duke of Portland, April 20, 1796, in Anne Barnard, *Lives of the Lindsays, or a Memoir of the Houses of Crawford and Balcarres by Lord Lindsay, of Which Are Added Extracts from the Official Correspondence of Alexander Sixth Earl of Balcarres, During the Maroon War; Together with Personal Narratives by His Brothers, the Hon. Robert Colin, James, John,*

and Hugh Lindsay; and by His Sister, Lady Anne Barnard (London: John Murray, 1849), 126. He noted that of the 800, "200 may be runaway slaves and some women attending them."

5. R. C. Dallas, *The History of the Maroons, from Their Origin to the Establishment of Their Chief Tribe at Sierra Leone, Including the Expedition to Cuba for the Purpose of Procuring Spanish Chasseurs and the State of the Island of Jamaica for the Last Ten Years with a Succinct History of the Island Previous to That Period* (London: Frank Cass, 1968), 1:88; David Geggus, "The Enigma of Jamaica in the 1790s: New Light on the Causes of Slave Rebellions," *William and Mary Quarterly* 44, no. 2 (1987): 284. The Jamaicans could distinguish runaways from Maroons. As Lieutenant Colonel Jenkins observed in March 1796, "The runaways are not as yet selected from the Maroons, lest it should cause an alarm" (447). See T. Jenkins, Lieutenant-Colonel commanding at St. Ann's barrack, March 1, 1796, *Journals of the Assembly of Jamaica*, JCB; Supplement to *The Royal Gazette*, November 28, 1795, to December 5, 1795, NLJ; Supplement to *The Royal Gazette*, October 31 to November 7, 1795, NLJ. This was Mr. Nash of Utility Plantation.

6. Supplement to *The Royal Gazette*, Saturday, April 16, 1796, to Saturday, April 23, 1796, NLJ. This was the last time the Maroons, as a community, launched a violent resistance against Jamaica's slave society.

7. Journal Assembly Records, March 22, 1796, 456, NLJ; Supplement to *The Royal Gazette*, April 30 to May 7, 1796, NLJ; Lieut-Gov Alexander, earl of Balcarres, April 29, 1796, *Journals of the Assembly of Jamaica*, JCB; *St. James's Chronicle or the British Evening Post* (London), April 23, 1796–April 26, 1796; Journal Assembly Records, March 22, 1796, 456; Journal Assembly Records, April 14, 1796, 489. Over the next three years Robertson created three maps, one of each county, to increase knowledge of frontier regions, open the door for the extension of cultivation, and promote the increase of white people in the island. All Journal Assembly records in NLJ. On the British colonization of the Caribbean, see B. W. Higman, "Economic and Social Development of the British West Indies from Settlement to ca. 1850," in *The Cambridge Economic History of the United States*, vol. 1, ed. Stanley L. Engerman and Robert E. Gallman (Cambridge: Cambridge University Press, 1996).

8. Balcarres to Duke of Portland, March 26, 1796, in Barnard, *Lives of the Lindsays*, 122; Walpole to Balcarres, March 11, 1796, Proceedings of the Governor and Assembly of Jamaica, JCB; Balcarres to Duke, April 17, 1796, in Barnard, *Lives of the Lindsays*, 125.

9. *Journals of the Assembly of Jamaica*, March 11, 1796, and March 23, 1796, 9:465, JCB.

10. Postscript to *The Royal Gazette,* Saturday, May 7, 1796, to Saturday, May 14, 1796, NLJ. The newspaper reported the merits of two free men of color who had distinguished themselves in the war; Douglas Hall, "Jamaica," in *Neither Slave nor Free: The Freedmen of African Descent in the Slave Societies of the New World,* ed. David W. Cohen and Jack P. Greene (Baltimore: Johns Hopkins University Press, 1972), 197–98.

11. Petition from the Free People of Color in Jamaica, Relating to Jamaica, 1792, Add MS 12431, BL. It appears that free blacks petitioned in contractual terms whereas the Maroons continued to employ the language of paternalism. Both forms had become customary legal protocol in the British Empire of the late eighteenth century; ibid.; Postscript to *The Royal Gazette,* Saturday, August 8, 1795, to Saturday, August 15, 1795, NLJ. A man of "yellow complexion," Trophane, aged forty, belonged to the estate of a man in Saint Domingo. He was, in fact, sold for "transportation" fifteen years previously by Rebecca Colt, a woman of color. His sister in Jamaica was a free black woman named Phillip.

12. Lieutenant-Governor Message, March 24, 1796, in Journal Assembly Records, NLJ; in 1798 there were 290 Maroons in Charles-Town, see Votes of the Assembly of Jamaica, 1798–99, Return of Maroons from Charles-Town, November 20, 1798, JARD, 266 Maroons in Moore-Town, see Votes of the Assembly of Jamaica, 1798–99, Return of Maroons from Moore-Town, November 20, 1798 (81), JARD; fewer than 200 Accompongs, see Votes of the Assembly of Jamaica, 1798–99, Return of Maroons from Accompong-Town, November 20, 1798; and only 47 in Scots-Hall, see Votes of the Assembly of Jamaica, 1798–99, Return of Maroons from Scott's Hall, November 20, 1798, all in JARD. Some in Trelawney town in response to Balcarres's proclamation surrendered on August 8, 1795, *Journals of the Assembly of Jamaica,* 9:397, JCB; they included Sukey Martin, for self and child named Wm. Martin; Mary Sterling; Mimba and her daughter, Mary Fisher; Maria, for self and child, named Thomas Morris; Patience; Juba, for self and child, named Quamina; Amelia Palmer; Susanna Palmer, for self and three children named Eleanor Palmer, Emily Montague, and John Pendril; Ann Sewell; Lilly Allen; Rosanna Scarlett, for self and four children named John Quick, Elizabeth Quick, Wm Scarlet Earle, and John Anglin Earle; Elizabeth Borthwick, for self and child, named Mary Sharp; Ann Maclachlan; James Allen; Sarah Saunders; Elizabeth Sewell Walcott, for self and two children named Ann Weir and Wm. Walcott; Betty Cole (397–98). The motivations for these surrenders remain elusive; June 3, 1796, Balcarres to Hardwicke, Hardwicke Papers, vol. 568, Add MS 35916, British Library; Balcarres expected that "civil policy will produce the extinction of the rest by mixing them in the mass of the free people."

13. Out-Letters of Jamaica, Committee of Correspondence, National Archives, May 15, 1797. As the numbers of free blacks increased, Jamaicans had begun to question their service in the militia; James Stephen, MHS, The crisis of the sugar colonies; or, An enquiry into the objects and probable effects of the French expedition to the West Indies: and their connection with the colonial interests of the British empire. To which are subjoined, sketches of a plan for settling the vacant lands of Trinidad. In four letters to the Right Hon. Henry Addington, 1802, Box E187, 119, MHS. Stephen worried, "It is impossible that the black soldier should regard the extreme and degrading bondage of his brethren without disgust"; Mr. Batty, Resolution of the House, December 14, 1795, *Journals of the Assembly of Jamaica,* 9:421, JCB.

14. Geggus, "Slavery, War and Revolution," 24. On opposition to slave troops, see Elsa V. Goveia, *Slave Society in the British Leeward Islands at the End of the Eighteenth Century* (New Haven: Yale University Press, 1965), and essays in Christopher Leslie Brown and Philip D. Morgan, eds., *Arming Slaves: From Classical Times to the Modern Age* (New Haven: Yale University Press, 2006). Also see Wayne E. Lee, *Empires and Indigenes: Intercultural Alliance, Imperial Expansion, and Warfare in the Early Modern World* (New York: New York University Press, 2011). The role of marginalized people in the making of empires is discussed in Jane Burbank and Frederick Cooper, *Empires in World History: Power and Politics of Difference* (Princeton: Princeton University Press, 2010); *St. James's Chronicle or the British Evening Post* (London), November 7, 1795–November 10, 1795, Issue 5910. The Maroon population had grown from 600 in 1739 to 1,507 in 1794.

15. James Stephen, The crisis of the sugar colonies, 1802, Box E187, notes from all four letters, 64–69, MHS.

16. Unlike slaves, who saw an opportunity to gain their freedom in the British army, free and colored blacks had less incentive. If captured, they risked enslavement; Roger Norman Buckley, *Slaves in Red Coats: The British West India Regiments, 1795–1815* (New Haven: Yale University Press, 1979), 53–55; despite heavy opposition from Jamaica's slaveholders, the empire recruited slave regiments and distributed them across the Caribbean. During the late 1790s it moved from purchasing slaves from planters to buying them directly from Africa, where they were cheaper and in large supply. Between 1795 and 1808 the army bought 13,400 slaves, about 7 percent of the total slaves imported into the British West Indies.

17. Balcarres to Duke of Portland, July 17, 1796, in Hardwicke Papers, vol. 568, Add MS 35916, BL; Balcarres to Walpole, March 16, 1796, Proceedings of the Governor and Assembly of Jamaica, London, November 1796, JCB. Here Balcarres

distinguished artificially between voluntary and coerced surrender. Because the Maroons had "capitulated" and not surrendered, their punishment would have to be more severe; Decision about Maroons by Mr. Grant and Mr. McLean, April 20, 1796, Votes of Assembly of Jamaica, JARD.

18. Balcarres to Walpole, March 9, 1796, Proceedings of the Governor and Assembly of Jamaica, JCB; Vincent Brown, *The Reaper's Garden: Death and Power in the World of Atlantic Slavery* (Cambridge: Harvard University Press, 2008), 20.

19. Walpole to Balcarres, March 11, 1796, Proceedings of the Governor and Assembly of Jamaica, JCB; *Journals of the Assembly of Jamaica,* March 11, 1796, 465, JCB; Walpole to Balcarres, March 11, 1796, Proceedings of the Governor and Assembly of Jamaica, JCB; he echoed the views of the antideportation councilors. He believed the Trelawney Town Maroons had maintained the peace in Jamaica and, indeed, a Trelawney-like group of loyal blacks would have halted the slave rebellion at Saint-Domingue; Walpole to Balcarres, March 7, 1796, Hardwicke Papers, vol. 568, Add MS 35916, BL; Walpole to Balcarres, April 29, 1796, and undated, Hardwicke Papers, Add MS 35916, BL.

20. Balcarres to Duke, December 31, 1795, in Barnard, *Lives of the Lindsays,* 103; Letter, January 30, 1796, in Barnard, *Lives of the Lindsays,* 114.

21. Balcarres to Duke, December 31, 1795, in Barnard, *Lives of the Lindsays,* 103; Michael Duffy, "The French Revolution and the British Attitudes to the West Indian Colonies," in *A Turbulent Time,* 98.

22. Balcarres to Hardwicke, July 17, 1796, in Hardwicke Papers, Add MS 35916, BL; Balcarres to Walpole, May 14, 1796, in Hardwicke Papers, Add MS 35916, BL; also Walpole to Balcarres, April 29, 1796, and undated, Hardwicke Papers, Add MS 35916, BL; George Walpole to Lord Balcarres, May 16, 1796, in Hardwicke Papers, Add MS 35916, BL. Smith would not leave without his extended family. As Walpole wrote, Smith "does not want to remain; he understands that his wife and children were to remain with him but not his father and his brothers, that is to say Joe Williams, Cope, Charles Samuels and Genslete (?)"; Decision made by special committee, April 20, 1796, Journals of Assembly, JCB; Walpole to Balcarres, April 2, 1796, April 29, 1796, and undated, Hardwicke Papers, Add MS 35916, BL; Walpole did not forget Samuels and would try to rescue him from England. But by this time Samuels was in Nova Scotia.

23. Supplement to *The Royal Gazette,* November 28 to December 5, 1795, NLJ; George Walpole, Private, Proceedings of the Assembly of Jamaica, December 25, 1795, JCB. We know very little about Montague James's involvement in the war. We

know he was reported to be sick, and medicines were sent to him in January. Supplement to *The Royal Gazette,* Saturday, January 2, 1796 to Saturday, January 9, 1796, NLJ.

24. This number is reported by Mavis C. Campbell, ed., *Nova Scotia and the Fighting Maroons: A Documentary History* (Williamsburg, Va.: College of William and Mary Press, Studies in Third World Societies, 1990), xi. Repeatedly, between 150 and 160 Maroon men are listed in the records for Sierra Leone. Other Trelawney Town Maroons in the northeastern part of the island, in Westmoreland Parish, who had lived outside of Trelawney Town before the war and who stayed out of the rebellion continued to live separately from both Maroons and white society; Journal Assembly Records, March 29, 1796, NLJ; Supplement to *The Royal Gazette,* November 19, 1796, to November 26, 1796, NLJ; see the related essay on the relationship between poverty and slavery: Philip D. Morgan, "The Poor: Slaves in Early America," in *Slavery in the Development of the Americas,* ed. Frank D. Lewis, David Eltis, and Kenneth L. Sokoloff (Cambridge: Cambridge University Press, 2004), 288–323.

25. Supplement to *The Royal Gazette,* August 27, 1796, to September 3, 1796; Supplement to *The Royal Gazette,* June 4, 1796, to June 11, 1796; Supplement to *The Royal Gazette,* June 25, 1796, to July 2, 1796, all in NLJ. Pope was another of Francklyn's slaves; Proceedings of the Governor and Assembly of Jamaica, December 20, 1795, and November 1796; *Journals of the Assembly of Jamaica,* March 22, 1796, JCB. To compare the punishment meted out to rebellious slaves and to white convicts during this time, see Colin Forster, "Convicts: Unwilling Migrants from Britain and France," in *Coerced and Free Migration: Global Perspectives* (Stanford: Stanford University Press, 2002). For a perspective on a nation's rationale for deportation, see Daniel Kanstroom, *Deportation Nation* (Cambridge: Harvard University Press, 2010).

26. Proceedings of the Assembly of Jamaica, April 23, 1796, JCB. Those who voted yes were Redwood, Bryan, Halsted, Campbell, Foulks, Cockburn, Ross, Johnstone, Taylor, Thompson, Cuthbert, McLean, Wedderburn, White, Vaughan, Murray, Christie, Fuller, Shirley, Edwards. Those who voted no were Quarrell, Fuller, Hodges, Galbraith, Fitch, Mathison, Woolfrys, Stewart, Grant, Anderson, Osborn, Henckell, Deans; Balcarres writing to Forster Barham, Esq, May 23, 1796, in Hardwicke Papers, vol. 568, Add MS 35916, BL; Balcarres to Dundas, January 30, 1796, in Barnard, *Lives of the Lindsays,* 116; Journal Assembly Records, March 17, 1796, NLJ.

27. Votes of Assembly of Jamaica, June 2, 1796, JARD.

28. Some hounds remained; some were bought by slave owners who used them instead of the deported Maroons as a warning to slaves.

29. Balcarres letter, May 3, 1796, MS 606, Private and Confidential, NLJ. He writes, "The Negroes [slaves] hold us in high estimation, having conceived that the Maroons were not only invincible, but invulnerable"; Thomas Munro to Mr. Brodie, August 16, 1796, in Hardwicke Papers, Add MS 35916, BL.

30. Votes of Assembly of Jamaica, June 12, 1798, JARD; Supplement to *The Royal Gazette*, April 30 to May 7, 1796, NLJ; Votes of Assembly of Jamaica, June 13, 1798, JARD; Votes of Assembly of Jamaica, May 15, 1798, JARD. In addition to their families, the terms of the 1738–39 treaties had isolated the Maroons in one location.

31. Walpole to Balcarres, April 29, 1796, Proceedings of the Governor and Assembly of Jamaica, London, JCB; *True Briton* (London), Wednesday, May 2, 1798, Issue 1671.

32. *St. James's Chronicle or the British Evening Post* (London), August 27, 1796–August 30, 1796; *Morning Chronicle* (London), Saturday, July 30, 1796; announces publication of proceedings.

33. David Patrick Geggus, *Slavery, War, and Revolution: The British Occupation of Saint Domingue, 1793–1798* (New York: Oxford, 1982), 178; by restricting the issue of slavery to the Maroons, the antislavery agitators could support a single cause and believe they had won a small victory. Their exhaustive supposed rescue of the Maroons has compelled historians too to locate the Maroons solely as "resisters" of slavery, not as intermediaries who found the means to survive in a slave society; *Lloyd's Evening Post* (London), November 4, 1795–November 6, 1795, Issue 5959. This slippage between Maroons as "Negroes" and "Indians" and the racial assumptions that go with each category remain part of the Maroon heritage.

34. Balcarres letter, May 3, 1796, MS 606, Private and Confidential, NLJ; *Journals of the Assembly of Jamaica,* December 7, 1796, JCB; Balcarres to Duke, October 1, 1796, in Hardwicke Papers, Add MS 35916, BL.

35. Balcarres letter, May 3, 1796, MS 606, Private and Confidential, NLJ; Journals of the House of Assembly, August 3, 1799, 325.

36. Proceedings of the Governor and Assembly of Jamaica, December 24, 1795, JCB; it is difficult to say definitively what motivated Walpole. In his ever-thoughtful works, B. W. Higman notes that "individuals can act inconsistently without changing the beliefs themselves." See Higman, "Methodological Problems in the Study of the Slave Family," in *Comparative Perspectives on Slavery in New World Plantation Societies,* 371.

37. George Wilson Bridges, *Annals of Jamaica by the Reverend George Wilson Bridges, A.M.* (London: John Murray, 1828), 250, 221.

38. Andrew Smith, Captain of Maroons to Charles Samuels, date Maroon Hall, June 3, 1797, Colonial Office Papers, MG II N.S. "A," vol. 127 (Microfilm C9137), NSA; also see Mrs. A. C. Carmichael, *Domestic Manners and Social Condition of the White, Coloured and Negro Population of the West Indies,* 2 vols. (London: Whittaker, Treacher, 1833), 1:321. Carmichael wrote, "Negroes do not regard England and Scotland in the same light: this I believe proceeds from two causes. Scotchmen are proverbially active and economical, abroad as well as at home: and perhaps there are not two qualities which the majority of Negroes dislike more thoroughly"; Robert Sewell to Duke of Portland, April 5, 1798, *Journals of the Assembly of Jamaica,* JCB.

Chapter 4. Conversion

1. Much of the content in this chapter was published in a slightly different format in *Acadiensis* 2017. "Slavery in Nova Scotia" (long green folder with clippings), MG 1, vol. 356, #10, LAC. The exact number is debatable. Another report indicates that 568 Maroons reached Nova Scotia. See *Columbia Centinel,* December 16, 1797; John Wentworth to Lord Balcarres, August 4, 1797, RG 1, vol. 52, 1337-N, LAC. Wentworth reported that one "sensible man," John Jarrett, lamented the loss of his property in Jamaica; another Maroon complained about a "well-furnished house and cellar" he had left behind. See John Wentworth to Duke of Portland, April 21, 1797, RG 1, vol. 52, 1337-N, LAC. One Maroon woman who reached Sierra Leone, Sylvia Harding, came without a "mother or father." Harding noted that she was brought "as one of the family of Mrs. Connor of the Maroons of which nation petitioner also was." Harding raises the possibility that Maroon women may have owned female slaves. That Sylvia Harding refers to the Maroon woman as "Mrs. Connor" is striking, the only case in the sources where a Maroon woman is referred to as "Mrs." Sierra Leone Council, 1813–15, CO 270/14, TNA; Balcarres to Duke of Portland, April 17, 1796, in Anne Barnard, *Lives of the Lindsays, or a Memoir of the Houses of Crawford and Balcarres by Lord Lindsay, of Which Are Added Extracts from the Official Correspondence of Alexander Sixth Earl of Balcarres, During the Maroon War; Together with Personal Narratives by His Brothers, the Hon. Robert Colin, James, John, and Hugh Lindsay; and by His Sister, Lady Anne Barnard* (London: John Murray, 1849), 126; the war cost over £350,000 in just eight months; Graeme Wynn, "On the Margins of Empire, 1760–1840," in *The Illustrated History of Canada,* ed. Craig Brown (Toronto: Key Porter Books, 2002), 189–278; Graeme Wynn, "A Region of Scattered Settlements and Bounded Possibilities: Northeastern North America, 1775–1800," *Canadian Geographer* 31, no. 4 (December 1987): 319–38; Julian Gwyn, *Excessive Expectations:*

Maritime Commerce and the Economic Development of Nova Scotia, 1740–1870 (Montreal: McGill-Queen's University Press, 1998); John N. Grant, *The Maroons in Nova Scotia* (Halifax: Formac, 2002).

2. M. C. F. Easmon, "Sierra Leone's Connection with Royalty," *Sierra Leone Studies* 16 (1962); Prince Edward letter to "My Lord Duke," August 25, 1796, CO 217/71, LAC; in his letter he noted that 540 Maroons had arrived; Dr. John Oxley to John Wentworth, May 31, 1797, enclosure in letter from John Wentworth to Duke of Portland dated June 2, 1797, C9137, MG II N.S. "A," vol. 125 (154), LAC. Oxley notes the long confinement and the bad water in Jamaica: "[They] can do us no harm . . . nor do they seem disposed to evil"; John Wentworth to G. Hammond, August 16, 1796, RG 1, vol. 50–51, 1337-N, LAC. This demographic difference—the large number of women and children—distinguished the Maroons' relocation from the middle passage. It also highlights that the Maroons were deported for political, not economic, reasons. Of the 3,000 black Loyalists who moved to Nova Scotia after the War of American Independence, 1,336 were men, 914 women, and 750 children. See Robin W. Winks, *The Blacks in Canada: A History* (Montreal: McGill-Queen's University Press, 1971), 33; Disposition of Thomas Barclay of Annapolis in the County of Annapolis, May 23, 1799, CO 217/37, LAC.

3. John Wentworth to Admiral Murray, June 24, 1795, RG 1, vol. 50–51, 1337-N, LAC; one contemporary noted, "It appears they have brought some MONEY with them and the project is likely to be useful to this country, should the Maroons prove industrious," in *True Briton* (London), September 2, 1796; John Wentworth to Duke of Portland, July 25, 1796, MG II N.S., "A," vol. 123, LAC; the Citadel had remained in a state of disrepair since 1783. Some sentries apparently conducted themselves as "unarmed banditti." See June 11, 1783, and July 1, 1783, in MG 12, HQ 1, LAC; John Wentworth to Dr. Morris, May 1, 1799, RG 1, vol. 52, 1337-N, LAC.

4. Arrangement with Prince Edward, July 25, 1796, Microfiche 232 (CIHM no. 47614 ICMH no), BL; John Wentworth to Henry Dundas, May 7, 1794, RG 1, vol. 48, 1336-N, LAC.

5. Prince Edward letter to "My Lord Duke," August 25, 1796, CO 217/71, LAC; John Wentworth to Duke of Portland, September 20, 1796, RG 1, vol. 50–51, 1337-N, LAC; John Wentworth to Duke of Portland, September 20, 1796, Microfiche 232 (CIHM no. 47614 ICMH no), BL.

6. For the discussion of African Americans in the Maritimes I am indebted to Harvey Amani Whitfield's work. See his "Reviewing Blackness in Atlantic Canada and the African Atlantic Canadian Diaspora," *Acadiensis* 37, no. 2 (2008), 130–39, and

"The Struggle over Slavery in the Maritime Colonies," *Acadiensis* 41, no. 2 (2012): 17–44; also see his book *North to Bondage: Loyalist Slavery in the Maritimes* (Vancouver: University of British Columbia Press, 2016). The Maroons' dependent status foreshadowed the large-scale importation of indentured servants to the Americas in the early nineteenth century. Although these laborers came willingly to work in the Caribbean colonies and had legal freedom as well as social status above slaves, they oftentimes lived a marginal existence; as O. Nigel Bolland notes, "Approximately 28 million East Indians left their homelands between 1846 and 1932 to work as 'coolie' laborers in the American tropics." See Bolland, "Colonization and Slavery in Central America," 6; from newspaper clipping in 1773 (1772?): "Ran away from her master, John Rock, on Monday, a negro girl named Thursday, about four and a half feet high, broad set, with a lump over her right eye. Had on, when she went away, a red cloth petticoat, a red baize bed gown, and a red ribbon about her head." Thursday is mentioned in Rock's will in 1776. See MG 1, vol. 356, #10, "Slavery in Nova Scotia" (long green folder with clippings), excerpts, LAC; Ken Donovan, "Slavery and Freedom in Atlantic Canada's African Diaspora: Introduction," *Acadiensis* 43, no. 1 (Winter/Spring 2014): 109–15. Donovan notes that 3,550 black people eventually emigrated from the American colonies to Nova Scotia, of whom approximately 34 percent remained slaves, 111; on legal protection by the British Empire, see Winks, *The Blacks in Canada,* 26; Whitfield, "The Struggle over Slavery," 20; the black Loyalist influx included 1,200 people designated as "servants," who arrived with the white Loyalists; Whitfield, "The Struggle over Slavery," 27.

7. *Nova Scotia Magazine,* April 1790, AP EUH, Akins Collection, NSA.

8. Whitfield, *North to Bondage;* Robin Winks, "A Sacred Animosity: Abolition in Canada," in *The Antislavery Vanguard: New Essays on the Abolitionists,* ed. Martin Duberman (Princeton: Princeton University Press, 1965), 302. Winks notes that some slaves escaped to the New England states to find freedom; David G. Bell, "Slavery and the Judges of Loyalist New Brunswick," *University of New Brunswick Law Journal* 31 (1982): 9–42; Barry Cahill, "Habeas Corpus and Slavery in Nova Scotia: *R v. Hect, ex parte Rachel, 1798,*" *University of New Brunswick Law Journal* 44 (1995): 179–209; Barry Cahill, "Slavery and the Judges of Loyalist Nova Scotia," *University of New Brunswick Law Journal* 43 (1994): 73–135; Barry Cahill, "The Antislavery Polemic of Rev. James MacGregor: Canada's Proto-Abolitionist as 'Radical Evangelical,'" in *The Contribution of Presbyterianism to the Marine Provinces of Canada,* ed. Charles H. H. Scobie and G. A. Rawlyk (Montreal: McGill-Queen's University Press, 1997). In addition, Chief Justices Thomas Strange and Sampson S. Blowers made it difficult for

slave owners to prove legal ownership of slaves; Whitfield, "The Struggle over Slavery," 17–44. Slavery faded in Nova Scotia during the 1820s, about a decade before imperial emancipation; slavery died out in the Maritimes for three reasons: the challenge presented by slave runaways, the voice of key antislavery chief justices who ruled against slave owners, and the repeated denial by the Nova Scotia legislature (in 1787, 1789, 1801, and 1808) to give statutory recognition to slavery. See Whitfield, *North of Bondage,* chap. 5.

9. John Wentworth does not explicitly mention Loyalist slaves in his correspondence. His family owned slaves in New Hampshire; although blacks worked in his household in Nova Scotia, their precise status remains unclear. See Brian C. Cuthbertson, *The Loyalist Governor: Biography of Sir John Wentworth* (Halifax: Petheric Press, 1983), 78; we do know that Wentworth sent a shipment of nineteen slaves from Nova Scotia to Suriname, see *North of Bondage,* 52; appointed as surveyor general of woods in the early 1790s, Wentworth knew of the black Loyalists and their subsequent exile; John Wentworth to John King, Esq., September 14, 1792, RG 1, vol. 48, 1336-N, LAC; John Wentworth to Duke of Portland, October 29, 1796, MG II N.S. "A," vol. 124, LAC. In the British army during the war they exchanged "obedience for provisioned subsistence"; Nova Scotia, Miscellaneous, No. 7, October 29, 1796, CO 217/69, LAC; John Wentworth to Henry Dundas, March 22, 1793, RG 1, vol. 48, 1336-N, LAC; John Wentworth to John King, December 13, 1792, RG 1, vol. 48, 1336-N, LAC; this phrase is mine. John Wentworth treated the Maroons, like the Mi'kmaq, as an autonomous community. He did not intervene in cases where Maroons committed offenses against other Maroons. Just two months after their arrival in Nova Scotia he stipulated that three Maroon captains should, under the supervision of Alexander Ochterloney and William Dawes Quarrell, decide on a sentence. See John Wentworth to Duke of Portland, September 20, 1796, RG 1, vol. 50–51, 1337-N, LAC; on the Loyalists who remained in Nova Scotia, see James W. St. G. Walker, "The Establishment of a Free Black Community in Nova Scotia, 1783–1840," in *The African Diaspora: Interpretive Essays,* ed. Martin L. Kilson and Robert I. Rotberg (Cambridge: Harvard University Press, 1976).

10. Duke of Portland to John Wentworth, July 15, 1796, CO 218/27, TNA.

11. William Dawes Quarrell to Sewell, Halifax, January 15, 1797, *Journals of the Assembly of Jamaica,* 10:547, JCB; Quarrell mentioned 530 Maroons.

12. Sir William Young, *Historical Survey of the Island of Saint Domingo together with an account of the Maroon negroes in the island of Jamaica; and a history of the war in the West Indies, in 1793 and 1794; also a tour through the several islands of Barbados,*

St. Vincent, Antigua, Tobago, and Grenada in the Years 1791 and 1792 (London, 1801). Young notes that his account of the Maroons is taken from Edward Long, *The History of Jamaica: Reflections on Its Situation, Settlements, Inhabitants, Climate, Products, Commerce, Laws, and Government* (Montreal: McGill-Queen's University Press, 2002), written in 1774, 317–18; *Journals of the Assembly of Jamaica,* July 2, 1799, JCB.

13. *Journals of the Assembly of Jamaica,* March 4, 1801, JCB; John Wentworth to Lord Balcarres, June 13, 1798, RG 1, vol. 52, 1337-N, LAC; I am deeply thankful to John G. Reid and Harvey A. Whitfield for their critical feedback at every stage of this chapter; Elizabeth Mancke's work on empire and loyalism remains foundational. Paul W. Wilderson, *Governor John Wentworth and the American Revolution: The English Connection* (Hanover, N.H.: University of New England Press, 1994), 99; Cuthbertson, *The Loyalist Governor;* John Wentworth fits Ann Gorman Condon's description of elite Loyalists who sought to reassert patriarchal hierarchy in a new context. See Condon, "Loyalist Style and the Culture of the Atlantic Seaboard," *Material History Bulletin* no. 25 (1987): 21–28, and "The Family in Exile: Loyalist Values After the Revolution," in *Intimate Relations: Family and Community in Planter Nova Scotia, 1759–1800,* ed. Margaret Conrad (Fredericton: Acadiensis Press, 1995). See also Patricia Rogers, "The Loyalist Experience in an Anglo-American Atlantic World," in *Planter Links: Community and Culture in Colonial Nova Scotia,* ed. Margaret Conrad and Barry Moody (Fredericton: Acadiensis Press, 2001), 165–74; Wentworth was an exile of war like the Maroons. The War of American Independence had uprooted him from his privileged place in the empire; the British war with the French uprooted the Maroons from their protected role in the empire.

14. Letter from Quarrell to Balcarres, November 27, 1798, in Votes of Assembly of Jamaica, 1798–99, JARD; *Journals of the Assembly of Jamaica,* October 10, 1796, JCB; John Wentworth to G. Hammond, August 16, 1796, RG 1, vol. 50–51, 1337-N, LAC; Jeffrey A. Fortrin, "Blackened Beyond Our Native Hue: Removal, Identity and the Trelawney Maroons on the Margins of the Atlantic World, 1796–1800," *Citizenship Studies* 10, no. 1 (2006): 31; Cuthbertson, *The Loyalist Governor,* 83.

15. Michael Wallace, July 15, 1799, C9138, Colonial Office, Nova Scotia, "A," July–December, 1799, vol. 130 (41), LAC; Letter from William Dawes Quarrell to Earl of Balcarres, November 27, 1798, Votes of Assembly of Jamaica, 1798–99, JARD; John Wentworth to Duke of Portland, May 5, 1799, C9138, Colonial Office, Nova Scotia, "A," January–June, 1799, vol. 129 (104), LAC (also see mention of black Loyalists); John Wentworth to Duke of Portland, August 13, 1796, Microfiche 232 (CIHM no. 47614 ICMH no), BL.

16. The Maroons entered a diversified society. First, there was the backbone of the colony: the English, Scots, and Americans who had settled there since the 1750s. There were also Germans in Lunenburg and some Irish immigrants. A few hundred Acadian families—those not deported in 1755—remained. There was the group of black Loyalists, at least two thousand free blacks, who had been granted refuge in Nova Scotia after the Revolution (the remaining twelve hundred had left Nova Scotia for Sierra Leone in 1792, about four years before the Maroons arrived). There were slaves, many of whom had accompanied the white Loyalists who had arrived in Nova Scotia after the war. And there were Mi'kmaw families. See Wynn, "A Region of Scattered Settlements." Also Graeme Wynn, "A Province Too Much Dependent on New England," *Canadian Geographer* 31, no. 2 (June 1987): 98–113; and Philip A. Buckner, "Was There a 'British' Empire? *The Oxford History of the British Empire* from a Canadian Perspective," *Acadiensis* 32, no. 1 (Autumn 2002): 110–28; Cuthbertson, *The Loyalist Governor,* 32.

17. William C. Wicken, *Mi'kmaq Treaties on Trial: History, Land and Donald Marshall Junior* (Toronto: University of Toronto Press, 2002), 130; William C. Wicken, *Colonization of Mi'kmaw Memory and History, 1794–1928* (Toronto: University of Toronto Press, 2012), 8, 97; extract of Observations on Halifax to Granville, September 8, 1790 (from Inglis?); the population before Loyalist migration was fourteen thousand; John G. Reid shows how the demographic shift that occurred with Loyalist immigration impacted the Mi'kmaq: see "Pax Britannica or Pax Indigena? Planter Nova Scotia (1760–1782) and Competing Strategies of Pacification," *Canadian Historical Review* 85, no. 4 (2004). As Reid writes, "The loyalist emigration extended into Nova Scotia a weight of settlement that was incompatible with Aboriginal economies" (673).

18. L. F. S. Upton, *Micmacs and Colonists: Indian–White Relations in the Maritime Provinces, 1713–1867* (Vancouver: University of British Columbia Press, 1979), 36; Wicken, *Mi'kmaq Treaties on Trial,* 40; Stephen Patterson also argues that the "interaction of indigenous and colonial peoples is best understood from the inside" (24). See Stephen Patterson, "Indian–White Relations in Nova Scotia, 1749–61: A Study in Political Interaction," *Acadiensis* 23, no. 1 (1993): 24; Wicken, *Mi'kmaq Treaties on Trial,* 175, 192; Johan Seume, "Mein Lebin," in *The Old Man Told Us: Excerpts from Micmac History, 1500–1950,* ed. Ruth Holmes Whitehead (Halifax: Nimbus, 1991), 175. The Mi'kmaq spoke an Eastern Algonquian language. See Robert M. Leavitt, *Maliseet Mi'kmaq: First Nations of the Maritimes* (Fredericton: New Ireland Press, 1995), 41.

19. John G. Reid must be credited for his observation that "a new and demonstrably different phase of settler colonization began during the later years of the Revolution, with the Loyalist migration." See John G. Reid, "'In the Midst of Three Fires, a French one, an American one, and an Indian one': Imperial-Indigenous Negotiations during the War of 1812 in Eastern British America" (paper presented at "The War of 1812: Memory and Myth, History and Historiography" conference, University of London, July 12–14, 2012). Like Harvey A. Whitfield, Catherine M. A. Cottreau-Robins calls the Loyalist period in Nova Scotia an age of slavery. See Cottreau-Robins, "Searching for the Enslaved in Nova Scotia's Loyalist Landscape," *Acadiensis* 43, no. 1 (Winter/Spring 2014): 125–36; Cole Harris, *The Reluctant Land: Society, Space, and Environment in Canada before Confederation* (Vancouver: University of British Columbia Press, 2008), 179; Reid, "Empire, the Maritime Colonies, and the Supplanting of Mi'kma'ki/Wulstukwik, 1780–1820," *Acadiensis* 28, no. 2 (Summer/Autumn 2009): 83. Reid notes the effects of smallpox and dysentery, diseases brought directly by the settlers in 1801 and 1803; Upton, *Micmacs and Colonists,* 145, 139, 140.

20. Leavitt, *Maliseet Mi'kmaq,* 82; Upton, *Micmacs and Colonists,* 128, 133–34; one petition in 1831 described how the sound of the axe had scared away game and how the sale of baskets and buckets did not substitute for hunting; according to Council Minutes of March 9, 1790, nine thousand moose were killed in Cape Breton during 1789 only for the sake of their skins. See Seume, "Mein Lebin," 178. In a recent essay Jason Hall complicates our understanding of precolonial cultivation; his close study suggests that both the Maliseet and Mi'kmaq managed land—they grew Jerusalem artichokes, ground nuts, and maize—well before contact with the Europeans. See Hall, "Maliseet Cultivation and Climatic Resilience on the Wəlastəkw/St. John River During the Little Ice Age," *Acadiensis* 44, no. 2 (Summer/Autumn 2015): 3–25; Wicken, *Colonization of Mi'kmaw Memory and History,* 102.

21. Grant, *The Maroons in Nova Scotia,* chap. 3; John Wentworth to Henry Dundas, May 3, 1793, RG 1, vol. 48, 1336-N, LAC; John Wentworth to Henry Dundas, July 23, 1793, RG 1, vol. 48, 1336-N, LAC; John Wentworth to Henry Dundas, May 19, 1794, RG 1, vol. 48, 1336-N, LAC; John Wentworth to Duke of Portland, December 21, 1796, RG 1, vol. 52, 1337-N, LAC.

22. From January 12, 1770. See Wilderson, *Governor John Wentworth,* 128; Upton, *Micmacs and Colonists,* 130; quoted in Ellen Gibson, *John Clarkson and the African Adventure* (London: Macmillan, 1980), 69–70.

23. In her recent essay in *Acadiensis,* Mary McCarthy cites Zainab Amadahy, a writer of African, Cherokee, and European descent, who writes that the process of

colonization has left him "clanless" with no "familiar relationship with the land." See McCarthy, "Mixed Race Identity: Black and Maliseet: My Personal Narrative," *Acadiensis* 43, no. 1 (2014): 122; also see Trudy Sable and Bernie Francis, *The Language of This Land: Mi'kma'ki* (Sydney, Nova Scotia: Cape Breton University Press, 2012); Andrew Parnaby, "The Cultural Economy of Survival: The Mi'kmaq of Cape Breton in the Mid-19th Century," *Labour/Le Travail* 61 (Spring 2008): 73; Patterson, "Indian–White Relations," 24; Parnaby, "The Cultural Economy of Survival"; also see Wicken, *Colonization of Mi'kmaw Memory and History,* 112.

24. Duke of Portland to John Wentworth, MG II N.S. "A," vol. 124, LAC. He spent £656 between 1795 and 1796; John Wentworth to Duke of Portland, April 21, 1797, RG 1, vol. 52, 1337-N, LAC; Proceedings of His Majesty's Council in Court Assembly Session, July 4, 1798 (136), CO 217/73, LAC; Journal and Proceedings of the House of Assembly of Jamaica (transcribed), June 9, 1798, CO 217/73, LAC; Journal and Proceedings of the House of Assembly of Jamaica, June 7, 1799, CO 217/73, LAC.

25. Extract from letter from a gentleman at Halifax in *True Briton* (London), September 2, 1796. As reported, "About 700 of the Maroon Negroes from Jamaica arrived here, in two transports, convoyed by the Dover, of 44 guns"; *Oracle and Public Advertiser* (London), March 28, 1796. This includes the sentence on aborigines; see Second Address, delivered in 1814, of the "Deplorable State of the Indians in Halifax, Nova Scotia" (Hathi Trust online). Four topics would be covered: Natural disposition and intellectual powers of the Indians; Causes of their jealousy and suspicion of the integrity of the Europeans; Their fidelity and strict observance of the treaties of peace with the English; The probability of their acceding to any wise plan that may be proposed for their civilization, and lastly the cause of failure hereby adopted; for a deep contextualization of the Mi'kmaw world, see Reid, "Empire, the Maritime Colonies, and the Supplanting of Mi'kma'ki/Wulstukwik, 1780–1820," 78–97.

26. John Wentworth's initial attitude toward the Maroons echoed Walpole's in Jamaica.

27. *Times* (London), October 22, 1796; Benjamin Gerrish Gray, Preston, June 18, 1798, sent in enclosure (like the rest of these letters) to Duke of Portland from John Wentworth on June 23, 1798, MG II N.S. "A," vol. 127, LAC.

28. Wentworth's deep knowledge of Mi'kmaw acculturation to Catholicism possibly prevented him from attempting this experiment with them. See Judith Fingard, "English Humanitarianism and the Colonial Mind: Walter Bromley in Nova Scotia, 1813–1825," *Canadian Historical Review* 54 (1973): 144; Nova Scotia, Miscellaneous, September 20, 1796, CO 217/69, LAC; Wentworth to Duke of Portland, Halifax,

September 20, 1796, Microfiche 232, BL; Nova Scotia, Miscellaneous, No. 5, September 24, 1796, CO 217/69, LAC.

29. Like Wentworth, other Loyalists believed an inextricable link existed between loyalty to the empire and Anglican worship. To ensure deeper allegiance, Charles Inglis, another Loyalist who had lived in British-occupied New York City during the war years, was appointed as the first bishop of Nova Scotia in 1787. John Frederick Wolverton, *Colonial Anglicanism in North America* (Detroit: Wayne State University Press, 1984); John Wolfe Lydekker, *The Life and Letters of Charles Inglis: His Ministry in America and Consecration as First Colonial Bishop, from 1759 to 1787* (London: Society for Promoting Christian Knowledge, 1936); Stanley Boyd Schlenter, "Religious Faith and Commercial Empire," in *The Oxford History of the British Empire,* ed. P. J. Marshall (London: Oxford, 1998); *Nova Scotia Magazine,* April 1790, AP EUH, Akins Collection, NSA; *Nova Scotia Magazine,* essay by "Columella," November 25, 1789, NSA; *St. James's Chronicle or the British Evening Post* (London), October 20, 1796–October 22, 1796.

30. *Journals of House of Assembly,* August 3, 1799, JCB. Here they are referred to as "600 pagans"; see Statement of Facts respecting the settling of Maroons in Nova Scotia referred to by the Lieutenant-Governor of that Province, May 30, 1799, Colonial Office, Nova Scotia, "A," January–June, 1799, vol. 129 (179), LAC; Nova Scotia, Miscellaneous, No. 7, October 29, 1796, CO 217/69, LAC; John Wentworth to Duke of Portland, August 13, 1796, MG II N.S., "A," LAC.

31. Extract of Observations on Halifax to Granville, September 8, 1790 (from Inglis?); the writer explained, "In this country which is so REMOTE from the parent state, principles of loyalty should be inculcated"; John Wentworth to Duke of Portland, August 13, 1796, MG II N.S., "A," LAC; John Wentworth, January 20, 1795, RG 1, vol. 50–51, 1337-N, LAC.

32. John Wentworth to Duke of Portland, September 20, 1796, Microfiche 232 (CIHM no. 47614 ICMH no), BL. He estimated the cost to be £240 annually; Nova Scotia, Miscellaneous, No. 4. September 20, 1796, CO 217/69, LAC; John Wentworth to Duke of Portland, September 20, 1796, CO 217/69, LAC; John Wentworth to Earl of Balcarres, October 10, 1796, RG 1, vol. 50–51, 1337-N, LAC; Wentworth noted that "all the Maroons understood English and many spoke it fluently"; see Wentworth to Duke of Portland, December 21, 1796, RG 1, vol. 52, 1337-N, LAC; Charles Bruce Fergusson, *Clarkson's Mission to America, 1791–92,* NSA, Publication no. 11, 1971, 138. *Nova Scotia Magazine,* April 1790 (AP EUH, Akins Collection); *Nova Scotia Magazine,* essay by "Columella," November 25, 1789, NSA.

33. George Ross, September 10, 1800, in Mavis C. Campbell, *Back to Africa: George Ross and the Maroons from Nova Scotia to Sierra Leone* (Trenton, N.J.: Africa World Press, 1993), 7.

34. John Wentworth to Duke of Portland, August 13, 1796, MG II N.S., "A," LAC; Benjamin Gerrish Gray (parson of Maroons) to John Wentworth, on June 18, 1798, MG II N.S. "A," vol. 127, LAC.

35. John Wentworth to Duke of Portland, June 23, 1798, RG 1, vol. 52, Reel 19, 1337-N, LAC; John Wentworth to Duke of Portland, July 10, 1797, MG II N.S. "A," vol. 125 (212), LAC; Michael Wallace, June 27, 1799, in *Journals of House of Assembly,* JCB; Wallace writes, "eventually good has resulted from it [Boydville]." Yet it occasioned an increased expense in the purchasing of lands, building of houses, extra expense transporting supplies with an additional superintendent; and similar expenses would have attended every detachment so settled, had it been put into practice.

36. Journal Assembly Records, March 23, 1796, NLJ; other families in the Boydville group included the following: George Lawrence, Taylor Moody, Robert Fowler, Pat O'Conner, G. G. Barrett, John Russia, Jobie Lawrence, Herbert Gerard, Capt. John Palmer, Quaco Leburque, Charles Samuel, Charles Downing.

37. Extract of letter to Walpole, January 10, 1797, 1b/5/14/2, NLJ (letter sent only in 1798?). Maroon Town, June 3, 1797, letter from Andrew Smith, Captain of Maroons, to Charles Samuels, date Maroon Hall, June 3, 1797, Colonial Office Papers, NSA, 1798, MG II N.S. "A," vol. 127 (Microfilm C9137), 40. Captain David Shaw, possibly the father of Charles Shaw, had helped Major General Walpole in Jamaica. See George Walpole to Lord Balcarres, March 13, 1796, Proceedings of the Governor and Assembly of Jamaica, November 1796, JCB.

38. June 8, 1797, Robert Sewell to Jamaica Committee, Committee of Correspondence Out-Letter book, 1b/4/14/2, National Archives of Jamaica; extract of letter to Walpole, January 10, 1797, 1b/5/14/2, National Archives of Jamaica; Letter from Halifax to Duke on April 23, 1797, in an attachment to Wentworth sent from England on March 8, 1798, Colonial Office Papers, NSA, 1798, MG II N.S. "A," vol. 127 (Microfilm C9137), 26; extract of letter to Walpole, January 10, 1797, 1b/5/14/2, National Archives of Jamaica; after the Maroons left Nova Scotia, Wentworth suggested that they protected their rituals through a secret oath, and, indeed, a Maroon could confront murder for divulging these. Wentworth to John King, August 6, 1800, CO 217/37, TNA.

39. Letter from Halifax to Duke on April 23, 1797, in an attachment to Wentworth sent from England on March 8, 1798, Colonial Office Papers, NSA, 1798, MG

II N.S. "A," vol. 127 (Microfilm C9137), 26; John Wentworth to Duke of Portland, October 22, 1799, RG 1, vol. 52, 1337-N, LAC.

40. Alexander Ochterloney, December 18, 1798, *Journals of the Assembly of Jamaica,* JCB. Most of the Caribs were women and children. See Nancie L. Gonzales, "The Garifuna of Central America," in *The Indigenous People of the Caribbean,* ed. Samuel M. Wilson (Gainesville: University Press of Florida, 1997), 203.

41. Thomas Strangeways, *Sketch of Mosquito Shore: Including the Territory of Poyais, Descriptive of the Country; with Some Information as to Its Productions, the Best Mode of Culture &C. Chiefly Intended for the Use of Settlers* (Edinburgh: William Blackwood, 1822), 39; Mavis C. Campbell, *Becoming Belize: A History of an Outpost of Empire Searching for Identity* (Kingston: University of West Indies Press, 2011), 112–26. Because the Caribs were not identified as a people of African ancestry, Sierra Leone did not emerge as an option for them as it had for the Maroons; following a slave rebellion in Barbados in 1816, the captured rebels were again shipped to Belize in Central America. The Caribs had set a precedent for disposing of dangerous enemies. See David Brion Davis, *Inhuman Bondage: The Rise and Fall of Slavery in the New World* (New York: Oxford University Press, 2006), 212.

42. Duke of Portland to Robert Sewall, March 30, 1798, *Journals of the Assembly of Jamaica,* 10:120, JCB; in 1840 Rattan was considered a home for liberated Africans. See the Liberated Negroes' Civilization Society, around 1840, CO 318/148, TNA.

43. At least one was expelled for attending a cockfight on a Sunday; Private and Confidential, John Wentworth to John King, April 14, 1799, C9138, Colonial Office, Nova Scotia, "A," January–June, 1799, vol. 129, LAC; Mavis C. Campbell cites other sentences in her edited volume *Nova Scotia and the Fighting Maroons: A Documentary History* (Williamsburg, Va.: College of William and Mary Press, Studies in Third World Societies, 1990), 138–39.

44. Wentworth's use of indigenous peoples and blacks as military allies drew from a long tradition. See Wayne E. Lee, *Empires and Indigenes: Intercultural Alliance, Imperial Expansion, and Warfare in the Early Modern World* (New York: New York University Press, 2011); Christopher Leslie Brown and Philip D. Morgan, eds., *Arming Slaves: From Classical Times to the Modern Age* (New Haven: Yale University Press, 2006). On black Loyalists, see James W. St. G. Walker, *The Black Loyalists: The Search for a Promised Land in Nova Scotia and Sierra Leone, 1783–1870* (New York: Africana, 1976). Also see Winks, *The Blacks in Canada,* Grant, *The Maroons in Nova Scotia,* and Mavis C. Campbell's three books on the maroons; *Journals of the House of Assembly,* December 18, 1798. As Ochterloney reported later, Wentworth thought of forming the Maroons

into a body and attaching them to "some riflemen to defend Cole Harbour road. He did give some commissions to the Maroons"; *Journals of the House of Assembly,* March 4, 1801. Quarrell wrote, "The alarm occasioned in Halifax by Richery's squadron—Wentworth proposed to embody the Maroons as a military corps—he applied to me to recommend such Maroons best deserving of commissions"; *Journals of the House of Assembly,* John Wentworth to Duke of Portland, October 8, 1796, JCB; John Wentworth to Duke of Portland, September 24, 1796, Microfiche 232 (CIHM no. 47614 ICMH no), BL; John Wentworth to Duke of Portland, October 8, 1796, RG 1, vol. 50–51, 1337-N, LAC; John Wentworth to Duke of Portland, April 21, 1797, RG 1, vol. 52, 1337-N, LAC.

45. John Wentworth to Henry Dundas, July 23, 1793, RG 1, vol. 48, 1336-N, LAC. The issue of allegiance to the French would also arise for the Acadians. See John Wentworth to Henry Dundas, November 9, 1793, RG 1, vol. 48, 1336-N, LAC; John Wentworth to Duke of Portland, September 24, 1796, Microfiche 232 (CIHM no. 47614 ICMH no), BL. In October, when the French fleet departed Newfoundland, the danger left the colony.

46. Duke of Portland to John Wentworth, June 12, 1797, *Journals of the Assembly of Jamaica,* JCB; John Wentworth to Duke of Portland, April 21, 1797, MG II N.S. "A," vol. 125, LAC; John Wentworth to G. Hammond, August 16, 1796, RG 1, vol. 50–51, 1337-N, LAC.

47. Harvey Amani Whitfield notes that "slavery lasted longer in Maritime Canada than in any New England state, and continued well into the early nineteenth century, as it did in New York and New Jersey." See Whitfield, "Black Loyalists and Black Slaves"; John Wentworth to G. Hammond, August 16, 1796, RG 1, vol. 50–51, 1337-N, LAC; Wentworth to Duke of Portland, September 20, 1796, RG 1, vol. 50–51, 1337-N, LAC; Duke of Portland to John Wentworth, December 16, 1796, MG II N.S. "A," vol. 124, LAC.

48. Young, *Historical Survey,* 319; sustained attention to the plight of the aboriginals came in the early nineteenth century, by British officers such as Walter Bromley.

Chapter 5. Winter

1. John Wentworth to Duke of Portland, May 7, 1797, RG 1, vol. 52, 1337-N, LAC; extracts of letter to Walpole, January 10, 1797, 1b/5/14/2, Committee of Correspondence Out-Letter Book, JARD. Assumptions about Canada's winters were evident in many contexts. In his fictional account of Jamaica, written in Canada, Cyrus Francis Perkins wrote, "A winter's sojourn in the province of Canada, and the leisure

necessarily entailed on an invalid in an algid climate, has at length enabled me to prosecute what I had long intended." See Perkins, *Busha's Mistress, or Catherine the Fugitive: A Stirring Romance of the Days of Slavery in Jamaica,* ed. Verene A. Shepherd, David V. Trotman, and Paul E. Lovejoy (Kingston: Ian Randle, 2003); and Ninette Kelley and Michael Trebilcock, *The Making of the Mosaic: A History of Canadian Immigration Policy* (Toronto: University of Toronto Press, 1998), 22–61. Eighteenth-century preoccupations with tropical climate are better known. See, for example, Philip D. Curtin, *The Image of Africa: British Ideas and Action, 1780–1850* (Madison: University of Wisconsin Press, 1964). For some of the literature related to climate, see Robert Claiborne, *Climate, Man, and History* (New York: Norton, 1970); Reid A. Bryon and Christine Padoch, "On the Climates of History," in *Climate and History: Studies in Interdisciplinary History,* ed. Robert I. Rotberg and Theodore K. Rabb (Princeton: Princeton University Press, 1981); John Gascoigne, *Joseph Banks and the English Enlightenment: Useful Knowledge and Polite Culture* (Cambridge: Cambridge University Press, 1994); Vladimir Jankovic, *Reading the Skies: A Cultural History of English Weather, 1650–1820* (Chicago: University of Chicago Press, 2000); Neville Brown, *History and Climate Change: A Eurocentric Perspective* (London: Routledge, 2001); Michael Chenoweth, *The Eighteenth-Century Climate of Jamaica* (Philadelphia: American Philosophical Society, 2003); Katharine Anderson, *Victorians and the Science of Meteorology* (Chicago: University of Chicago Press, 2005); Jan Golinski, *British Weather and the Climate of Enlightenment* (Chicago: University of Chicago Press, 2007); Malcom Walker, *History of the Meteorological Office* (Cambridge: Cambridge University Press, 2012); Andrea Wulf, *Founding Gardeners: The Revolutionary Generation, Nature, and the Shaping of the American Nation* (New York: Knopf, 2011).

2. Thomas Cooper, extract of a letter from a gentleman in America to a friend in England, On the subject of emigration, 1798, Sabin, 16611, E 187 box, MHS; this concern with the Maroons' deportation to a cold climate served as an indirect criticism of the power of planter elites. The shrill worry over the Maroons overlapped with the discovery of the urban poor and criminal classes in Britain. See C. A. Bayly, *Imperial Meridian: The British Empire and the World, 1780–1830* (London: Longman, 1989), 6–8.

3. Handbill cited in R. R. Kuczynski, *Demographic Survey of the British Colonial Empire,* vol. 1, *West Africa* (London: Oxford University Press, 1948), 41.

4. General Description of the Province of Nova Scotia, Lieutenant Colonel Morse, chief engineer in America, upon a tour of province in Autumn, 1783, under Carleton orders from New York received on July 28, 1783, WO 55/1558/2, TNA.

5. *Columbia Centinel,* December 16, 1797, Boston; *Commercial Advertiser,* June 2, 1798, New York City; *Telegraph* (London), August 15, 1796.

6. Nova Scotia, Miscellaneous, No. 5, August 12, 1797, CO 217/69, LAC; despite the recent history of the Trelawney war and the Saint-Domingue rebellion, Portland did not associate the Maroons with the rebels in Saint-Domingue.

7. Georgia was an earlier experiment. Christopher Leslie Brown, *Moral Capital: Foundations of British Abolitionism* (Chapel Hill: University of North Carolina Press, 2006); Starr Douglas and Felix Driver, "Imagining the Tropical Colony: Henry Smeathman and the Termites of Sierra Leone," in *Tropical Visions in an Age of Empire,* ed. Felix Driver and Luciana Martins, 91–112 (Chicago: University of Chicago Press, 2005); for considerations of destinations for white convicts from London at this time, see R. A. Swan, *To Botany Bay . . . If Policy Warrants the Measure* (Canberra: Roebuck Society Publications, 1973), and Marjory Harper, "British Migration and the Peopling of Empire," in *The Oxford History of the British Empire,* vol. 3, *The Nineteenth Century,* ed. Andrew Porter (Oxford: Oxford University Press, 1999); Forster, "Convicts"; Alan Frost, *Convicts and Empire: A Naval Question, 1776–1811* (Melbourne: Oxford University Press, 1980).

8. Kuczynski, *Demographic Survey,* 41. In earlier parliamentary hearings in 1785 Henry Smeathman recounted the terrible climate he found in the area and the high possibility of disease and death. But in 1787 Smeathman, seeing a chance to accompany the settlers and improve his own cash-strapped status, enthusiastically supported Sierra Leone; Henry Smeathman, Esq., "Plan of a Settlement to Be Made near Sierra Leone on the Grain Coast of Africa," Rare Books, THL (1786); Isaac Land and Andrew M. Schocket, "New Approaches to the Founding of Sierra Leone Colony, 1786–1808," *Journal of Colonialism and Colonial History,* 9, no. 3 (Winter 2008). During her visit to the island of St. Vincent, Mrs. Carmichael noted a plant she saw for the first time "growing wild by the road-side instead of being carefully cherished in a hot-house"; Mrs. A. C. Carmichael, *Domestic Manners and Social Condition of the White, Coloured and Negro Population of the West Indies,* 2 vols. (London: Whittaker, Treacher, 1833), 1:8; Gascoigne, *Joseph Banks and the English Enlightenment.* Gascoigne notes, "The idea of improvement came to embrace a wider and wider range of activities but its origins were closely linked with an activity which was at the heart of landed society: the practice of agriculture" (185).

9. Robin Hallett, *The Penetration of Africa: European Exploration in North and West Africa to 1815* (New York: Praeger, 1965), 270; Robin Hallett, ed., *Records of the African Association, 1788–1831* (London: Thomas Nelson, 1964), 8; Adams George

Archibald, "Story of Deportation of Negroes from Nova Scotia to Sierra Leone, Read by Ex-Governor Archibald," March 12, 1885, *Collections of NS Historical Society for the years 1889–1891,* 7:134.

10. Clarkson Papers, 1792, Report on Sierra Leone, THL. The vision for Sierra Leone followed earlier schemes for Georgia in 1732. Both were based on antislavery principles and imagined industrious, sober, moral farming families who would set a model for a new kind of British settlement. Both establishments fortified imperial presence in strategic regions and received large infusions of British public spending to sustain them. See Julian Gwyn, "Economic Fluctuations in Wartime Nova Scotia, 1755–1815," in *Making Adjustments: Change and Continuity in Planter Nova Scotia, 1759–1800,* ed. Margaret Conrad (Fredericton: Acadiensis Press, 1991), 86, 73. Nova Scotia and Cape Breton, in fact, would receive £152,300 sterling in the sixty years between 1756 and 1815.

11. This is from Quarrell's answer, March 4, 1801, in *Journals of the Assembly of Jamaica,* 10:543, JCB. He wrote that he was averse to sending the Maroons to Sierra Leone.

12. Robert Sewell, September 6, 1796, Committee of Correspondence Out-Letter Book, 1b/5/14/2, JARD.

13. Stiv Jakobsson, *Am I Not a Man and a Brother? British Missionaries and the Abolition of the Slave Trade and Slavery in West Africa and the West Indies, 1786–1838* (Lund: Gleerup, 1972), 31; African Office, July 8, 1796, CO 267/10, TNA; African Office, July 12, 1796, CO 267/10, TNA; instead, they recommended that the Maroons be shipped to Madagascar, a "fine fruitful and extensive island"; Duke of Portland to John Wentworth, July 15, 1796, CO 218/27, TNA; *Telegraph* (London), August 15, 1796.

14. John Wentworth to Duke of Portland, August 13, 1796, MG II N.S., "A," vol. 123, LAC; John Wentworth to Duke of Portland, October 29, 1796, *Journals of the Assembly of Jamaica,* JCB.

15. The winters in England elicited no discussion when the poor left London in 1787. From William Wilberforce, July 8, 1791, Rothley Temple near Leicester (to Lieutenant Clarkson?), A-1981 microfilm, LAC.

16. Granville Sharp to John Clarkson, July 24, 1792, LAC; Notebook of John Clarkson, AD MS 41262B, October 29, 1791 (other dates also possible, not clear), BL.

17. William Dawes Quarrell to James Wedderburn, October 29, 1796, *Journals of the Assembly of Jamaica,* JCB.

18. Précis of letters from His Royal Highness Prince Edward and John Wentworth, April 21 to May 24, 1797, CO 218/23, LAC; John Wentworth to Duke of Portland, June 2, 1797, C9137, MG II N.S. "A," vol. 125, LAC.

19. Sir William Young, *Historical Survey of the Island of Saint Domingo together with an account of the Maroon negroes in the island of Jamaica; and a history of the war in the West Indies, in 1793 and 1794; also a tour through the several islands of Barbados, St. Vincent, Antigua, Tobago, and Grenada in the Years 1791 and 1792* (London, 1801), 320, 327; John Wentworth to John King (Private), May 23, 1799, CO 217/37, TNA; Michael Wallace, July 15, 1799, Colonial Office, Nova Scotia, "A," July-December, 1799, vol. 130 (41), LAC.

20. John Wentworth to Mr. King, September 11, 1797, MG II N.S. "A," vol. 126, LAC. Wentworth too heard their "long storys"; John Wentworth to Earl of Balcarres, August 4, 1797, RG 1, vol. 52, 1337-N, LAC; Benjamin Gray, June 18, 1798, *Journals of the Assembly of Jamaica*, JCB. Reverend Gray lamented, "The spirit of the man has not departed with himself"; Letter from Halifax to Duke on April 23, 1797, in an attachment to Wentworth sent from England on March 8, 1798, Colonial Office Papers, 1798, MG II N.S. "A," vol. 127, LAC; Committee of Correspondence, Out-Letter Book, August 11, 1797, JARD.

21. Précis of letters from His Royal Highness Prince Edward and John Wentworth, April 21 to May 24, 1797, CO 218/23, LAC; extract of letter to Walpole, January 10, 1797, Committee of Correspondence Out-Letter Book, 1B/5/14/2, JARD.

22. *General Evening Post* (London), April 6, 1797–April 8, 1797; *True Briton* (London), April 7, 1797; *London Packet or New Lloyd's Evening Post* (London), April 5, 1797. On Walpole's background, see John N. Grant, *The Maroons in Nova Scotia* (Halifax: Formac, 2002), 28.

23. Letter to John Wentworth, April 4, 1798, Colonial Office Papers, NSA, 1798, MG II N.S. "A," vol. 127, LAC; John Wentworth to Duke of Portland, August 13, 1796, CO 217/67, LAC; Wentworth to Eginton?, August 15, 1796, RG 1, vol. 50–51, 1337-N, LAC.

24. *Journals of the Assembly of Jamaica*, December 20, 1797, JCB; *Journals of the Assembly of Jamaica*, December 18, 1798, JCB; *Journals of the House of Assembly*, December 19, 1798, JCB; précis of letters from His Royal Highness Prince Edward and John Wentworth, May 7 to May 31, 1797, CO 218/23, LAC; Robert Sewell, June 25, 1798, *Journals of the Assembly of Jamaica*, JCB.

25. William Dawes Quarrell, April 25, 1797, *Journals of the Assembly of Jamaica*, JCB.

26. *Journals of the Assembly of Jamaica*, January 8, 1796, JCB. Robert Sewell to Duke of Portland, April 5, 1798, *Journals of the Assembly of Jamaica*, 10:120, JCB; *Journals of the Assembly of Jamaica*, December 20, 1797, JCB.

27. John Wentworth to Duke of Portland, June 23, 1798, Colonial Office Papers, 1798, MG II N.S. "A," vol. 127, LAC; John Wentworth, October 10, 1796, *Journals of the Assembly of Jamaica,* JCB; John Wentworth to Duke of Portland, June 23, 1798, RG 1, vol. 52, 1337-N, LAC; John Wentworth to Duke of Portland, June 23, 1798, *Journals of the Assembly of Jamaica,* JCB; Grant, *Maroons in Nova Scotia,* chap. 9.

28. Duke of Portland to Earl of Balcarres, February 8, 1798, *Journals of the Assembly of Jamaica,* JCB; Duke of Portland to Earl of Balcarres, March 11, 1798, *Journals of the Assembly of Jamaica,* JCB.

29. John Wentworth to Earl of Balcarres, August 4, 1797, RG 1, vol. 52, 1337-N, LAC.

30. John Wentworth to King, April 24, 1797 (Private and Confidential), MG II N.S. "A," vol. 125, LAC; John Wentworth to Duke of Portland, April 10, 1799, RG 1, vol. 52, 1337-N, LAC. Wentworth writes that those at Preston remain deluded; John Wentworth to Duke of Portland, June 23, 1798, *Journals of the Assembly of Jamaica,* JCB.

31. John Wentworth to Earl of Balcarres, August 4, 1797, RG 1, vol. 52, 1337-N, LAC.

32. Antislavery discourse was obsessed with population decreases. In Britain, liberty had led to an increased workforce by the mid-eighteenth century; in the West Indies, slavery had led to starving conditions and a catastrophic drop in population. Nova Scotia's winter was likened to Caribbean slavery as being a hindrance to population growth. On the preoccupation with population in antislavery rhetoric, see B. W. Higman, "Slavery and Development of Demographic Theory in the Age of Industrial Revolution," in *Slavery and British Society, 1776–1846,* ed. James Walvin (Baton Rouge: Louisiana State University, 1982); John Wentworth to Dr. Morris, May 1, 1799, RG 1, vol. 52, 1337-N, LAC; Benjamin Gray to John Wentworth, June 18, 1798, *Journals of the House of Assembly*, JCB; John Wentworth to Duke of Portland, April 21, 1797, RG 1, vol. 52, 1337-N, LAC; précis of letters from His Royal Highness Prince Edward and Sir John Wentworth, June 2 to June 29, 1797, CO 218/23 (532 persons noted here), LAC; John Oxley to John Wentworth, May 31, 1797, CO 217/68, LAC; John Oxley, A Return of Sick and Numbers of Maroons from March 1 to April 1, 1798 by Surgeon, CO 217/69, LAC.

33. John Wentworth to Duke of Portland, June 23, 1798, RG 1, vol. 52, 1337-N, LAC; *Journals of the House of Assembly,* August 3, 1799, JCB; John Wentworth to Earl of Balcarres, June 13, 1798, *Journals of the House of Assembly,* JCB; *Journals of the House of Assembly,* March 4, 1801, JCB.

34. The convention of using petitions to appeal to British authorities has a long history. On Acadians, see N. E. S. Griffiths, *From Migrant to Acadian: A North American Border People, 1604–1755* (Montreal: McGill-Queens University Press, 2005), 410; on the Mi'kmaq, see William C. Wicken, *Colonization of Mi'kmaw Memory and History, 1794–1928* (Toronto: University of Toronto Press, 2012), 109; on free blacks in Belize, see Mavis C. Campbell, *Becoming Belize: A History of an Outpost of Empire Searching for Identity* (Kingston: University of West Indies Press, 2011), 112–26, 223. All black communities in Nova Scotia during the eighteenth and early nineteenth centuries used petitions to gain imperial protection. These included the black Loyalists in the 1780s, the Maroons in the 1790s, and the black refugees who fled to the region after the War of 1812. See Deirdre Coleman, *Romantic Colonization and British Anti-Slavery* (Cambridge: Cambridge University Press, 2005), 111; James W. St. G. Walker, *The Black Loyalists: The Search for a Promised Land in Nova Scotia and Sierra Leone, 1783–1870* (New York: Africana, 1976), 20; Harvey A. Whitfield, *Blacks on the Border: The Black Refugees in British North America, 1815–1860* (Burlington: University of Vermont Press, 2006). Black fidelity to the British Crown was part of the British Atlantic world. See Jerry Bannister and Liam Riordan, eds., *The Loyal Atlantic: Remaking the British Atlantic in the Revolutionary Era* (Toronto: University of Toronto Press, 2012).

Chapter 6. Resistance

1. John Wentworth to King, April 24, 1797 (Private and Confidential), MG II N.S. "A," vol. 125, LAC.

2. T. Chamberlain, June 20, 1798, sent in enclosure (like the rest of these letters) to Duke of Portland from John Wentworth on June 23, 1798, MG II N.S. "A," vol. 127, LAC. The Maroons may have asked for a Bible during the oath-taking ritual; Benjamin Gerrish Gray, June 18, 1798, sent in enclosure (like the rest of these letters) to Duke of Portland from John Wentworth, June 23, 1798, MG II N.S. "A," vol. 127, LAC. Also see Kenneth Bilby, "Swearing by the Past, Swearing to the Future: Sacred Oaths, Alliances, and Treaties among the Guianese and Jamaican Maroons," in *Origins of the Black Atlantic*, ed. Laurent Dubois and Julius S. Scott (New York: Routledge, 2010); Barbara K. Kopytoff, "Colonial Treaty as Sacred Charter of the Jamaican Maroons," *Ethnohistory* 26, no. 1 (Winter 1979); Henry Hoetink, "The Cultural Links," in *Africa and the Caribbean: The Legacies of a Link*, ed. Margaret E. Crahan and Franklin W. Knight (Baltimore: Johns Hopkins University Press, 1979). For the persistence of cultural patterns, see Sylviane A. Diouf, *Servants of Allah: African*

Muslims Enslaved in the Americas (New York: New York University Press, 1998). On Acadian oaths, see Jeffers Lennox, "Crossing Borders, Changing Worlds: Eighteenth-Century Nova Scotia's Atlantic Connections," *Journal of Canadian Studies* 42, no.1 (2008). On difficulties in incorporating a conquered people, see Robin F. A. Fabel, *Colonial Challenges: Britons, Native Americans, and Caribs, 1759–1775* (Gainesville: University Press of Florida, 2000).

3. T. Chamberlain, June 20, 1798, MG II N.S. "A," vol. 127, LAC; John Wentworth to King, April 24, 1797 (Private and Confidential), MG II N.S. "A," vol. 125, LAC; Wentworth thought that the number of women and children—double the number of men—made this scheme impossible: ibid.

4. Alexander Howe to John Wentworth, June 8, 1798, MG II N.S. "A," vol. 127, LAC; Andrew Smith to Charles Samuels, June 3, 1797, MG II N.S. "A," vol. 127, LAC.

5. T. Chamberlain, June 20, 1798, sent in enclosure (like the rest of these letters) to Duke of Portland from John Wentworth on June 23, 1798, *Journals of the House of Assembly*, JCB; Wentworth to Balcarres, August 4, 1797, RG 1, vol. 52, 1337-N, JCB; T. Chamberlain, June 20, 1798, sent in enclosure (like the rest of these letters), from John Wentworth to Duke of Portland, June 23, 1798, MG II N.S. "A," vol. 127, LAC.

6. John Wentworth to King, April 24, 1797 (Private and Confidential), MG II N.S. "A," vol. 125, LAC; Prince Edward to John King, June 1, 1797 (Private and Confidential), MG II N.S. "A," vol. 125, LAC.

7. John Wentworth to Duke of Portland, August 12, 1797, MG II N.S. "A," vol. 126, LAC.

8. Prince Edward to Duke of Portland, April 23, 1797 (PRIVATE), MG II N.S. "A," vol. 125, LAC; précis of letters from Prince Edward and John Wentworth, April 23 to May 24, 1797, CO 218/23, LAC; Prince Edward to Duke of Portland, April 23, 1797, CO 217/71, LAC. He said a war between the United States and France was possible. He complained that the force "at present here is by no means sufficient for the defense"; Wentworth to Maroons, May 28, 1797, MG II N.S. "A," vol. 125, LAC; Andrew Smith to Charles Samuels, June 3, 1797, MG II N.S. "A," vol. 127, LAC; William Dawes Quarrell disapproved of the bargain. On March 4, 1801, he wrote, "Yet I never could or did approve of any promise, which might furnish the Maroons with a plea for withholding the interests they should have taken in improving the lands which were allotted to them." See *Journals of the Assembly of Jamaica*, JCB; John Wentworth to Maroons, May 28, 1797, CO 217/68, LAC; John Wentworth to Duke of Portland, June 2, 1797, MG II N.S. "A," vol. 125, LAC.

9. *Journals of the Assembly of Jamaica,* March 4, 1801, JCB.

10. Disposition of Thomas Barclay of Annapolis in the County of Annapolis, May 23, 1799, CO 217/37, LAC; Charles Bruce Fergusson, *Clarkson's Mission to America, 1791–92,* 24, NSA, Publication no. 11, 1971; on Howe, see Lois K. Kernaghan's entry in the *Dictionary of Canadian Biography,* vol. 5 (University of Toronto, online); John N. Grant, *The Maroons in Nova Scotia* (Halifax: Formac, 2002), 97–98; Alexander Howe, August 9, 1797, MG II N.S. "A," vol. 126, LAC; John Wentworth to King, April 24, 1797 (Private and Confidential), MG II N.S. "A," vol. 125, LAC.

11. *Journals of the Assembly of Jamaica,* December 18, 1798, JCB; Sewell to Walpole, January 10, 1797, Committee of Correspondence Out-Letter Book, JARD.

12. John Wentworth to J. King, May 30, 1799, "A," January–June, 1799, vol. 129 (166), LAC; Alexander Howe to Wentworth, June 8, 1798, MG II N.S. "A," vol. 127, LAC. Their "made-up pains" potentially cost the colony three to four thousand bushels of potatoes annually; T. Chamberlain, June 20, 1798, MG II N.S. "A," vol. 127, LAC; *Journals of the Assembly of Jamaica,* December 18, 1798, JCB; Wentworth to John King (Private), May 23, 1799, CO 217/37, LAC; T. Chamberlain, June 20, 1798, MG II N.S. "A," vol. 127, LAC.

13. John Wentworth to Dr. Morris, May 1, 1799, RG 1, vol. 52, 1337-N, LAC; John Wentworth to John King (Private), May 23, 1799, CO 217/37, LAC; Alexander Howe to Wentworth, June 8, 1798, MG II N.S. "A," vol. 127, LAC.

14. Alexander Howe to John Wentworth, June 8, 1798, MG II N.S. "A," vol. 127, NSA; Thomas Chamberlain, June 20, 1798, sent in enclosure to the Duke of Portland from John Wentworth, June 23, 1798, MG II N.S. "A," vol. 127, NSA; John Wentworth to John King (Private), May 23, 1799, CO 217/37, LAC; Alexander Ochterloney also accused Lady Wentworth of keeping two Maroon men. Examination of Alexander Ochterloney, December 18, 1798, *Journals of the Assembly of Jamaica,* JCB; Brian C. Cuthbertson, *The Loyalist Governor: Biography of Sir John Wentworth* (Halifax: Petheric Press, 1983), 83.

15. Alexander Howe to Wentworth, June 8, 1798, MG II N.S. "A," vol. 127, LAC; Benjamin Gray to John Wentworth, June 18, 1798, *Journals of the Assembly of Jamaica,* JCB; Dr. Oxley, June 16, 1798, *Journals of the Assembly of Jamaica,* JCB.

16. T. Chamberlain, June 20, 1798, sent in enclosure (like the rest of these letters) to Duke of Portland from John Wentworth on June 23, 1798, MG II N.S. "A," vol. 127, LAC; T. Chamberlain to W. D. Quarrell, September 7, 1798, *Journals of the Assembly of Jamaica,* JCB.

17. John Fraser, July 2, 1799, *Journals of the Assembly of Jamaica,* JCB.

18. Michael Wallace, June 27, 1799, *Journals of the Assembly of Jamaica,* JCB.

19. Thomas Clarkson, in 1791, disapproved of military men as settlers. In November he wrote to William Wilberforce, "It is my opinion though I cannot be a sufficient judge that military men are very improper persons to govern any place, they generally speaking are debauched men and mind their bottle more than their duty." See Fergusson, *Clarkson's Mission,* 87; Thomas Ludlam to Directors, May 8, 1799, CO 267/10, TNA.

20. Seymour Drescher, *Capitalism and Antislavery: British Mobilization in Comparative Perspective* (New York: Oxford University Press, 1987), 4. See a partial list of the extensive literature on abolitionism in the bibliography; Samuel Thornton to Duke of Portland, January 4, 1799, Miscellaneous, end of CO 217/70, LAC; in petitioning the British government, the Maroons followed the conventions long established by the black Loyalists. As Harvey Whitfield notes, "I would say this [petitioning] makes them rather common in the history of black people in Nova Scotia. Indeed, the black Loyalists, Jamaican Maroons, and Black Refugees [who settled in Nova Scotia after the War of 1812] all pledged their allegiance to the Crown and used the Crown for their own ends. The Black Refugees liked to publicly proclaim their loyalty to the British crown. They even went around during Victoria's birthday with a banner reading 'Victoria and Freedom.' Indeed, in an 1841 petition, black people in [neighboring] New Brunswick claimed to be the most loyal subjects" (private correspondence).

21. Hale is mentioned by the Maroon Andrew Smith in the following: Letter from Halifax to Duke of Portland on April 23, 1797, in an attachment sent from England on March 8, 1798, Colonial Office Papers, MG II N.S. "A," vol. 127, LAC. Reverend Benjamin Gray noted Maroon sympathizers in the neighborhood; Maroon Petition: Maroons to Walpole, April 23, 1797, MG II N.S. "A," vol. 125, LAC; Letter from Halifax to Duke of Portland on June 8, 1798, sent from England on March 8, 1798, Colonial Office Papers, MG II N.S. "A," vol. 127, LAC; Captain Alexander Howe to Wentworth, MG II N.S. "A," vol. 127, LAC; Maroon Petition: Maroons to Walpole, April 23, 1797, MG II N.S. "A," vol. 125, LAC. Also see Mavis C. Campbell, "Montague James and the Maroons in Jamaica, Nova Scotia and Sierra Leone," in *People and Empires in African History: Essays in Memory of Michael Crowder,* ed. Michael Crowder, J. F. Ade Ajayi, J. D. Y. Peel (London: Longman, 1992).

22. Halifax, June 4, 1797, enclosed in letter, from William Dawes Quarrell to Walpole, MG II N.S. "A," vol. 127, LAC; Chief Montague James signed on behalf of 530 Maroons. The full petition reads as follows: "That your Majesty's petitioners having from the bad conduct of their superintendent and false misrepresentations of

malicious persons been induced to take up arms against their much beloved friends and countrymen the inhabitants of Jamaica the contest after much bloodshed was happily terminated by treaty with general Walpole by which treaty we your majesty's subjects held ourselves bound and did comply with as far as the nature of circumstances and our situation would admit of. We have nevertheless been transported from Jamaica in violation of that treaty and are now resident in Nova Scotia, a country so severely cold and so different in every production from our native climate that our existence even should it be prolonged must be attended with the utmost misery and wretchedness. We humbly beseech your Majesty that you would be graciously pleased to interpose your royal authority that if we are not permitted to return to Jamaica agreeable to the treaty we may be removed to some warmer climate where we may be enabled by our industry to maintain our wives and children and relieve them from those sufferings to which in this country we see no end."

23. Duke of Portland to John Wentworth, March 8, 1798, but original letter of November 4, 1797, from Maroons to Duke of Portland in MG II N.S. "A," vol. 127, LAC; Maroon Petition, unsigned, to General Walpole in London, August 1798, Miscellaneous, CO 217/70, LAC; this was signed by Andrew Smith, John Jarrett, and Bonny Baclie on behalf of all the Maroons. They did not trust the succession of new appointments by Wentworth. They missed the Jamaican superintendents Quarrell and Ochterloney and asked for their return; ibid.; Maroon Petition to Duke of Portland, August 12, 1797, Nova Scotia, Miscellaneous, CO 217/69, LAC; John Jarrett, signed for Montague James, on behalf of 600 Maroons; Maroon Petition, unsigned, to General Walpole, August 1798 in Nova Scotia, 1799, Miscellaneous, CO 217/70, LAC; this was signed by Andrew Smith, John Jarrett, and Bonny Baclie on behalf of all the Maroons. In Nova Scotia, they could never have happiness or comfort and "for the present every pleasing prospect is vanished."

24. Samuel Thornton to Duke of Portland, by January 4, 1799, "A," January–June, 1799, LAC; this was signed by the six men, the largest number of Maroon captains thus far: John Jarrett, Andrew Smith, James Barnet, James Lawrence, Thomas Johnston, and Charles Shaw, on behalf of the Maroons in Preston near Halifax in the province of Nova Scotia; Samuel Thornton to Duke of Portland, January 4, 1799, "A," January–June, 1799, LAC.

25. John Wentworth to John King (Private), May 23, 1799, CO 217/37, LAC; John Wentworth to Duke of Portland, April 10, 1799, RG 1, vol. 52, 1337, LAC.

26. T. Chamberlain to John Wentworth, June 20, 1797, *Journals of the Assembly of Jamaica*, JCB.

27. Wentworth to John King (Private), May 23, 1799, CO 217/37, LAC.

28. Alexander Howe to John Wentworth, June 8, 1798, *Journals of the Assembly of Jamaica,* JCB; John Wentworth to Duke of Portland, April 10, 1799, RG 1, vol. 52, 1337-N, LAC. The families were the two Jarretts, the two Shaws, and Harding.

29. John Wentworth to Duke of Portland, May 5, 1799, "A," January–June, 1799, vol. 129, LAC; John Wentworth to Duke of Portland, October 22, 1799, RG 1, vol. 52, 1337-N, LAC; John Wentworth to Duke of Portland, April 13, 1799, CO 217/270, NLJ; Wentworth referred to Captain David Shaw and Captain Charles Shaw. The relationship between the two men is not clear. David Shaw died on November 12, 1800, in Sierra Leone. See Mavis C. Campbell, *Back to Africa: George Ross and the Maroons from Nova Scotia to Sierra Leone* (Trenton, N.J.: Africa World Press, 1993), 36. It is unclear if the eight families included the five men who were troublemakers; John Wentworth to Duke of Portland, October 22, 1799, RG 1, vol. 52, 1337-N, LAC; John Wentworth to John King (PRIVATE), November 27, 1799, CO 217/73, LAC.

30. John Wentworth to John King, May 30, 1799, "A," January–June, 1799, vol. 129, LAC; John Wentworth to John King (Private), May 23, 1799, CO 217/37, LAC. As Wentworth wrote, "The Maroons by their committee, Jarrat, Smith, Shaw, and Harding, earnestly endeavored to construct and engage with the merchants of Halifax, to furnish a large cargo of slaves from Sierra Leone in four or six months after their disembarkation in that country. They were exceedingly sanguine in their ability and prowess to supply four hundred captives which they will certainly attempt if they meet any encouragement and can obtain firearms, from any slave traders, on the coast, altho' our merchants would not engage with them here."

31. Wentworth to John King (Private), May 23, 1799, CO 217/37, LAC. There were only nineteen boys by 1799—it is not clear how many there were originally; Fraser, May 31, 1799, "A," January–June, 1799, vol. 129 (212), LAC. Fraser describes them as being "strong and capable"; Grant, *The Maroons in Nova Scotia,* 8.

32. John Wentworth to Duke of Portland, June 23, 1798, RG 1, vol. 52, 1337-N, LAC; Alexander Howe to John Wentworth, June 8, 1798, *Journals of Assembly* (Halifax), LAC; John Wentworth to Dr. Morris, May 1, 1799, RG 1, vol. 52, 1337-N, LAC.

33. Boydville Petition (Maroon Petition), May 5, 1799, Colonial Office, Nova Scotia, "A," January–June, 1799, vol. 129, LAC; in smaller letters, also signed by G. G. Barrett, John Russia, Jobie Lawrence, Herbert Gerard, Capt. John Palmer, Quaco Leburque, Charles Samuel, Charles Downing; this was signed by the Maroons who had separated from the other Trelawney Town Maroons: James Palmer, George Lawrence, Taylor Moody, Robert Fowler, and Pat O'Conner.

34. Wentworth to John King (Private), May 23, 1799, CO 217/3; Duke of Portland to John Wentworth, October 9, 1799, CO 218/27, LAC.

35. Duke of Portland to John Wentworth, October 8, 1799, CO 218/27, LAC.

36. The description in 1802 reads as follows: "He came over with the Maroons but is not reckoned among them." See July 31, 1802, list, WO 1/352, TNA; John Wentworth to Duke of Portland, August 6, 1800, RG 1, vol. 53, NSA. Wentworth reported, "Four have deserted to avoid going to Sierra Leone."

37. From September 9, 1800, in Campbell, *Back to Africa,* 6.

38. Mr. Thornton, October 5, 1799, Terms in which to receive the Maroons, CO 267/10, TNA.

39. Some Maroons owned slaves in Sierra Leone (private conversation with Paul E. Lovejoy, January 2017); some may have turned to slave trading. Suzanne Schwarz and Paul E. Lovejoy, with funding from the British Library's Endangered Archives Programme, are in the process of creating an electronic database of early nineteenth-century Sierra Leone records.

Chapter 7. Crisis

1. Interestingly, no women or children were associated with Martin Sewell. Sierra Leone Office, March 19, 1802, WO 1/352, TNA; Sierra Leone Council, September 30, 1800, CO 270/5, TNA; Appendix to the Minutes for the Year 1800, CO 270/5, TNA; the council had originally consisted of eight members, modeled after the East India Company. Philip D. Curtin, *The Image of Africa: British Ideas and Action, 1780–1850* (Madison: University of Wisconsin Press, 1964), 108; Rachel B. Herrmann recently called the black Loyalists' revolt a "food riot." See Herrmann, "Rebellion or Riot: Black Loyalist Food Laws in Sierra Leone," *Slavery and Abolition* 37, no. 4 (December 2016): 680–703; Wallace Brown, "The Black Loyalists in Sierra Leone," in *Moving On: Black Loyalists in the Afro-Atlantic World,* ed. John W. Pulis (New York: Garland, 1999), chap. 5; James W. St. G. Walker, *The Black Loyalists: The Search for a Promised Land in Nova Scotia and Sierra Leone, 1783–1870* (New York: Africana, 1976), 242–45.

2. The original purchase was twenty miles east and twenty miles south of the town. But it was later agreed that the company would occupy only land three miles to the east and twenty miles to the south. See BT 6/70, TNA; an island like Jamaica was much more easily fortified and defended than a peninsula in a vast continent; B. W. Hodder, "Periodic and Daily Markets in West Africa," in *The Development of Indigenous Trade and Markets in West Africa,* ed. Claude Meillassoux (Oxford: International African Institute, 1971).

3. Presents wanted for native chiefs, May 1, 1808, CO 267/24, TNA; in 1787 John Clarkson noted the fancy attire of a West African king: "His dress was a sky-blue silk jacket with silver lace, striped cotton trowsers, ruffled shirt, green morocco slippers, a cocked-hat with gold lace, and a white cotton cap, for which a large old judge's wig was afterwards substituted." Rev. E. G. Ingham, *Sierra Leone After a Hundred Years* (1894; repr. London: Frank Cass, 1968), 24; Winston McGowan, "The Establishment of Long-Distance Trade Between Sierra Leone and Its Hinterland, 1787–1821," *Journal of African History* 31 (1990): 35.

4. Thomas Ludlam to Court of Directors, May 8, 1799, CO 267/10, TNA.

5. Queries Proposed by Commodore Hallowell, January 12, 1803, WO 1/352, TNA; on confusions over the definitions of African slavery, see Winthrop D. Jordan's essay, written forty years ago, "Planter and Slave Identity Formation: Some Problems in the Comparative Approach," in *Comparative Perspectives on Slavery in New World Plantation Societies,* ed. Vera Rubin and Arthur Tuden (New York: New York Academy of Sciences, 1977); Christopher Fyfe, *Sierra Leone Inheritance* (London: Oxford, 1964), 10–11.

6. Suzanne Schwarz, "Zachary Macaulay and the Development of the Sierra Leone Company, 1793–94" (Part 2: Journal, October–December, 1793), in *University of Leipzig Papers on Africa, History and Cultural Series,* No. 9, 2002, xi. Between 1780 and 1807 about fifty-three thousand slaves were shipped from Sierra Leone. This accounted for 6 percent of slaves embarked on British vessels during this period. Ibid., 109.

7. Walker, *Black Loyalists,* 233; James Campbell, *Middle Passages: African American Journeys to Africa, 1787–2005* (New York: Penguin, 2006), 26; John Peterson, *Province of Freedom: A History of Sierra Leone, 1787–1870* (Evanston: Northwestern University Press, 1969), 43.

8. Matthew Tilly to John Clarkson, July 4, 1827, Clarkson Papers, 1824–1842, Box 3, THL; the Nova Scotians also objected to the Maroons' arrival in Sierra Leone without payment. See August 31, 1799: "All *forrenners* [*sic*] *coming into the Colony of SL* for to live as a seetlor [*sic*] they shall pay a sum of money for the good of the Colony and the sum of money that they shall pay is to be fixed by Hundredors and Tythingmen and the Governor and Council," in Claude George, *The Rise of British West Africa, Comprising the Early History of The Colony of Sierra Leone, The Gambia, Lagos, Gold Coast, etc. etc., with a Brief Account of Climate, the Growth of Education, Commerce, and Religion and a Comprehensive History of the Bananas and Bunce Islands* (London: Houlston and Sons, 1904), 44; T. Ludlam, November 11, 1801, CO 270/6, TNA; Fyfe, *Sierra Leone Inheritance,* 13–18.

9. Sierra Leone Council, September 25, 1800, CO 270/5, TNA; Sierra Leone Council, December 24, 1800, CO 270/5, TNA; General Court of Proprietors of The Sierra Leone Company, held at the New London Tavern, Cheapside, London, on Thursday, the 26th March, 1801 with Henry Thornton Chair, BL. Until 1799 the company had no legal title to enforce their authority, as was known to the Nova Scotians. Only on July 5, 1799, did the company receive a charter granting them the power to make laws "not repugnant to those of England." See Thomas Nelson Goddard, *The Handbook of Sierra Leone* (London: G. Richards, 1925), 28; Sierra Leone Council, December 24, 1800, CO 270/5, TNA; Queries Proposed by Commodore Hallowell, with the Governor, January 12, 1803, WO 1/352, TNA. This was the smallest number since 1796.

10. Sierra Leone Council, December 24, 1800, CO 270/5, TNA; Mavis C. Campbell, *Back to Africa: George Ross and the Maroons from Nova Scotia to Sierra Leone* (Trenton, N.J.: Africa World Press, 1993), 12. On September 18, 1800, George Ross wrote, "I gave the hint to Captain Smith of the Maroons and told him if he heard a Pistol go off, it was the alarm and he was to rouse the Maroons instantly and repair to Lieutenant Smith's cabin, and mine for arms."

11. George Ross, September 14, 1800, in Campbell, *Back to Africa,* 9. On this day Ross noted, "No prayers today." He mentions scholars twice: on September 14 and September 20, 1800; George Ross, September 18, 1800, in Campbell, *Back to Africa,* 11; in Preston, Elsy Jarrett had complained about abuse from a Maroon named Barnett; George Ross, September 10, 1800, and September 14, 1800, in Campbell, *Back to Africa,* 7, 9; Sierra Leone Council, 1813–1815, CO 270/14, TNA.

12. George Ross, September 14, 1800, in Campbell, *Back to Africa,* 9; George Ross, September 25, 1800, in Campbell, *Back to Africa,* 13; Ross would gift him a bottle of port wine; Campbell, *Back to Africa,* November 2, 1800, 32. Ross mentions Rozey for the first time when her sister dies and her father is drunk at the funeral.

13. Sierra Leone Council, April 13, 1797, CO 270/4, TNA. In the Court of Directors meeting held on December 10, 1795, Ross was designated as "servant of the Company." In August 1797 he was asked to take over as cashier but refused for health reasons. In June 1798 he asked to leave Sierra Leone to avoid the "present rainy season"; George Ross, September 30, 1800, in Campbell, *Back to Africa,* 15; Appendix to the Minutes for the Year 1800, CO 270/5, TNA; Sierra Leone Council, October 2, 1800, CO 270/5, TNA. Gen. Montague James, Col. Johnstone, Major Bailey (apparently drunk), Captains Smith, Shaw, Palmer, and others attended; the officers chose to exclude "Old Jarrett."

14. See October 1, 1800, entry in Campbell, *Back to Africa,* 16; Christopher Fyfe, "Introduction," in "*Our Children Are Free and Happy*": *Letters from Black Settlers in Africa in the 1790s,* ed. Christopher Fyfe (Edinburgh: Edinburgh University Press, 1991), 15; Eveline C. Martin, *The British West African Settlements, 1750–1821* (New York: Longmans, Green, 1927), 131; R. A. Austen and W. D. Smith, "Images of Africa and British Slave-Trade Abolition: The Transition to Imperialist Ideology, 1787–1807," *African Historical Studies* 2 (1969): 331.

15. The list of Sierra Leone's governors included the following: Lieut. John Clarkson, 1792–93; Lt. William Dawes, R.N., 1794–95; Zachary Macaulay, 1795–96; William Dawes, 1796–99; Zachary Macaulay, 1799; John Gray, 1799–1800; Thomas Ludlam, 1800; Gray, 1801–3; William Dawes, 1803; Capt. William Day, R.N., 1803–5; Thomas Ludlam, 1805; Captain William Day, 1806–8; Thomas Ludlam, 1808–10. See Cyril P. Foray, *Historical Dictionary of Sierra Leone,* African Historical Dictionaries 12 (Metuchen, N.J.: Scarecrow Press, 1977), 80; Suzanne Schwarz, "Zachary Macaulay and the Development of the Sierra Leone Company, 1793–94" (Part 1: Journal, June–October 1793), in *University of Leipzig Papers on Africa, History and Cultural Series,* no. 4, 2000, iii, ix; Peterson, *Province of Freedom,* 29; Zachary Macaulay to Jean (Macaulay) Babington, February 9, 1795, Macaulay Papers, Box 1, THL.

16. Henry Thornton to John King, March 11, 1799, Miscellaneous CO 217/70, LAC. This is also paraphrased in pages 97–98 of Mavis C. Campbell, ed., *Nova Scotia and the Fighting Maroons: A Documentary History* (Williamsburg, Va.: College of William and Mary Press, Studies in Third World Societies, 1990).

17. John Gray and Thomas Ludlam, June 10, 1799, CO 267/10, TNA; J. Gray and Ludlam to Duke of Portland, May 6, 1799, CO 267/10, TNA; Thomas Ludlam to Court of Directors, May 8, 1799, CO 267/10, TNA; Charmilly, Answer by way of letter to Bryan Edwards, Esq., 167; R. R. Kuczynski, *Demographic Survey of the British Colonial Empire,* vol. 1, *West Africa* (London: Oxford University Press, 1948), 58, 65.

18. John Gray and Ludlam to Duke of Portland, May 6, 1799, CO 267/10, TNA; also see Martin, *British West African Settlements,* 105–20; the company expected to make a profit through land revenue from quitrents, a tax on the produce of the country, profits from land reserved to the company, and profits on trade with the interior. For the most recent study on expectations of West Africa, see the essays in Robin Law, Suzanne Schwarz, and Silke Strickrodt, eds., *Commercial Agriculture: The Slave Trade and Slavery in Atlantic Africa* (London: Boydell and Brewer, 2013).

19. Duke of Portland to John Wentworth, January 20, 1800, CO 218/27, LAC; Governor and Council of Sierra Leone, March, 1799, CO 267/10, TNA.

20. Mr. Hermitage, sometime in 1799, CO 267/10, TNA; John Gray and Thomas Ludlam to Duke of Portland, May 6, 1799, CO 267/10, TNA.

21. J. J. Crooks, *A History of the Colony of Sierra Leone, Western Africa* (London: Frank Cass, 1903), 57; the company paid £45 annually, or £900 sterling. See Thomas Ludlam to Court of Directors, May 8, 1799, CO 267/10, TNA; Schwarz, "Zachary Macaulay" (Part 2), xxv; Thomas Ludlam to Court of Directors, May 8, 1799, CO 267/10, TNA; Campbell, *Back to Africa,* 15–16.

22. Campbell, *Back to Africa,* 16; George Ross Journal, October 1, 1800, *Back to Africa,* 16; Sierra Leone Council, October 2, 1800, CO 270/5, TNA. The Maroons had also stood by British royalty in Nova Scotia, agreeing to build fortifications in Halifax at the behest of Prince Edward, Duke of Kent, the son of George III.

23. John Gray and Thomas Ludlam to Directors, June 10, 1799, 267/10, TNA.

24. Appendix to the Minutes for the Year 1800, CO 270/5, TNA; Appendix Minutes, October 1 (?), 1800 Council, CO 270/5, TNA; Appendix Minutes, October 3, 1800, CO 270/5, TNA.

25. Appendix Minutes, October 3, 1800, CO 270/5, TNA; Sierra Leone Council, December 24, 1800, CO 270/5, TNA.

26. General Court of Proprietors of The Sierra Leone Company, held at the New London Tavern, Cheapside, London, on Thursday, the 26th March, 1801, BL; George Ross to Council, June 17, 1801, CO 270/6, TNA; Council, December 24, 1800, CO 270/5, TNA; Campbell, *Back to Africa,* 18.

27. Appendix Minutes, October 3, 1800, CO 270/5, TNA; Appendix to the Minutes for the Year 1800, CO 270/5, TNA; this was King Firama; Sierra Leone Council, December 31, 1800, CO 270/5, TNA; seven rebels regarded as irredeemable were sent to Goree Island; Walker, *Black Loyalists,* 234, 241.

28. Campbell, *Back to Africa,* 18.

29. Appendix to the Minutes for the Year 1800, CO 270/5, TNA; John Gray and Thomas Ludlam to Directors, June 10, 1799, CO 267/10, TNA.

30. General Court of Proprietors of The Sierra Leone Company, held at the New London Tavern, Cheapside, London, on Thursday, the 26th March, 1801, BL; Council Minutes, March 7, 1801, CO 270/5, TNA; George Ross to Council, June 17, 1801, CO 270/6, TNA; Sierra Leone Council, November 3, 1800, CO 270/5, TNA.

31. Campbell, *Back to Africa,* 15.

32. Sierra Leone Council, September 22, 1801, CO 270/6, TNA.

33. In December 1799 the council had noted the precarious balance maintained with natives. As the minutes recorded, "We are at present forced to make [sacrifices] in

submitting to costly and tedious palavers [conferences] as well as frequent encroachment and unwarrantable pretensions [from the natives]." See Sierra Leone Council Minutes, December 10, 1799, CO 270/4, TNA; C. W. Newbury, *British Policy Towards West Africa: Select Documents, 1786–1874* (Oxford: Clarendon Press, 1965), 182.

34. Walker, *Black Loyalists,* 243; Zachary Macaulay to Dr. Thorpe, published 1815, in "Letters to his Royal Highness the Duke of Gloucester," 11, Rare Books, THL; Zachary Macaulay, June 7, 1797, Box 20, THL. As Macaulay wrote, the English had no "constraining power over the natives."

35. J. Wilson, James Carr, Michael Macmillan to Sierra Leone Council, January 24, 1802, CO 270/8, TNA; Walker, *Black Loyalists,* 243; Goddard, *Handbook of Sierra Leone,* 29.

36. David Geggus, "The Enigma of Jamaica in the 1790s: New Light on the Causes of Slave Rebellions," *William and Mary Quarterly* 44, no. 2 (1987): 294; copy of letter from Governor and Council of Sierra Leone to Commodore Hallowell, when he was there in January 1803, January 12, 1803, BT 6/70, TNA; Colonel Fraser, February 27, 1802, Goree, Inclosure, CO 268/7, TNA; Observations on the Situation of Sierra Leone with respect to the surrounding Natives, William Dawes, November, 1811, CO 267/29, TNA; Goddard, *Handbook of Sierra Leone,* 30; Appendix to Report from the Committee on the Sierra Leone Company's Petition, February 27, 1804, BT 6/70, TNA.

37. Report of the Sierra Leone Company—Committee on the Petition of the Court of Directors, May 25, 1802, WO 1/352, TNA.

38. Letter from Governor and Council to Court of Directors, October 19, 1802, WO 1/352, TNA.

39. Peregrine Thorne to John Sullivan, April 4, 1803, WO 1/352, TNA; Geoff Quilley, "The Lie of the Land: Slavery and the Aesthetics of Imperial Landscape in Eighteenth-Century British Art," in *Representing Slavery: Art, Artefacts, and Archives in the Collections of the National Maritime Museum,* ed. Douglas Hamilton and Robert J. Blyth (Aldershot, England: Lund Humphries, 2007), 122; Schwarz, "Zachary Macaulay" (Part 2), viii; Macaulay especially was interested in this effort.

40. List of Maroons, Nova Scotians, and Europeans, October 4, 1802, WO 1/352, TNA. There were 891 Nova Scotians, of whom almost 50 percent (443) were children.

Chapter 8. Accommodation

1. Periodic journeys into the interior were planned. For example, in 1794 James Watt went north to the Futa Jalon. See Robin Hallett, *The Penetration of Africa:*

European Exploration in North and West Africa to 1815 (New York: Praeger, 1965), 271; Report of the Sierra Leone Company—Committee on the Petition of the Court of Directors, May 25, 1802, WO 1/352, TNA. On the Treaty of Amiens, see François Crouzet, "America and the Crisis of the British Imperial Economy, 1803–1807," in *The Early Modern Atlantic Economy,* ed. John J. McCusker and Kenneth Morgan (Cambridge: Cambridge University Press, 2009), 291; John Gascoigne, *Joseph Banks and the English Enlightenment: Useful Knowledge and Polite Culture* (Cambridge: Cambridge University Press, 1994), 246; Roger Norman Buckley, *Slaves in Red Coats: The British West India Regiments, 1795–1815* (New Haven: Yale University Press, 1979), 258. Napoleon did not fully adhere to the terms of the treaty: the French acquired Louisiana from Spain, expanded their navy, and moved to increase their presence in Algiers.

2. Thomas Clarkson to Sir Charles MacCarthy, November, 1817, Clarkson Papers, 1787–1818, Box 2, THL; the treaty referred to was signed September 23, 1817 (the Friendly Society of Sierra Leone was defunct by 1818); Zachary Macaulay to Dr. Thorpe, published 1815 in "Letters to his Royal Highness the Duke of Gloucester, president of the African Association," Rare Books, THL.

3. Kehinde Olabimtan, "Church Missionary Society Projects of Agricultural Improvement in Nineteenth-Century Sierra Leone and Yorubaland," in *Commercial Agriculture: The Slave Trade and Slavery in Atlantic Africa,* ed. Robin Law, Suzanne Schwarz, and Silke Strickrodt (London: Boydell and Brewer, 2013), 214; THL; A. L. Mabogunje, "The Land and Peoples of West Africa," in *History of West Africa,* ed. J. F. A. Ajayi and Michael Crowder (New York: Columbia University Press, 1976), 1:11; John Peterson, "The Enlightenment and the Founding of Freetown," in *Freetown: A Symposium,* ed. Christopher Fyfe and Eldred Jones (Freetown: Sierra Leone University Press, 1968), 14; R. J. Olu-Wright, "The Physical Growth of Freetown," in *Freetown: A Symposium,* 25; J. McKay, "Commercial Life in Freetown," in *Freetown: An Interpretation of Sierra Leone History, 1787–1816,* ed. Christopher Fyfe and Eldred Jones (Freetown: Sierra Leone University Press, 1968), 65; A. P. Kup, *A History of Sierra Leone, 1400–1787* (Cambridge: Cambridge University Press, 1961), 120; Christopher Fyfe, *Sierra Leone Inheritance* (London: Oxford, 1964), 5.

4. Howard Temperley, "Anti-Slavery as Cultural Imperialism," in *Anti-Slavery, Religion and Reform: Essays in Memory of Roger Anstey,* ed. Christine Bolt and Seymour Drescher (Kent: Dawson, 1980), 346; Zachary Macaulay, June 7, 1797, Macaulay Papers, THL.

5. Speech used in forming the committees in 1823 and 1824, Clarkson Papers, 1787–1818, Box 2, THL.

6. The image of West Africa as the "white man's grave" would not emerge until the 1820s. Philip D. Curtin, *The Image of Africa: British Ideas and Action, 1780–1850* (Madison: University of Wisconsin Press, 1964), 180; Smeathman, *Plan of a Settlement,* 12, Rare Books, THL; one historian calls Australia Sierra Leone's twin sister, for both settlements were launched at the same time, in 1787. See N. A. Cox-George, *Finance and Development in West Africa: The Sierra Leone Experience* (London: Dennis Dobson, 1961), 129.

7. R. R. Kuczynski, *Demographic Survey of the British Colonial Empire,* vol. 1, *West Africa* (London: Oxford University Press, 1948), 43. The first 439 settlers (of whom 70 were women) came from among the thousands of free black poor in London, numbered to be over 14,000; Granville Sharp to Dr. Lehsom, October 13, 1788, Clarkson Papers, THL. Initially, 700 people had volunteered to go to the settlement; they left on April 8, 1787, and arrived on May 9, 1787; Eveline C. Martin, *The British West African Settlements, 1750–1821* (New York: Longmans, Green, 1927), 106; Granville Sharp to Dr. Lehsom, October 13, 1788, Clarkson Papers, THL; in 1787 the black poor were not sent to Botany Bay. See James Belich, "The Rise of the Angloworld: Settlement in North America and Australia, 1784–1918," in *Rediscovering the British World,* ed. Philip Buckner and R. Douglas Francis (Alberta: University of Calgary Press, 2005); R. A. Swan, *To Botany Bay . . . If Policy Warrants the Measure* (Canberra: Roebuck Society Publications, 1973); and Isaac Land and Andrew M. Schocket, "New Approaches to the Founding of Sierra Leone Colony, 1786–1808," *Journal of Colonialism and Colonial History* 9, no. 3 (Winter 2008).

8. They left Halifax on January 15, 1792, and arrived in Sierra Leone on March 6, 1792. See Kuczynski, *Demographic Survey,* 66; Adam Afzelius, *Sierra Leone Journal, 1795–96,* ed. Alexander Peter Kup (Uppsala: Almqvist and Wiksells, 1967), 2; Fyfe, *Sierra Leone Inheritance,* 120–122; Clarkson Letter Book, Narrative for Dr. Charles Taylor, MS 41264, BL.

9. The Sierra Leone Company advised against their arrival in the rainy season, between the months of May and November, but this never became a topic of concern; Campbell, *Back to Africa,* 27; one child died on November 15 and the second on December 24; Campbell, *Back to Africa,* 30; Campbell, *Back to Africa,* 34, 38; Campbell, *Back to Africa,* November 22, 41; Campbell, *Back to Africa,* November 24, 43; Campbell, *Back to Africa,* 41; Campbell, *Back to Africa,* 48.

10. General Court of Proprietors of The Sierra Leone Company, held at the New London Tavern, Cheapside, London, on Thursday, the 26th March, 1801, BL, 25; Campbell, *Back to Africa,* 21, 24; Some Maroons tried to escape the illness by fleeing

to the mountains. Lieutenant Jack Jarrett left Freetown to "try the effect of change of air on his health." See Sierra Leone Council, June 25, 1801, CO 270/6, TNA.

11. Dr. Chadwick, December 12, 1800, CO 270/6, TNA; J. Gray, December 12, 1800, Council Minutes, CO 270/5, TNA; in Jamaica the Maroons accepted medicine from plantation doctors and herbs prescribed by older Maroon women. R. C. Dallas, *The History of the Maroons, from Their Origin to the Establishment of Their Chief Tribe at Sierra Leone, Including the Expedition to Cuba for the Purpose of Procuring Spanish Chasseurs and the State of the Island of Jamaica for the Last Ten Years with a Succinct History of the Island Previous to That Period* (London: Frank Cass, 1968), 1:119.

12. Curtin, *Image of Africa,* 192; Journal of Zachary Macaulay, June 20, 1797, Macaulay Papers, Box 20, January 18–May 20, 1797 folder, THL; also see Philip D. Curtin, *Economic Change in Precolonial Africa: Senegambia in the Era of the Slave Trade* (Madison: University of Wisconsin Press, 1975).

13. J. Gray, January 8, 1801, Council Minutes, CO 270/5, TNA. In the first week, two hundred were reported sick; ibid. Of the three Maroons who had died, one was a woman supposed to be one hundred years old; Council Minutes, January 10, 1801, CO 270/5, TNA; in 1803 the surgeon Charles Spencer would note that the Maroons "by color or former residence, are becoming in some measure naturalized to the climate." See January 1, 1803, Health of the Colony, Surgeon Charles Spencer, Council Minutes, Sierra Leone, CO 270/8, TNA.

14. Council Minutes, January 6, 1801, CO 270/5, TNA; Council Minutes, January 27, 1801, CO 270/5, TNA; T. Ludlam, November 11, 1801, CO 270/6, TNA.

15. Council Minutes, April 27, 1801, CO 270/5, TNA; Council Minutes, April 29, 1801, CO 270/5, TNA; one person claimed land abandoned by a Maroon who "had proved contumacious and had departed from the colony." See December 19, 1812, CO 270/13, TNA; Letter from Governor and Council to Court of Directors, Freetown, October 19, 1802, WO 1/352, TNA.

16. Council Minutes, April 27, 1801, CO 270/5, TNA; Council Minutes, March 31, 1801, CO 270/5, TNA; Henry Thornton reporting to Lord Hobart on the Sierra Leone House, February 26, 1802, WO 1/352, TNA; the Maroons received four acres of land for each male twenty-one years of age and older, two for his wife, and one for each child. See Thomas Nelson Goddard, *The Handbook of Sierra Leone* (London: G. Richards, 1925), 29; Council Minutes, October 2, 1800, CO 270/5, TNA.

17. Report from the Committee on the Petition of the Court of Directors of the Sierra Leone Company, reported by Viscount Castlereagh, May 25, 1802, Williams

Collection, #DT 516.G7, BC; Report of the Sierra Leone Company—Committee on the Petition of the Court of Directors, May 25, 1802, WO 1/352, TNA.

18. George Ross to Council, May 26, 1801, CO 270/6, TNA. Ross asked for twenty muskets and ten pounds of gunpowder, which were denied by the council; on June 25, 1801, when George Ross gave Jack Jarrett a week's worth of provisions, Jarrett told him "in an insolent manner that I might keep it"; ibid.; Ross, June 6, 1801, in Campbell, *Back to Africa,* 65; Campbell, *Back to Africa,* 55; Campbell, *Back to Africa,* 106ff; Ross, June 16, 1801, in Campbell, *Back to Africa,* 94.

19. George Ross to Council, May 26, 1801, CO 270/6, TNA; Council Minutes, September 29, 1802, CO 270/8, TNA; Henry Adlum reached Sierra Leone on January 6, 1801. He would become alderman of Freetown by January 1803; Henry Adlum, September 10, 1801, CO 270/6, TNA; Examination of Benjamin Hallowell, BT 6/70, TNA. He was sent to Sierra Leone at the beginning of January 1803; Appendix to Report from the Committee on the Sierra Leone Company's Petition, February 27, 1804, BT 6/70, TNA.

20. Appendix to Report from the Committee on the Sierra Leone Company's Petition, February 27, 1804, BT 6/70, TNA; Maroon List, April 1, 1802—list of Maroons as returned by their superintendent, WO 1/352, TNA. Captain Andrew Smith had seven adults and eight children in his family. See CO 140/33, TNA.

21. Health of colony, Surgeon Charles Spencer, January 1, 1803, CO 270/8, TNA; Council Minutes, February 28, 1803, CO 270/9, TNA; the Sierra Leone Company did provide a pension to Colonel Montague James starting on March 26, 1801, and continuing at least until July 13, 1807; see Council Minutes, March 26, 1801, CO 270/5, TNA; and Zachary Macaulay to Edward Coke, July 13, 1807, WO 1/352, TNA; also see Gerald W. Hartwig and K. David Patterson, "The Disease Factor: An Introductory Overview," in *Disease in African History: An Introductory Survey and Case Studies,* ed. Gerald W. Hartwig and K. David Patterson (Durham: Duke University Press, 1978); Philip D. Curtin, "The End of the 'White Man's Grave'? Nineteenth-Century Mortality in West Africa," *Journal of Interdisciplinary History* 21, no. 1 (Summer 1990): 63–88; Philip D. Curtin, "Epidemiology and the Slave Trade," in *Migration and Mortality in Africa and the Atlantic World, 1700–1900,* ed. Philip D. Curtin (Aldershot, England: Ashgate, 2001); Philip D. Curtin, "The Epidemiology of Migration," in *Coerced and Free Migration: Global Perspectives* (Stanford: Stanford University Press, 2002); David P. Geggus observes that "the starkly different susceptibility to tropical disease displayed by Europeans and Africans during the St. Domingue conflict may have encouraged the growth of biological racism." See

Geggus, *The Haitian Revolution: A Documentary History* (Indianapolis: Hackett, 2014), xxxiv.

22. Maroon List, April 1, 1802—list of Maroons as returned by their superintendent, WO 1/352, TNA; Answers of the Governor and Council of Sierra Leone, Appendix F, 1803, BT 6/70, TNA; Abstract of Dispatches received from Sierra Leone dated at Freetown the 29th of October, 1806—laid before proprietors on January 8, 1807, BT 6/70, TNA.

23. Report of the Sierra Leone Company: Committee on the Petition of the Court of Directors, May 25, 1802, WO 1/352, TNA; Queries Proposed by Commodore Hallowell, with the Governor, January 12, 1803, WO 1/352, TNA; Extracts from Captain William Day to Mr. Thornton, February 18, 1803, WO 1/352, TNA; Governor Day to Henry Thornton, July 8, 1803, WO 1/352, TNA; William Day became governor in February 1803. Ludlam remained as councilor and then succeeded him again as governor. See James W. St. G. Walker, *The Black Loyalists: The Search for a Promised Land in Nova Scotia and Sierra Leone, 1783–1870* (New York: Africana, 1976), 248.

24. Appendix to Report from the Committee on the Sierra Leone Company's Petition, February 27, 1804, BT 6/70, TNA; Council meeting, May 6, 1799, CO 270/4, TNA; J. J. Crooks, *A History of the Colony of Sierra Leone, Western Africa* (London: Frank Cass, 1903), 57; General Court of Proprietors of The Sierra Leone Company, held at the New London Tavern, Cheapside, London, on Thursday, the 26th March, 1801, BL; the Bananas formed a group of three islands and were three miles from the mainland; the largest island was only twelve miles in circumference. See Claude George, *The Rise of British West Africa, Comprising the Early History of The Colony of Sierra Leone, The Gambia, Lagos, Gold Coast, etc. etc., with a Brief Account of Climate, the Growth of Education, Commerce, and Religion and a Comprehensive History of the Bananas and Bunce Islands* (London: Houlston and Sons, 1904), 64; J. Gray and Ludlam to Duke of Portland, May 6, 1799, CO 267/10, TNA; Council Meeting, May 13, 1799, CO 270/4, TNA; Thomas Ludlam to Court of Directors, May 8, 1799, CO 267/10, TNA.

25. This would become another scheme like Philip Beaver's in the Bulama Islands that had resulted in no permanent establishment. See P. E. H. Hair, "Sierra Leone and Bulama, 1792–94," *Sierra Leone Bulletin of Religion* 6, no. 1 (June 1964); Bruce Mouser, "Continuing British Interest in Coastal Guinea-Conakry and Fuuta Jaloo Highlands (1750 to 1850)," *Cahiers d'Etudes Africaines* 43, no. 172 (2003): 767; P. E. H. Hair, "'Elephants for Want of Towns': The Interethnic and International History of

Bulama Island, 1456–1870," *History in Africa* 24 (1997): 177–93; Deirdre Coleman, *Romantic Colonization and British Anti-Slavery* (Cambridge: Cambridge University Press, 2005), 70; and Philip Beaver, "African Memoranda" (1805), THL; for a Danish experiment in colonization in West Africa, see Per Hernaes, "A Danish Experiment in Commercial Agriculture on the Gold Coast, 1788–93," in *Commercial Agriculture.*

26. Report of the Sierra Leone Company—Committee on the Petition of the Court of Directors, May 25, 1802, WO 1/352, TNA.

27. Report from the Committee on the Petition of the Court of Directors of the Sierra Leone Company, reported by Viscount Castlereagh, May 25, 1802, Williams Collection, #DT 516. G7, 743, BC.

28. Thomas Clarkson, December 6, 1842, on how to set up a settlement in Africa, Clarkson Papers, 1824–42, Box 3, THL; the Church Missionary Society was established in 1799, see Olabimtan, *Church Missionary Society Projects;* Report of the Sierra Leone Company—Committee on the Petition of the Court of Directors, May 25, 1802, WO 1/352, TNA.

29. Statement of Directors, February 20, 1805, BT 6/70, TNA; Christopher Fyfe, *A History of Sierra Leone* (Oxford: Oxford University Press, 1962), 97; Statement of Directors, February 20, 1805, BT 6/70, TNA.

30. E. J. Wright, "Remarks on the Early Monetary Position in Sierra Leone with a Description of the Coinage Adopted," *Sierra Leone Studies* 1 (1953): 141; Goddard, *Handbook of Sierra Leone,* 30. After the French plundered the colony in 1794, the company turned to paper currency of dollars, half-dollars, and shillings; Henry Thornton, Esq., to Governor Ludlam, Feb. 7, 1807, Rare Books, THL.

31. *Royal Gazette and Sierra Leone Advertiser,* 1817–20. The August 9, 1817, issue notes 1803 as a turning point; questions asked of Hallowell and then of Macaulay, BT 6/70, TNA; also see F. B. Spilsbury, *Account of a Voyage to the Western Coast of Africa; Performed by His Majesty's Sloop "Favourite" in the Year 1805* (London: J. G. Barnard, 1807), 10; Governor Day to Mr. Macaulay, July 9, 1803, WO 1/352, TNA. The potential of a French attack is mentioned last in February 1803 in a letter from Henry Thornton to Lord Hobart, February 12, 1803, WO 1/352, TNA. The company avoided an attack from more powerful neighbors when Governor William Day appointed the successor to the dead king, doing so on the basis of the company's ownership of land in the Bullom Shore. See July 3, 1803, Governor Day to Henry Thornton, WO 1/352. Day writes, "I crowned Pa Jack under the title of 'King George Banna' king for the Sierra Leone people"; Council, March 14, 1803, CO 270/9, TNA; Council, April 18, 1803, CO 270/9, TNA; in January, the council reported that the

Maroon families could not maintain themselves and would not be able to provision themselves until they received their own land. See Council, January 13, 1803, CO 270/9, TNA.

32. Council Minutes, December 10, 1799, CO 270/4, TNA; Governor Day to Henry Thornton, July 8, 1803, WO 1/352, TNA; there is evidence of this in council minutes starting July 1, 1802, CO 270/8, TNA.

33. This seems to be the last time the Maroons used the same military titles as they had in Jamaica and Nova Scotia; Dallas, *History of the Maroons,* 2:244; in 1813 one Maroon in Sierra Leone went by the name of William Dawes Quarrell—see January 5, 1813, List of Houses in Sierra Leone, CO 270/13, TNA. Coincidentally, Jamaica lifted restrictions against the Maroons in 1805. After the Trelawney war, three of the remaining four Maroon communities were disarmed. In December 1805 they were again entrusted with arms. See G. Nugent to Eyre Coote, December 27, 1805, CO 137/14, TNA.

34. Letter received by General Nugent from correspondent in London, August 1804, CO 137/112, TNA; William Day to Court of Directors of Sierra Leone, February 27, 1805, WO 1/352, TNA. Apparently, Col. William Dawes Quarrell had sent a letter to the Maroons on June 14, 1804, which was received on January 23, 1805, when William Day, Governor, returned to Freetown (but this letter could not be located in the archives); Copy of letter from Captain Andrew Smith and Captain Charles Schaw [*sic*] (Maroons) to Col. William Dawes Quarrell, February 24, 1805, WO 1/352, TNA; Sierra Leone Council Minutes, November 11, 1808, CO 270/11, TNA. The maroons also named two streets based on regions and counties in Jamaica: Trelawney and Westmoreland Streets; William Day to Court of Directors, February 27, 1805, WO 1/352, TNA; Copy of letter from Captain Andrew Smith and Captain Charles Schaw (Maroons) to Col. William Dawes Quarrell, February 24, 1805, WO 1/352, TNA.

35. William Day arrived in Sierra Leone in February 1803 (Walker, *Black Loyalists,* 248) and returned at the end of the year to England; Day returned to Sierra Leone in 1805 and would die in office on November 4, 1805 (Fyfe, *A History of Sierra Leone,* 94), and Ludlam would again take over the office of governor. Abstract of Dispatches received from Sierra Leone dated at Freetown the 29th of October, 1806—laid before proprietors on January 8, 1807, BT 6/70, TNA; T. Thompson to Castlereagh, August 9, 1808, CO 267/24, TNA; William Day to Court of Directors, February 27, 1805, WO 1/352, TNA; Robert Jarrett was a carpenter: see Council Session, September 24, 1816, CO 270/14, TNA; see Sierra Leone Council, November 27, 1820, CO 270/15, TNA; the Maroons may also have worked as dispensers with the surgeon—see Letter

of Dr. James Higgins, December 30, 1810. Higgins discusses "black young men" who dispensed medicine without qualifications; Sierra Leone Council, November 27, 1820, CO 270/15, TNA. A petition from John Smith, carpenter, begins, "eldest son and heir of Andrew Smith, deceased."

36. Sierra Leone Council, September 28, 1815, CO 270/15, TNA. Charles Shaw also took care of an "ideotic" by the name of Dora Lawson. We know nothing else about his relationship with her. See Sierra Leone Council, January 11, 1813, CO 270/13, TNA; Sierra Leone Council, June 28, 1816, CO 270/14, TNA; John Thorpe, March 8, 1822, CO 270/16, TNA; Walker, *Black Loyalists,* 253; Francis A. J. Utting, *The Story of Sierra Leone* (Freeport: Books for Libraries Press, 1931), 106; William Day to Court of Directors, March 15, 1805, WO 1/352, TNA; Sierra Leone Council, 1813–15, CO 270/14, TNA; it is possible that Maroon men who were not within the military ranks had fewer options and so moved toward farming.

37. T. Thompson to London, 1808, CO 267/24, TNA. Thompson noted that the Maroons "as a body" had not professed Christianity. As was evident during the 1795–96 Maroon War, the Maroons held multiple and contradictory views and expressed a range of loyalties to the empire. The other two men were John Harding and William Libert, Sierra Leone Council, 1808, CO 267/24, TNA; T. Thompson to Castlereagh, August 9, 1808, CO 267/24, TNA; quoted in Campbell, *Back to Africa,* 36.

38. T. Thompson to London, 1808, CO 267/24, TNA; Abstract of Dispatches received from Sierra Leone dated at Freetown the 29th of October, 1806—laid before proprietors on January 8, 1807, BT 6/70, TNA; Campbell, *Back to Africa,* 26.

39. Christopher Fyfe, "The Countess of Huntington's Connexion in 19th Century Sierra Leone," *Sierra Leone Bulletin of Religion* 4, no. 1 (1962): 55. As Africanists have noted, African-rooted religions tended to be additive, not exclusive, in orientation; Campbell, *Back to Africa,* 24; Campbell, *Back to Africa,* October 23, 1800, 29; Remarks on List of Nova Scotians, July 31, 1802, WO 1/352, TNA. The daughter of Catherine Duncan married a Maroon man; some evidence points to Maroon women who remained single all their lives; there were many more women than men in the black settler population. Many black men also died in 1801 and 1802 defending the settlement. See Council Session July 25, 1816, CO 270/14, TNA; visit to Freetown, Sierra Leone, March 2016; Fyfe dates the chapel to 1822, *A History of Sierra Leone,* 139; the chapel is still standing in Freetown. At least until 1816 the Maroons continued to live in neighborhoods separate from those of the Nova Scotian settlers. See Council Session, September 9, 1816, CO 270/14, TNA.

40. Zachary Macaulay to Edward Coke, answering inquiries on Sierra Leone, July 13, 1807, WO 1/352, TNA; from October 23. See Campbell, *Back to Africa,* 29; Barnet was not alone in his violence toward women. The Maroon Tom Campbell gave his wife a "thrashing" that caused her to die three weeks later. Tom Tharpe went too far with a "too young" native girl and received a "thrashing" from his brother, Sam. See Campbell, *Back to Africa,* 45, 26.

41. Campbell, *Back to Africa,* 27 (child); Campbell, *Back to Africa,* 30 (six gallons for Palmer); Campbell, *Back to Africa,* 32, 29, 27, 30; to this day, some residents of Preston note the custom of drinking after funerals, which is not prevalent elsewhere in Nova Scotia.

42. Philip D. Curtin, "The Atlantic Slave Trade, 1600–1800," in *History of West Africa,* ed. J. F. A. Ajayi and Michael Crowder (New York: Columbia University Press, 1976), 1:317; some Maroons served as police officers by 1808. See May 1, 1808, CO 267/24, TNA. The Maroons were Charles Shaw, John Harding, and William Libert.

43. The act was passed on March 25, 1807. It forbade British subjects to trade in slaves after May 1, 1807. Fyfe, *A History of Sierra Leone,* 97. On paper, the Parliament took over Sierra Leone on August 8, 1807, and officially took it over on January 1, 1808. Interestingly, the British did not take over Bance Island, and it was subsequently abandoned. In 1808 Governor Ludlam preached to Muslims to give up the slave trade around Sierra Leone. In February he wrote, "I think the Koran does not tell you to sell any of your prisoners to the Christians." See Governor Letter book, 1808 to 1811, FBC; the colony no longer feared an internal attack: see letter from Thomas Ludlam, April 4, 1808, CO 324/69, TNA. Ludlam noted the friendly relations the colony had established with the Susoo, Bullom, and Timmaney nations. The Mandingoes to the north, he wrote, would be formidable, but they were occupied by their "internal dissensions and fear of insurrection among their slaves"; Council Minutes, November 11, 1808, CO 270/11, TNA; the only liberated slaves sanctioned in the colony were brought from European ships; African domestic slavery presumably arose from ancient custom, not avarice or immorality, and required tolerance. See Proclamation, February 26, 1811, CO 270/12, TNA; Clarkson to Friendly Society at Sierra Leone, 1811 (?), Clarkson Papers, 1787–1818, Box 1, THL; T. Thompson to Castlereagh, August 9, 1808, CO 267/24, TNA; T. Thompson to London, CO 267/24, TNA; Rosanne Marion Adderley, *New Negroes from Africa: Slave Trade Abolition and Free African Settlement in the Nineteenth-Century Caribbean* (Bloomington: Indiana University Press, 2006), 3. Note that this atonement did not apply to ending the

domestic slave trade in Africa. In 1811 the government promised not to interfere with the "ancient customs of Africa." See Proclamation, February 26, 1811, CO 270/12, TNA. Unlike previous governors, Thompson did not favor expenditures in promoting English or Christian conversion: it was costly and "utterly unnecessary," he believed, to encourage laboring Africans to adopt "European manners of living." See T. Thompson, December 31, 1808, CO 267/24, TNA; but in 1811 the black Quaker from the United States Paul Cuffee observed the transformations in Sierra Leone. He saw twelve natives in a Methodist church in Sierra Leone. He wrote, "They seemed to have some of the movements of truths to tuch [*sic*] their minds. They betook themselves to the mode of English mode of Cloathing." See Rosalind Cobb Wiggins, ed., *Captain Paul Cuffee's Logs, 1808–1817: A Black Quaker's "Voice from within the Veil"* (Washington, D.C.: Howard University Press, 1996), 172; List of Maroons and Nova Scotians, April 1811, under order of Governor Columbine, FBC. This included 165 men, 195 women, and 447 children. The Nova Scotians had 982 members, and there were just 28 Europeans in the colony; the Maroon Charles Shaw oversaw those who settled in Leicester. Fyfe, *A History of Sierra Leone*, 115.

44. Thomas Ludlam, April 13, 1808, CO 267/24, TNA. Also cited in Nemata Amelia Blyden, *West Indians in West Africa, 1808–1880: The African Diaspora in Reverse* (Rochester: University of Rochester Press, 2000), 11; Mr. Ludlam, April 4, 1808, CO 324/69, TNA; March 31, 1808, in CO 267/24. Also see Blyden, *West Indians in West Africa,* 10; dispatches were sent to the Secretary of State, from April 3, 1809, to November 24, 1812, FBC. This was written sometime after July 1810; Governor Thompson captured his understanding of the relationship between black troops and white supervisors by remarking that "disciplined heads" were needed among the "nervous arms" of the black population. See T. Thompson to Castlereagh, August 9, 1808, CO 267/24, TNA; also see Gad J. Heuman, *Between Black and White: Race, Politics and the Free Coloreds in Jamaica, 1792–1865* (Westport, Conn.: Greenwood Press, 1981), 24–27.

Epilogue

1. John Ewart (agent of Jamaica on immigration), September 30, 1841, CO 140/33, TNA. The exact number of Maroons who reached Kingston cannot be determined, but enough disembarked to be noticed as a group. Curiously, the Maroon John Thorpe, possibly the Maroon who went to Christian school in Nova Scotia four decades earlier, requested the Maroons' return to Jamaica in 1839 but was denied. See Sierra Leone Council, April 11, 1839, CO 270/21, TNA; Frederick Knight observes,

the Caribbean epochs "are not divided by dynastic changes, parliamentary dissolutions and wars. Instead narrations of slavery, emancipation, and post-emancipation replace the conventional political indicators." Franklin W. Knight and Margaret E. Crahan, "The African Migration and the Origins of an Afro-Caribbean Society and Culture," in *Africa and the Caribbean: The Legacies of a Link,* ed. Franklin W. Knight and Margaret E. Crahan (Baltimore: Johns Hopkins University Press, 1979), ix.

2. An unverifiable report from 1841 suggests that all but 70 Maroons left for Jamaica. See Report of His Majesty's Commissioners on the State of our Settlements on the western coast of Africa, Sierra Leone, August 26, 1841, CO 267/172, TNA. No other evidence corroborates that so many Maroons and their descendants returned to Jamaica; John Wentworth had singled out five men as troublemakers—"two Jarratts, two Shaws, and one Harding"—who should be sent to some remote place. John Wentworth to Duke of Portland, April 13, 1799, CO 217/270, NLJ; Return of immigrants who have arrived in the Island of Jamaica from Sept 30, 1840 to Sept 30, 1841 under the Immigration Act, CO 140/133, TNA; it is difficult to know if this was the same Rosey who had relations with George Ross in 1800. We know there was also a Rosey Hamilton among the Maroons. One Maroon by the name of Ann Williams, the mother of William Douglas Gray, "paid her debt to nature" soon after her arrival in Sierra Leone. See Sierra Leone Council, 1813–15, 270/14, TNA; Ana Williams (same person as Ann Williams) petitioned as a widow in Sierra Leone Council, September 26, 1812, CO 270/13, TNA; Sophie Rickett petitioned as a widow in 1819; see Sierra Leone Council, April 21, 1819, CO 270/15, TNA; unlike Nova Scotia's black Loyalists, Maroon women entered Sierra Leone as wives, mothers, and daughters, not as potential landholders. All land was initially titled to Maroon men and, at their death, to the next male head of the family; this deficiency stayed with Maroon women for four decades. See Christopher Fyfe, *A History of Sierra Leone* (Oxford: Oxford University Press, 1962), 100; between 1802 and 1811 the Trelawney population grew by almost 60 percent to 807 members. See Census of Freetown only in April 1811. By the 1840s the Maroons and their descendants would have increased but would have formed a tiny percentage of the population dominated by liberated Africans; the sources identify one woman, Sylvia Harding, who came without a husband or parents. In an 1816 petition she writes that she was "brought to colony without mother or father—brought as one of the family of Mrs. Connor [O'Connor] of the Maroons of which nation Petitioner also was." Sylvia Harding could have been a relative of Mrs. Connor—or her slave; a visible manifestation of the Maroons' family structure comes to us by way of lists kept by Maroon superintendents in each colony:

the names of Maroon men, with their military ranks, were listed in long columns to the left, and across each row were the numbers of wives, sons, daughters, and other kin; unlike the Maroon returnees, the free blacks in Jamaica were predominantly young and women.

3. Captain H. Turner of the *West Indian,* December 10, 1841, CO 318/155, TNA. Turner unintentionally pointed to the Maroons' unwillingness to resign to local conditions in Sierra Leone: the Maroons, he said, "are a proud idle set of people, a burthen to this colony than otherwise." They were less "easily managed" and less "satisfied" than liberated Africans. See Captain H. Turner, December 8, 1841, CO 318/155, TNA.

4. Sierra Leone Council, 1813–15, May 23, 1816, CO 270/14, TNA; both John Libert and John Gray wanted land to the west of the city; Betsy Shaw petition, September 6, 1813; Nancy Jarrett petition, January 11, 1813, and September 9, 1816; Petition of John Gray, May 23, 1816; Petition of John Libert, May 23, 1816; Mary Brown, February 3, 1819; Daniel Parkinson, February 29, 1820. All in CO 270/14, TNA.

5. *Royal Gazette and SL Advertiser,* "Interesting Event" section, January 13, 1821, paper, CO 270/12, TNA.

6. Fyfe, *A History of Sierra Leone,* 88–104; Commander Bedford Pim, "The Negro and Jamaica," read before the Anthropological Society of London, February 1, 1866, at St. James Hall, London (Special Number of *Popular Magazine of Anthropology*), in MHS, 65.

7. It is difficult to assess the extent to which Maroon descendants remained loyal to King George.

8. Just two years earlier John Thorpe, on behalf of the "Maroon inhabitants of the colony," petitioned a return to Jamaica and was denied. See John Thorpe, April 11, 1839, CO 270/21, TNA; Franklin W. Knight, "The Disintegration of the Caribbean Slave Systems, 1772–1886," in *General History of the Caribbean: The Slave Societies of the Caribbean,* ed. Pieter C. Emmer (London: UNESCO/Macmillan, 1997), 339.

9. Proclamation, May 23, 1835, CO 137/198/76, TNA.

10. Proclamation by the Governor, June 1835, CO 137/198, TNA (emphasis added). Also see Sidney W. Mintz, "Epilogue: The Divided Aftermaths of Freedom," in *Between Slavery and Free Labor: The Spanish-Speaking Caribbean in the 19th Century,* ed. Charles H. Vance (Baltimore: Johns Hopkins University Press, 1985).

11. Edward Panton, April 11, 1840, CO 137/252, TNA; see also Speech of Governor, October 26, 1841; see *Journal of Assembly Records,* October 1842, CO 140/134,

TNA. In April 1840 the Jamaican assemblyman Edward Panton announced that the only "hope which now remains for the colony rests upon a large increase of the laboring population."

12. T. Thompson to Castlereagh, August 9, 1808, CO 267/24, TNA. Some liberated Africans suffered the punishment earlier meted out to slaves. In 1808 an eight-year-old African girl accused a British official of burning her on the back with a hot iron. Reportedly, it left marks that would shame a European executioner. In defense, the official observed that he would do what he pleased "with his own." He had, after all, redeemed her from a life of enslavement; Frederick Elliot, Robert Torrens, Edward E. Villiers to James Stephen, July 29, 1840, Colonial Land and Emigration Office (copy sent to Governor of Sierra Leone) CO 137/252, TNA; also see Rosanne Marion Adderley, *New Negroes from Africa: Slave Trade Abolition and Free African Settlement in the Nineteenth-Century Caribbean* (Bloomington: Indiana University Press, 2006); C. T. Metcalfe to Lord Stanley, October 27, 1841, CO 137/256, TNA; some Jamaicans expressed concerns that the arrival of free "heathen" might prove injurious to Jamaica; these rescued Africans were not allowed to return to their own towns. See Sierra Leone, 1837–42, March 10, 1838, in CO 270/21, TNA. When Dirk Andy and John Dunkannah asked to return to their own country on the river Niger, for example, the board ruled unanimously that "granting such an indulgence as that solicited would lead to endless applications of the like nature, and therefore rejected the passage of the petition."

13. Return of immigrants who have arrived in the Island of Jamaica from September 30, 1840, to September 30, 1841, under the Immigration Act, CO 140/133, TNA; the Maroons were not particularly sought after as laborers by Jamaican planters. See Nathaniel Isaacs to W. I. Emigration Society in London, August 18, 1841, CO 318/155, TNA.

14. House of Assembly, speech, October 24, 1843, CO 140/135, TNA. It provided a convenient harbor, fertile soil, and a varied climate, factors that were suitable for coffee and sugar as well as "the most delicate and highly prized vegetables and fruits of Europe."

15. J. M. Higginson, Report on Emigrants September 30, 1841, CO 140/133, TNA; Governor McDonald, November 24, 1842, CO 267/176, TNA; in November 1842 Jamaica's governor blamed the failure directly on the *Commissioner Barclay.*

16. October 18, 1844, Sierra Leone, CO 140/36, TNA; William A. Green, "Plantation Society and Indentured Labour: The Jamaican Case, 1834–1865," in *Colonialism and Migration: Indentured Labour Before and After Slavery,* ed. P. C. Emmer (Dordrecht:

Martinus Nijhoff, 1986), 171; the labor shortage in the British West Indies was solved by transporting laborers from Cuba, China, and India. The permeability of the Maroon community in Sierra Leone remains unclear. In 1816, when one Maroon woman, Sylvia Harding, petitioned for land, she argued that she was a member of the "nation" of the Maroons. See September 3, 1816, Council Session, CO 270/14, TNA.

17. Ira Berlin, "The Development of Plantation Systems and Slave Societies: A Commentary," in *Comparative Perspectives on Slavery in New World Plantation Societies,* ed. Vera Rubin and Arthur Tuden (New York: New York Academy of Sciences, 1977), 70. Berlin notes that the maturation of Afro-American culture correlates with the emergence of African American families. Because Mavis C. Campbell ends her first book on the Trelawney Town Maroons with their deportation from Jamaica, she gives heavy weight to the 1795–96 war. She writes, "The Trelawney Town War was the denouement of a process that began with the Treaties" (259).

18. Both the white Loyalist John Wentworth and the Maroon captain Andrew Smith named their sons after King George III. Mavis C. Campbell cautions against adopting a Marxist framework to understand the Maroons, see Mavis C. Campbell, *The Maroons of Jamaica, 1655–1796: A History of Resistance, Collaboration, and Betrayal* (Granby, Conn.: Bergin and Garvey, 1988), 13; Eric Foner and Manning Marable, *Herbert Aptheker on Race and Democracy* (Urbana: University of Illinois Press, 2006), 19. Aptheker uses this term to describe the Maroons in the context of the United States; Nadine Hunt and Olatunji Ojo, "Introduction," in *Slavery in Africa and the Caribbean: A History of Enslavement and Identity Since the Eighteenth Century,* ed. Olatunji Ojo and Nadine Hunt (New York: I. B. Tauris, 2012). The British never used marriages as a customary means for integrating themselves into the local African societies; on the "hypervisibility" of resistance, see Christine Chivallon, "Representing the Slave Past: The Limits of Museographical and Patrimonial Discourses," in *At the Limits of Memory: Legacies of Slavery in the Francophone World,* ed. Nicola Frith and Kate Hodgson (Liverpool: Liverpool University Press, 2015); Bogumil Jewsiewicki notes that our idea of slavery—borrowed from early abolitionists—is symbolized by chains. Therein lies our difficulty in reconciling the Trelawney Town Maroons' accommodation as a form of resistance. See Bogumil Jewsiewicki, "In the Empire of Forgetting: Collective Memory of the Slave Trade and Slavery," in *Crossing Memories: Slavery and African Diaspora,* ed. Mariana C. Candido, Ana Lucia Araujo, and Paul E. Lovejoy (Trenton, N.J.: Africa World Press, 2011), 3–5.

19. Jeff Forret, review of "The Long Emancipation: The Demise of Slavery in the U.S.," *Slavery and Abolition* 37, no. 4 (2016): 763–64. Foret suggests that we consider

slave abolition not as one extended process that began somewhere in the eighteenth century and culminated with the emancipation of slaves in Brazil in 1888, but as "discrete mini-emancipations."

20. In the Maroon context it is helpful to consider emancipation as separation from the rule of whites and as belonging inside an alternate community. See the discussion by Igor Kopytoff and Suzanne Miers, "African Slavery as an Institution of Marginality," in *Slavery in Africa: Historical and Anthropological Perspectives,* ed. Suzanne Miers and Igor Kopytoff (Madison: University of Wisconsin Press, 1977). Also see David Eltis, "Migration and Agency in Global History," in *Coerced and Free Migration: Global Perspectives,* ed. David Eltis (Stanford: Stanford University Press, 2002), 3. Outside of a history of slavery and emancipation, it is also useful to situate the Maroons' return to Jamaica in the larger history of labor migration. Eltis writes, "In a larger canvas, the ethnic composition of free and coerced migration in the four centuries before 1900 is a template for migration in the twentieth and twenty-first centuries"; Jeffrey A. Fortrin, in "Blackened Beyond Our Native Hue: Removal, Identity and the Trelawney Maroons on the Margins of the Atlantic World, 1796–1800," *Citizenship Studies* 10, no. 1 (February 2006), explains that the Maroons were marginal in three ways: (1) in the British Empire; (2) in the periphery of Jamaican plantation society; and (3) as dissidents within the Maroon societies (25). The Maroons operated in the context of humanitarianism, not of human rights. See William Mulligan and Maurice Bric, eds., *A Global History of Anti-Slavery Politics in the Nineteenth Century* (London: Palgrave Macmillan, 2013), 6–8.

21. Christopher Schmidt-Nowara, "Age of Democratic Revolutions," in Miller, ed., *Princeton Companion to Atlantic History,* 129–31. Schmidt-Nowara redefines R. R. Palmer's Democratic revolutions as "liberation from various forms of domination, not only from the formal political institutions of empire, bulwarks of aristocratic privilege, at the heart of Palmer's study." For another way to conceptualize this era, see James Belich, "The Rise of the Angloworld: Settlement in North America and Australia, 1784–1918," in *Rediscovering the British World,* ed. Philip Buckner and R. Douglas Francis (Alberta: University of Calgary Press, 2005). One historian, A. D. Dridzo, mentioned by Mavis C. Campbell, called the 1795–96 war a plot instigated by the plantocracy to advance their own interests. This clearly became an issue after the war started, but I have not found evidence of this in the first weeks. See Campbell, *Maroons of Jamaica,* 263.

22. Lovejoy observes that the response of an enslaved population depended foremost on the contexts in which individuals found themselves. Not only creolization

but also the pace of creolization affected strategies for survival. Paul E. Lovejoy, "Narratives of Trans-Atlantic Slavery in the Life Stories of Two Muslims," in *Africa and Trans-Atlantic Memories: Literary and Aesthetic Manifestations of Diaspora and History,* ed. Paul E. Lovejoy, Naana Opoku-Agyemang, and David V. Trotman (Trenton, N.J.: Africa World Press, 2008), 7, 15; Campbell notes that their survival in the most extreme circumstances has led them to see themselves today as a chosen people. *Maroons of Jamaica,* 260. Also see Bev Carey, *The Maroon Story: The Authentic and Original History of the Maroons in the History of Jamaica, 1490–1880* (New York: Agouti Press, 1997); Carey Robinson, *The Fighting Maroons of Jamaica* (Kingston: William Collins and Sangster, 1969); and Kenneth M. Bilby, *True-Born Maroons* (Kingston: Ian Randle, 2006).

23. The British also made use of African elites. Placing the Maroons or Africans in positions of authority over whites remained unthinkable. See C. A. Bayly, *Imperial Meridian: The British Empire and the World, 1780–1830* (London: Longman, 1989), 10–12, 122; Frederick Cooper, "Empirical Futures: Anthropologists and Historians Engage the Work of Sidney W. Mintz," in *Space, Time and History: The Conceptual Limits of Globalization,* ed. Frederick Cooper (Chapel Hill: University of North Carolina Press, 2009); Sidney W. Mintz, "Labor Needs and Ethnic Ripening in the Caribbean Region," Woodrow Wilson Lectures, #137 (1982); Winks emphasizes that imperial history can benefit only from the wider perspectives offered by area studies and cultural studies. To this we can add Maroon histories. See Robin W. Winks, "Future of Imperial History," in *The Oxford History of the British Empire: Historiography,* ed. Robin W. Winks (New York: Oxford University Press, 1999); Jerry Bannister, in "Atlantic Canada in an Atlantic World? Northeastern North America in the Long 18th Century," *Acadiensis* 43, no. 2 (Summer/Autumn 2014): 3–30, has more recently extended Winks's argument about the importance of studying the British Empire from its Atlantic peripheries.

Bibliography

Reconstructing the migrations of the Maroons required research in multiple libraries and archives across the world. It also meant consulting hundreds of secondary sources related to black migrations, Atlantic revolutions, slavery, and abolitionism. This lists the sources I consulted; not all the sources listed here are cited in the body of the work.

Primary Manuscript Sources

United States

Clements Library (Ann Arbor, Michigan)
The Huntington Library (San Marino, California)
John Carter Brown Library (Brown University, Rhode Island)
John J. Burns Library (Boston College)
Massachusetts Historical Society (Boston)

Britain

British Library (London)
The National Archives (Kew)

Sierra Leone

Fourah Bay College Archives (Freetown)

Jamaica

Jamaican Archives and Records Department (Spanish Town)
National Library of Jamaica (Kingston)

Canada

Nova Scotia Archives (Halifax)
Library and Archives Canada (Ottawa)

Primary Printed Sources

Afzelius, Adam. *Sierra Leone Journal, 1795–96.* Edited by Alexander Peter Kup (Studia Ethnographica Upsaliensia, 1967). Printed by Almqvist and Wiksells, Uppsala, 1967.

An Account of Jamaica and Its Inhabitants by a gentleman, long resident in the West Indies, London. Printed for Longman, Nurst, Rees, and Orme, by G. Woodfall, 1808, BL.

Anonymous. The importance of Jamaica to Great-Britain, consider'd. With some account of that island, from its discovery in 1492 to this time: . . . An account of their fruits, drugs, timber and dying-woods, . . . With an account of their trade and produce; . . . In a letter to a gentleman. 1740. THL.

Archibald, Adams George. "Story of Deportation of Negroes from Ns to Sierra Leone, Read by Ex-Governor Archibald," March 12, 1885, *Collections of NS Historical Society for the years 1889–1891.* Vol. 7. 1891.

Barnard, Anne. *Lives of the Lindsays or a Memoir of the Houses of Crawford and Balcarres by Lord Lindsay, of Which Are Added Extracts from the Official Correspondence of Alexander Sixth Earl of Balcarres, During the Maroon War; Together with Personal Narratives by His Brothers, the Hon. Robert Colin, James, John, and Hugh Lindsay; and by His Sister, Lady Anne Barnard.* Vol. 3. London: John Murray, 1849.

Barrington, George. "History of New South Wales." 1802. Rare Books, THL.

Beaver, Philip. "African Memoranda." 1805. Rare Books, THL.

Blome, Richard. "A Description of the Island of Jamaica; with the Other Isles and Territories in America, to Which the English Are Related, Viz. Barbadoes, St. Christophers, Nievis, or Mevis, Antego, St. Vincent. Dominica, Montserrat, Anguilla. Barbada, Bermudes, Carolina." 1678. Rare Books, THL.

Bridges, George Wilson. *Annals of Jamaica by the Reverend George Wilson Bridges, A.M.* Vol. 2. London: John Murray, 1828.

Browne, Patrick, M.D. "Civil and Natural History of Jamaica." 1756. Rare Books, JCB.

———. "Civil and Natural History of Jamaica." 1789. Rare Books, JCB.

Carmichael, Mrs. A. C. *Domestic Manners and Social Condition of the White, Coloured and Negro Population of the West Indies.* 2 vols. London: Whittaker, Treacher, 1833.

Charmilly, Venault de. Answer to Bryan Edwards (1797). Rare Books, JCB.

Dallas, R. C. *The History of the Maroons, from Their Origin to the Establishment of Their Chief Tribe at Sierra Leone, Including the Expedition to Cuba for the Purpose of Procuring Spanish Chasseurs and the State of the Island of Jamaica for the Last Ten Years with a Succinct History of the Island Previous to That Period.* 2 vols. 1803.

Dicker, Samuel. "A Letter to a Member of Parliament, Concerning the Importance of Our Sugar-Colonies to Great Britain. By a Gentleman, Who Resided Many Years in the Island of Jamaica." 1745. Rare Books, THL.

Edwards, Bryan. *The History Civil and Commercial of the British Colonies in the West Indies,* 3 vols. 1801. Rare Books, CL.

Falconbridge, Alexander. "An Account of the Slave Trade on the Coast of Africa." 1792.

Fergusson, Charles Bruce. *Clarkson's Mission to America, 1791–92.* NSA, Publication no. 11, 1971.

Hansard, *The Parliamentary History of England from the Earliest Period to the Year 1803, from Which Last-Mentioned.* Vol. 32, from May 27, 1795, to March 2, 1797. London: Hansard, 1818.

Hickeringill, Edmund. "Jamaica Viewed: With All the Ports, Harbours, and Their Several Soundings, Towns, and Settlements Thereunto Belonging Together, with the Nature of It's Climate, Fruitfulnesse of the Soile, and It's Suitableness to English Complexions." 1661. Rare Books, THL.

———. "Jamaica Viewed." 1705. Rare Books, JCB.

Leslie, Charles. A new and exact account of Jamaica, wherein the antient and present state of that colony, its importance to Great Britain, laws, trade, manners and religion, together with the most remarkable and curious animals, plants, trees, &c. are described: with a particular account of the sacrifices, libations, &c. at this day in use among the negroes. The third edition. To which is added, an appendix. 1740. Rare Books, THL.

Long, C. E. "Papers Relating to Jamaica, Presented by C. E. Long." 1730s. BL.

Long, Edward. *The History of Jamaica: Reflections on Its Situation, Settlements, Inhabitants, Climate, Products, Commerce, Laws and Government*, 3 vols. 1774.

Macdonald, James S. "North British Society of Halifax." 1894. Rare Books, THL.

Matthews, John. "Voyage to the River Sierra Leone." In *Voyage to the River Sierra Leone on the coast of Africa; containing an account of the trade and productions of the country, and of the civil and religious customs and manners of the people; in a series of letters to a friend in England by John Matthews, Lieut in the Royal Navy; during his residence in that country in the years 1785, 1786, and 1787 with an additional letter on the subject of the Slave Trade.* Printed in London in 1788. Rare Books, THL.

Newbury, C. W. *British Policy Towards West Africa: Select Documents, 1786–1874.* Oxford: Clarendon Press, 1965.

Pim, Commander Bedford. "The Negro and Jamaica," by Commander Bedford Pim, of Royal Navy, read before the anthropological society of London, February 1, 1866, at St. James Hall, London. Special Number of the Popular Magazine of Anthropology, 1866. MHS.

Pinckard, George, M.D. "Notes on the West Indies." 1806. Rare Books, JCB.

Rainsford, Marcus. *An Historical Account of the Black Empire of Hayti (1805).* Edited by Paul Youngquist and Gregory Pierrot. Durham: Duke University Press, 2013.

Roberts, Orlando W. *Narrative of Voyages and Excursions on the East Coast and in the Interior of Central America; Describing a Journey up the River*

San Juan, and Passage across the Lake of Nicaragua to the City of Leon: Pointing out the Advantages of a Direct Commercial Intercourse with the Natives. Narrative of Voyages and Excursions, C2 1827 Ro. Edited by Orlando W. Roberts, many years a resident trader, with notes and observations by Edward Irving. Edinburgh: Constable, 1827.

Sharp, Granville. "Extract of a Letter to a Gentleman in Maryland." 1797. Rare Books, THL.

———. "Serious Reflections on the Slave Trade & Slavery." 1797. Rare Books, THL.

Smeathman, Henry, Esq. "Plan of a Settlement to Be Made near Sierra Leone on the Grain Coast of Africa." 1786. Rare Books, THL.

Stanford, George. "Obi; or the History of Three-Fingered Jack in a Series of Letters." In *Rare Books.* 1804. Rare Books, THL.

Strangeways, Thomas. *Sketch of the Mosquito Shore, Including the Territory of Poyais, Descriptive of the Country; with Some Information as to Its Productions, the Best Mode of Culture &C. Chiefly Intended for the Use of Settlers.* Edinburgh: William Blackwood, 1822.

Thicknesse, Philip. *Memoirs and Anecdotes of Philip Thicknesse, Late Lieutenant Governor of Land Guard Fort and Unfortunately Father to George Touchet, Baron Audley.* Dublin: Graisberry and Campbell, 1790.

Uring, Nathaniel. "A History of the Voyages and Travels of Capt. Nathaniel Uring." 1726. Rare Books, CL.

Wadstrom, Carl. "An Essay on Colonization, Particularly Applied to the Western Coast of Africa, . . ." By C. B. Wadstrom. In Two Parts. . . . Vol. 2. 1794. Rare Books, THL.

Williamson, Hugh. Observations on the Climate in Different Parts of America, Compared with the Climate in Corresponding Parts of the Continent to Which Address Remarks on the Different Complexions of the Human Race with Some Account of the Aborigines of America, by Hugh Williamson, M.D., Member of the Holland Society of Sciences. 1811.

Willyams, Cooper. "Account of the Campaign in the West Indies in the Year 1794." Rare Books, THL.

Winterbottom, Thomas, M.D. "Account of the Native Africans." 2 vols. In *Account of the Native Africans in the Neighborhood of Sierra Leone to which is added an account of the present state of medicine among them.* 1803. Rare Books, THL.

Young, William. *Historical Survey of the Island of Saint Domingo Together with an Account of the Maroon Negroes in the Island of Jamaica; and a History of the War in the West Indies, in 1793 and 1794; Also a Tour through the Several Islands of Barbados, St. Vincent, Antigua, Toabo, and Grenada in the Years 1791 and 1792.* London: John Stockdale, 1801.

———. "An Account of the Black Charaibs in the Island of St. Vincent, Part II." 1795. Rare Books, JCB.

Secondary Sources

The study of slavery and the Maroons has grown tremendously in recent years. All the sources listed below have informed my thinking and have shaped the overlapping fields of Atlantic history most pertinent to this project. This list, which is not exhaustive, is divided into readings by sections: British Empire, Black Migrations, and Historical Memory; Maroons; Caribbean; Jamaica; Nova Scotia; West Africa; Sierra Leone; Abolition; and After Abolition. Any omission of important works is inadvertent.

British Empire, Black Migrations, and Historical Memory

On migrations in the British colonies, see R. R. Kuczynski, *Demographic Survey of the British Colonial Empire,* vol. 1, *West Africa* (London: Oxford University Press, 1948); Philip D. Curtin, *The Atlantic Slave Trade: A Census (*Madison: University of Wisconsin Press, 1969); Henry Hoetink, *Slavery and Race Relations in the Americas: Comparative Notes on Their Nature and Nexus* (New York: Harper and Row, 1973); Philip D. Curtin, "The Atlantic Slave Trade, 1600–1800," in *History of West Africa,* ed. J. F. A. Ajayi and Michael Crowder (New York: Columbia University Press, 1976), vol. 1; Ellen Gibson Wilson, *The Loyal Blacks* (New York: Capricorn Books, 1976); Winthrop D. Jordan, "Planter and Slave Identity Formation: Some Problems in the Comparative Approach," in

Comparative Perspectives on Slavery in New World Plantation Societies, ed. Vera Rubin and Arthur Tuden (New York: New York Academy of Sciences, 1977); Franklin W. Knight and Margaret E. Crahan, "The African Migration and the Origins of an Afro-Caribbean Society and Culture," in *Africa and the Caribbean: The Legacies of a Link,* ed. Franklin W. Knight and Margaret E. Crahan (Baltimore: Johns Hopkins University Press, 1979); Eugene Genovese, *From Rebellion to Revolution: Afro-American Slave Revolts in the Making of the Modern World* (Baton Rouge: Louisiana State University Press, 1979); Henry Hoetink, "The Cultural Links," in *Africa and the Caribbean: The Legacies of a Link,* ed. Margaret E. Crahan and Franklin W. Knight (Baltimore: Johns Hopkins University Press, 1979); Alan Frost, *Convicts and Empire: A Naval Question, 1776–1811* (Melbourne: Oxford University Press, 1980); David Patrick Geggus, "British Opinion and the Emergence of Haiti, 1791–1805," in *Slavery and British Society, 1776–1846* (Baton Rouge: Louisiana State University Press, 1982); Rosalind Cobb Wiggins, *Captain Paul Cuffee's Logs and Letters, 1808–1817: A Black Quaker's "Voice from within the Veil"* (Washington, D.C.: Howard University Press, 1996); David Patrick Geggus, "Slavery, War and the Revolution in the Greater Caribbean, 1789–1815," in *A Turbulent Time: The French Revolution and the Greater Caribbean,* ed. David Barry Gaspar and David Patrick Geggus (Bloomington: Indiana University Press, 1997); Sylviane A. Diouf, *Servants of Allah: African Muslims Enslaved in the Americas* (New York: New York University Press, 1998); David Northrup, "Migration: Africa, Asia, the Pacific," in *The Oxford History of the British Empire,* vol. 3, *The Nineteenth Century,* ed. Andrew Porter (Oxford: Oxford University Press, 1999); Marjory Harper, "British Migration and the Peopling of Empire," in *The Oxford History of the British Empire,* vol. 3, *The Nineteenth Century,* ed. Andrew Porter (Oxford: Oxford University Press, 1999); Paul E. Lovejoy, "Identifying Enslaved Africans in the African Diaspora," in *Identity in the Shadow of Slavery* (London: Continuum, 2000); Jan Vasina, "Foreword," in *Central Africans and Cultural Transformations in the African Diaspora,* ed. Linda M.

Heywood (New York: Cambridge University Press, 2002); David Northrup, *Africa's Discovery of Europe, 1450–1850* (Oxford: Oxford University Press, 2002); on the range of "unfreedoms," see Paul E. Lovejoy and Nicholas Rogers, eds., *Unfree Labour in the Development of the Atlantic World* (Portland: Frank Cass, 1994); David Eltis, ed., *Coerced and Free Migration: Global Perspectives* (Stanford: Stanford University Press, 2002); David Eltis, "Migration and Agency in Global History," in *Coerced and Free Migration: Global Perspectives,* ed. David Eltis (Stanford: Stanford University Press, 2002); Colin Forster, "Convicts: Unwilling Migrants from Britain and France," in *Coerced and Free Migration: Global Perspectives,* ed. David Eltis (Stanford: Stanford University Press, 2002); Philip D. Morgan and Sean Hawkins, eds., *Black Experience and the Empire* (New York: Oxford University Press, 2004); Toyin Falola and Matt D. Childs, *The Yoruba Diaspora in the Atlantic World* (Bloomington: Indiana University Press, 2004); Keith Mason, "The American Loyalist Diaspora and the Reconfiguration of the British Atlantic World," in *Empire and Nation: The American Revolution in the Atlantic World,* ed. Eliga H. Gould and Peter S. Onuf (Baltimore: Johns Hopkins University Press, 2005); Michael A. Gomez, *Reversing Sail: A History of the African Diaspora* (Cambridge: Cambridge University Press, 2005); Simon Schama, *Rough Crossings: Britain, the Slaves, and the American Revolution* (New York: Harper-Collins, 2006); Jeffrey A. Fortrin, "Blackened Beyond Our Native Hue: Removal, Identity and the Trelawney Maroons on the Margins of the Atlantic World, 1796–1800," *Citizenship Studies* 10, no. 1 (February 2006): 5–34; Cassandra Pybus, *Epic Journeys of Freedom: Runaway Slaves of the American Revolution and Their Global Quest for Liberty* (Boston: Beacon Press, 2006); James Campbell, *Middle Passages: African American Journeys to Africa, 1787–2005* (New York: Penguin, 2006); Christopher Leslie Brown and Philip D. Morgan, eds., *Arming Slaves: From Classical Times to the Modern Age* (New Haven: Yale University Press, 2006); Alexander X. Byrd, *Captives and Voyagers: Black Migrants Across the Eighteenth-Century British Atlantic World* (Baton Rouge: Louisiana State University Press,

2008); Maya Jasanoff, "Revolutionary Exiles: The American Loyalist and French Émigré Diasporas," in *The Age of Revolutions in Global Context, c. 1760–1840,* ed. David Armitage and Sanjay Subrahmanyam (London: Palgrave Macmillan, 2010); Bogumil Jewsiewicki, "In the Empire of Forgetting: Collective Memory of the Slave Trade and Slavery," in *Crossing Memories: Slavery and African Diaspora,* ed. Mariana C. Candido, Ana Lucia Araujo, and Paul E. Lovejoy (Trenton, N.J.: Africa World Press, 2011); Christine Chivallon, "Representing the Slave Past: The Limits of Museographical and Patrimonial Discourses," in *At the Limits of Memory: Legacies of Slavery in the Francophone World,* ed. Nicola Frith and Kate Hodgson (Liverpool: Liverpool University Press, 2015).

Maroons

Carey Robinson, *The Fighting Maroons of Jamaica* (Kingston: William Collins and Sangster, 1969); Orlando Patterson, "Slavery and Slave Revolts: A Socio-Historical Analysis of the First Maroon War in Jamaica, 1655–1740," *Social and Economic Studies* 19, no. 3 (September 1970): 289–325; Gerald W. Mullin, *Flight and Rebellion: Slave Resistance in Eighteenth-Century Virginia* (New York: Oxford University Press, 1972); for the still-persistent Maroon interpretive framework, see Richard Price, *Maroon Societies: Rebel Slave Communities in the Americas* (Garden City, N.Y.: Anchor Books, 1973); Leslie F. Manigat, "The Relationship Between Marronage and Slave Revolts and Revolution in St. Domingue-Haiti," in *Comparative Perspectives on Slavery in New World Plantation Societies,* ed. Vera Rubin and Arthur Tuden (New York: New York Academy of Sciences, 1977); Barbara K. Kopytoff, "Colonial Treaty as Sacred Charter of the Jamaican Maroons," *Ethnohistory* 26, no. 1 (Winter 1979): 45–64; Richard Price, *First Time: The Historical Vision of an Afro-American People* (Baltimore: Johns Hopkins University Press, 1983); Gordon K. Lewis, *Main Currents in Caribbean Thought: The Historical Evaluation of Caribbean Society in Its Ideological Aspects, 1492–1900* (Baltimore: Johns Hopkins University Press, 1983); Herbert S. Klein, *African Slavery in Latin America and the Caribbean* (New York: Oxford, 1986);

Sylvia W. de Groot, "A Comparison Between the History of Maroon Communities in Surinam and Jamaica," in *Out of the House of Bondage: Runaways, Resistance and Marronage in Africa and the New World,* ed. Gad Heuman (London: Frank Cass, 1986); Richard B. Sheridan, "The Maroons of Jamaica, 1730–1830: Livelihood, Demography and Health," in *Out of the House of Bondage: Runaways, Resistance and Marronage in Africa and the New World,* ed. Gad Heuman (London: Frank Cass, 1986); David Patrick Geggus, "The Enigma of Jamaica in the 1790s: New Light on the Causes of Slave Rebellions," *William and Mary Quarterly* 44, no. 2 (April 1987); Mavis C. Campbell, *The Maroons of Jamaica, 1655–1796: A History of Resistance, Collaboration, and Betrayal* (Granby: Bergin and Garvey, 1988); Mavis C. Campbell, "Montague James and the Maroons in Jamaica, Nova Scotia and Sierra Leone," in *People and Empires in African History: Essays in Memory of Michael Crowder,* ed. Michael Crowder, J. F. Ade Ajayi, J. D. Y. Peel (London: Longman, 1992); Mavis C. Campbell, ed., *Nova Scotia and the Fighting Maroons: A Documentary History* (Williamsburg, Va.: College of William and Mary Press, Studies in Third World Societies, 1990); Mavis C. Campbell, *Back to Africa: George Ross and the Maroons from Nova Scotia to Sierra Leone* (Trenton, N.J.: Africa World Press, 1993); Bev Carey, *The Maroon Story: The Authentic and Original History of the Maroons in the History of Jamaica, 1490–1880* (New York: Agouti Press, 1997); Sylvia W. de Groot, Catherine A. Christen, and Franklin W. Knight, "Maroon Communities in the Circum-Caribbean," in *General History of the Caribbean: The Slave Societies of the Caribbean,* ed. Pieter C. Emmer (London: UNESCO/Macmillan, 1997); Werner Zips, *Black Rebels: African-Caribbean Freedom Fighters in Jamaica* (Princeton: Markus Wiener, 1998); Richard Price, *The Guiana Maroons: A Historical and Bibliographical Introduction* (Baltimore: Johns Hopkins University Press, 1998); Karla Gottlieb, *The Mother of Us All: A History of Queen Nanny, Leader of the Windward Jamaican Maroons* (Trenton, N.J.: Africa World Press, 2000); Maureen Warner-Lewis, "The Character of African-Jamaican Culture," in *Jamaica in Slavery and Freedom: History, Heritage and Culture,* ed. Kathleen E. A. Monteith and Glen Richards (Kingston: University of West Indies Press, 2002); Kenneth M. Bilby, *True-Born Maroons* (Kingston: Ian Randle, 2006); E. Kofi Agorsah, "Scars of Brutality: Archaeology of the Maroons in the Caribbean," in *Archaeology of Atlantic Africa and the African Diaspora,* ed. Akinwumi Ogundiran and Toyin Falola (Bloomington: Indiana University Press, 2007); Timothy Lockley, *Maroon Communities in South Carolina: A Documentary Record* (Charleston: University of South Carolina Press, 2009); Kenneth Bilby, "Swearing by the Past, Swearing to the Future: Sacred Oaths, Alliances, and Treaties among the Guianese and Jamaican Maroons," in *Origins of the Black Atlantic,* ed. Laurent Dubois and Julius S. Scott (New York: Routledge, 2010); Mariana C. Candido, Ana Lucia Araujo, and Paul E. Lovejoy, eds., *Crossing Memories: Slavery and African Diaspora* (Trenton, N.J.: Africa World Press, 2011); Nathaniel Millett, *The Maroons of Prospect Bluff and Their Quest for Freedom in the Atlantic World* (Gainesville: University Press of Florida, 2013); Sylviane Diouf, *Slavery's Exiles: The Story of the American Maroons* (New York: New York University Press, 2014).

Caribbean

The influence of Atlantic history has increasingly shifted our focus from the land-based West Indies to the ocean-based Caribbean. For studies that are still important, see F. W. Pitman, *The Development of the British West Indies, 1700–1763* (New Haven: Yale University Press, 1917); Lillian Penson, *The Colonial Agents of the British West Indies: A Study in Colonial Administration Mainly in the Eighteenth Century* (London: University of London Press, 1924); W. L. Burn, *The British West Indies* (London: Hutchinson's University Library, 1951); Elsa V. Goveia, *Slave Society in the British Leeward Islands at the End of the Eighteenth Century* (New Haven: Yale University Press, 1965); Elsa V. Goveia, *West Indian Laws of the Eighteenth Century* (Barbados: Caribbean University Press, 1970); Cyril Hamshere, *The British in the Caribbean* (Cambridge: Harvard University Press, 1972); Richard Sheridan, "Mortality and Medical Treatment of Slaves in the British West Indies," in *Race and Slavery in the Western Hemisphere: Quantitative Studies,* ed. Stanley L. Engerman and Eugene D. Genovese (Stanford: Center for Advanced Study in the Behavioral Sciences, 1975); Richard Price and Sidney W. Mintz, *An Anthropological Approach to the Afro-American Past: A Caribbean Perspective* (Philadelphia: Institute for the Study of Human Issues, 1976); Ira Berlin, "The Development of Plantation Systems and Slave Societies: A Commentary," in *Comparative Perspectives on Slavery in New World Plantation Societies,* ed. Vera Rubin and Arthur Tuden (New York: New York Academy of Sciences, 1977); B. W. Higman, "Methodological Problems in the Study of the Slave Family," in *Comparative Perspectives on Slavery in New World Plantation Societies,* ed. Vera Rubin and Arthur Tuden (New York: New York Academy of Sciences, 1977); Franklin W. Knight and Margaret E. Crahan, eds., *Africa and the Caribbean: The Legacies of a Link* (Baltimore: Johns Hopkins University Press, 1979); Robin F. A. Fabel, *Colonial Challenges: Britons, Native Americans, and Caribs, 1759–1775* (Gainesville: University Press of Florida, 2000); B. W. Higman, "African and Creole Slave Family Patterns in Trinidad," in *Africa and the Caribbean: The Legacies of a Link,* ed. Margaret E. Crahan and Franklin W. Knight (Baltimore: Johns Hopkins University Press, 1979); Elsa V. Goveia, *A Study on the Historiography of the British West Indies to the End of the Nineteenth Century* (Washington, D.C.: Howard University Press, 1980); B. W. Higman,"Slavery and Development of Demographic Theory in the Age of Industrial Revolution," in *Slavery and British Society, 1776–1846,* ed. James Walvin (Baton Rouge: Louisiana State University Press, 1982); David Patrick Geggus, *Slavery, War, and Revolution: The British Occupation of Saint Domingue, 1793–1798* (New York: Oxford, 1982); O. Nigel Bolland, "Colonization and Slavery in Central America," in *Unfree Labour in the Development of the Atlantic World,* ed. Paul E. Lovejoy and Nicholas Rogers (London: Frank Cass, 1994); Bryan Edwards, *Historical Survey of the Island of Saint Domingo Together with an Account of the Maroon Negroes in the Island of Jamaica and a History of the War in the West Indies in 1793 and 1794* (Salt Lake City: Filmed by the Genealogical Society of Utah, 1995); B. W. Higman, "Economic and Social Development of the British West Indies, from Settlement to ca. 1850," in *The Cambridge Economic History of the United States,* ed. Stanley L. Engerman and Robert E. Gallman, vol. 1 (Cambridge: Cambridge University Press, 1996); Michael Craton, "The Black Caribs of St. Vincent: A Reevaluation," in *The Lesser Antilles in the Age of European Expansion,* ed. Robert L. Paquette and Stanley L. Engerman (Gainesville: University Press of Florida, 1996); Michael Duffy, "The French Revolution and the British Attitudes to the West Indian Colonies," in *A Turbulent Time: The French Revolution and the Greater Caribbean,* ed. David Barry Gaspar and David Patrick Geggus (Bloomington: Indiana University Press, 1997); Franklin W. Knight, "The Disintegration of the Caribbean Slave Systems, 1772–1886," in *General History of the Caribbean,* vol. 3: *The Slave Societies of the Caribbean,* ed. Franklin W. Knight (London: Unesco, 1997); David Patrick Geggus, "Slavery, War and the Revolution in the Greater Caribbean, 1789–1815," in *A Turbulent Time: The French Revolution and the Greater Caribbean,* ed. David Barry Gaspar and David Patrick Geggus (Bloomington: Indiana University Press, 1997); Stanley L. Engerman and B. W. Higman, "The Demographic Structure of the Caribbean Slave Societies in the Eighteenth and Nineteenth Centuries," in *General History of the Caribbean,* vol. 3: *The Slave Societies of the Caribbean,* ed. Franklin W. Knight (London: Unesco, 1997); J. Paul Thomas, "The Caribs of St. Vincent: A Study of Imperial Maladministration, 1763–1773," in *Caribbean Slavery in the Atlantic World: A Student Reader,* ed. Verene A. Shepherd and Hilary McD. Beckles (Princeton: Markus Wiener, 2000); Hilary McD. Beckles, "Kalinago (Carib) Resistance to European Colonization of the Caribbean," in *Caribbean Slavery in the Atlantic World: A Student Reader,* ed. Verene A. Shepherd and Hilary McD. Beckles (Princeton: Markus Wiener, 2000); Claire Robertson and Marsha Robinson, "Re-Modeling Slavery as If Women Mattered," in vol. 2, *Women and Slavery: The Modern Atlantic* (Athens: Ohio University Press, 2008); Kenneth Morgan, "The Struggle for Survival: Slave Infant Mortality in the British Caribbean in the Late Eighteenth and Nineteenth Centuries," in *Children in Slavery Through the Ages,* ed. Suzanne

Miers, Gwyn Campbell, and Joseph C. Miller (Athens: Ohio University Press, 2009); Heather Cateau, "Beyond Planters and Plantership," in *Beyond Tradition: Reinterpreting the Caribbean Historical Experience,* ed. Heather Cateau and Rita Pemberton (Kingston: Ian Randle, 2006); Juanita de Barros, Audra Diptee, and David V. Trotman, "Introduction," in *Beyond Fragmentation: Perspectives on Caribbean History,* ed. Audra Diptee, Juanita de Barros, and David V. Trotman (Princeton: Markus Wiener, 2006); Sidney Mintz, *Three American Colonies: Caribbean Themes and Variations* (Cambridge: Harvard University Press, 2010); Jerry Bannister and Liam Riordan, eds., *The Loyal Atlantic: Remaking the British Atlantic in the Revolutionary Era* (Toronto: University of Toronto Press, 2012); Matthew Mulcahy, *Hubs of Empire: The Southeastern Lowcountry and British Caribbean* (Baltimore: Johns Hopkins University Press, 2014); David P. Geggus, *The Haitian Revolution: A Documentary History* (Indianapolis: Hackett, 2014); Richard Price, "Creolization," in *The Princeton Companion to Atlantic History,* ed. Joseph C. Miller (Princeton: Princeton University Press, 2015).

Jamaica

On colonial Jamaica, see Frank Cundall, *The Governors of Jamaica in the First Half of the Eighteenth Century* (London: West India Committee, 1937); W. J. A. Gardner, *History of Jamaica from Its Discovery by Christopher Columbus to the Year 1872: Including an Account of Its Trade and Agriculture; Sketches of the Manners, Habits, and Customs of All Classes of Its Inhabitants; and a Narrative of the Progress of Religion and Education in the Island* (London: Frank Cass, 1971); Edward Brathwaite, *The Development of Creole Society in Jamaica, 1770–1820* (Oxford: Clarendon Press, 1971); Sidney W. Mintz and Douglas Hall, "The Origins of the Jamaican Internal Marketing System," in *Papers in Caribbean Anthropology* 57, ed. Sidney W. Mintz (New Haven: Yale University Press, 1960); Philip D. Curtin, *Two Jamaicas: The Role of Ideas in a Tropical Colony, 1830–1865* (Cambridge: Harvard University Press, 1955); Jane Burbank and Frederick Cooper, *Empires in World History: Power and Politics of Difference* (Princeton: Princeton University Press, 2010); Clinton V. Black, *The*

Story of Jamaica: From Prehistory to the Present (London: Collins, 1965); George Metcalf, *Royal Government and Political Conflict in Jamaica, 1729–1783* (London: Royal Commonwealth Society, 1965); Douglas Hall, "Jamaica," in *Neither Slave nor Free: The Freedmen of African Descent in the Slave Societies of the New World*, ed. David W. Cohen and Jack P. Greene (Baltimore: Johns Hopkins University Press, 1972); Michael Craton, "Jamaican Slavery," in *Race and Slavery in the Western Hemisphere: Quantitative Studies*, ed. Stanley L. Engerman and Eugene D. Genovese (Stanford: Advanced Study in the Behavioral Sciences, 1975); Gad J. Heuman, *Between Black and White: Race, Politics and the Free Coloreds in Jamaica, 1792–1865* (Westport, Conn.: Greenwood Press, 1981); B. W. Higman, "Slavery and the Development of Demographic Theory in the Age of Industrial Revolution," in *Slavery and British Society, 1776–1846*, ed. James Walvin (Baton Rouge: Louisiana State University Press, 1982); Richard B. Sheridan, *Doctors and Slaves: A Medical and Demographic History of Slavery in the British West Indies, 1680–1834* (New York: Cambridge University Press, 1985); B. W. Higman, *Jamaica Surveyed: Plantation Maps and Plans of the Eighteenth and Nineteenth Centuries* (Kingston: Institute of Jamaica Publications, 1988); B. W. Higman, "Jamaican Port Towns in the Early Nineteenth Century," in *Atlantic Port Cities: Economy, Culture, and Society in the Atlantic World, 1650–1850*, ed. Franklin W. Knight and Peggy K. Liss (Knoxville: University of Tennessee Press, 1991); Roderick A. McDonald, *The Economy and Material Culture of Slaves: Goods and Chattels on the Sugar Plantations of Jamaica and Louisiana* (Baton Rouge: Louisiana State University Press, 1993); Trevor Burnard, "Not a Place for Whites? Demographic Failure and Settlement in Comparative Context: Jamaica, 1655–1780," in *Jamaica in Slavery and Freedom: History, Heritage and Culture*, ed. Kathleen E. A. Monteith and Glen Richards (Kingston: University of West Indies Press, 2002); Kathleen Monteith, "The Labor Regimen on Jamaica Coffee Plantations During Slavery," in *Jamaica in Slavery and Freedom: History, Heritage and Culture*, ed. Kathleen E. A. Monteith and Glen Richards (Kingston: University of West Indies Press, 2002);

Maureen Warner-Lewis, "The Character of African-Jamaican Culture," in *Jamaica in Slavery and Freedom: History, Heritage and Culture,* ed. Kathleen E. A. Monteith and Glen Richards (Kingston: University of West Indies Press, 2002); Jean Besson, *Martha Brae's Two Histories: European Expansion and Caribbean Culture-Building in Jamaica* (Chapel Hill: University of North Carolina Press, 2002); Verene A. Shepherd, "Questioning Creole: Domestic Producers in Jamaica's Plantation Economy," in *Questioning Creole: Creolisation Discourses in the Caribbean Culture, in Honour of Kamau Brathwaite,* ed. Verene A. Shepherd and Glen L. Richards (Kingston: Ian Randle, 2002); Lorna Elaine Simmonds, 'The Afro-Jamaican and the Internal Marketing System: Kingston, 1780–1834," in *Jamaica in Slavery and Freedom: History, Heritage and Culture,* ed. Kathleen E. A. Monteith and Glen Richards (Kingston: University of West Indies Press, 2002); Trevor Burnard, "'The Grand Mart of the Island': The Economic Function of Kingston, Jamaica, in the Mid Eighteenth Century," in *Jamaica in Slavery and Freedom: History, Heritage and Culture,* ed. Kathleen E. A. Monteith and Glen Richards (Kingston: University of West Indies Press, 2002); B. W. Higman, *Plantation Jamaica, 1750–1850: Capital and Control in a Colonial Economy* (Kingston: University of West Indies Press, 2005); Verene Shepherd, "Work, Culture, and Creolization: Slavery and Emancipation in Eighteenth- and Nineteenth-Century Jamaica," in *Art and Emancipation in Jamaica: Isaac Mendes Belisario and His Worlds,* ed. Gillian Forrester, Tim Barringer, and Barbaro Martínez-Ruiz (New Haven: Yale University Press, 2007); Vincent Brown, *The Reaper's Garden: Death and Power in the World of Atlantic Slavery* (Cambridge: Harvard University Press, 2008); Christer Petley, *Slaveholders in Jamaica: Colonial Society and Culture During the Era of Abolition* (London: Pickering and Chatto, 2009).

Nova Scotia

Winthrop Pickard Bell, *The "Foreign Protestants" and the Settlement of Nova Scotia* (Toronto: University of Toronto Press, 1961); Robin Winks, "A Sacred Animosity: Abolition in Canada," in *The Antislavery*

Vanguard: New Essays on the Abolitionists, ed. Martin Duberman (Princeton: Princeton University Press, 1965); Robin W. Winks, *The Blacks in Canada: A History* (Montreal: McGill-Queen's University Press, 1971); John N. Grant, "Black Immigrants into Nova Scotia, 1776–1815," *Journal of Negro History* 58, no. 3 (July 1973): 253–70; Judith Fingard, "English Humanitarianism and the Colonial Mind: Walter Bromley in Nova Scotia, 1813–1825," *Canadian Historical Review* 54 (1973); James W. St. G. Walker, *The Black Loyalists: The Search for a Promised Land in Nova Scotia and Sierra Leone, 1783–1870* (New York: Africana, 1976); James W. St. G. Walker, "The Establishment of a Free Black Community in Nova Scotia, 1783–1840," in *The African Diaspora: Interpretive Essays,* ed. Martin L. Kilson and Robert I. Rotberg (Cambridge: Harvard University Press, 1976); L. F. S. Upton, *Micmacs and Colonists: Indian–White Relations in the Maritime Provinces, 1713–1867* (Vancouver: University of British Columbia Press, 1979); Brian C. Cuthbertson, *The Loyalist Governor: Biography of Sir John Wentworth* (Halifax: Petheric, 1983); Virginia Miller, "The Micmac: A Maritime Woodland Camp," in *Native Peoples: The Canadian Experience,* ed. R. Bruce Morrison and C. Roderick Wilson (Toronto: McClelland and Stewart, 1986); Harvey A. Whitfield, *Blacks on the Border: The Black Refugees in British North America, 1815–1860* (Burlington: University of Vermont Press, 2006); Graeme Wynn, "A Region of Scattered Settlements and Bounded Possibilities: Northeastern North America, 1775–1800," *Canadian Geographer* 31, no. 4 (December 1987): 319–38; Johan Seume, "Mein Lebin," in *The Old Man Told Us: Excerpts from Micmac History, 1500–1950,* ed. Ruth Holmes Whitehead (Halifax: Nimbus, 1991); Mavis C. Campbell, *From Nova Scotia to Sierra Leone: The Fighting Maroons* (Trenton, N.J.: Africa World Press, 1993); Stephen Patterson, "Indian–White Relations in Nova Scotia, 1749–61: A Study in Political Interaction," *Acadiensis* 23, no. 1 (1993); Paul Wilderson, *Governor John Wentworth and the American Revolution: The English Connection* (Hanover, N.H.: University of New England Press, 1994); Robert M. Leavitt, *Maliseet Mi'kmaq: First Nations of the Maritimes* (Fredericton: New Ireland Press, 1995); Julian

Gwyn, *Excessive Expectations: Maritime Commerce and the Economic Development of Nova Scotia, 1740–1870* (Montreal: McGill-Queen's University Press, 1998); Robin W. Winks, "Future of Imperial History," in *The Oxford History of the British Empire: Historiography,* ed. Robin W. Winks (New York: Oxford University Press, 1999); Laird Niven and Stephen A. Davis, "Birchtown: The History and Material Culture of an Expatriate African American Community," in *Moving On: Black Loyalists in the Afro-Atlantic World,* ed. John W. Pulis (New York: Garland, 1999); Graeme Wynn, "On the Margins of Empire, 1760–1840," in *The Illustrated History of Canada,* ed. Craig Brown (Toronto: Key Porter Books, 2002); William C. Wicken, *Mi'kmaq Treaties on Trial: History, Land and Donald Marshall Junior* (Toronto: University of Toronto Press, 2002); John N. Grant, *The Maroons in Nova Scotia* (Halifax: Formac, 2002); John G. Reid, "Pax Britannica or Pax Indigena? Planter Nova Scotia (1760–1782) and Competing Strategies of Pacification," *Canadian Historical Review* 85, no. 4 (2004): 669–92; Harvey A. Whitfield, "Black Loyalists and Black Slaves in Maritime Canada," *History Compass* 52, no. 10 (2007); Andrew Parnaby, "The Cultural Economy of Survival: The Mi'kmaq of Cape Breton in the Mid-19th Century," *Labour/Le Travail* 61 (Spring 2008); Jeffers Lennox, "Crossing Borders, Changing Worlds: Eighteenth-Century Nova Scotia's Atlantic Connections," *Journal of Canadian Studies* 42, no. 1 (2008): 213–19; Harvey A. Whitfield, "Reviewing Blackness in Atlantic Canada and the African Atlantic Canadian Diaspora," *Acadiensis* 37, no. 2 (2008); John G. Reid, "Empire, the Maritime Colonies, and the Supplanting of Mi'kma'ki/Wulstukwik, 1780–1820," *Acadiensis* 28, no. 2 (Summer/Autumn 2009): 78–97; Zainab Amadahy and Bonita Lawrence, "Indigenous Peoples and Black People in Canada: Settlers or Allies?" in *Breaching the Colonial Contract: Anti-Colonialism in the US and Canada,* ed. Arlo Kempf (Toronto: Springer, 2009), 105–36; John G. Reid, "Response—Historical Analysis and Indigenous Dispossession," in *Shaping an Agenda for Atlantic Canada,* ed. John G. Reid and Donald J. Savoid (Halifax: Fernwood, 2011), 60; Maya Jasanoff, *Liberty's Exiles: American Loyalists in the Revolutionary World* (New York: Vintage, 2012); Harvey A. Whitfield, "The Struggle over Slavery in the Maritime Colonies," *Acadiensis* 41, no. 2 (2012): 17–44; William C. Wicken, *Colonization of Mi'kmaw Memory and History, 1794–1928* (Toronto: University of Toronto Press, 2012); John G. Reid, "'In the Midst of Three Fires, a French One, an American One, and an Indian One': Imperial-Indigenous Negotiations during the War of 1812 in Eastern British America" (paper presented at "The War of 1812: Memory and Myth, History and Historiography" conference, University of London, July 12–14, 2012); Trudy Sable and Bernie Francis, *The Language of This Land: Mi'kma'ki* (Sydney, Nova Scotia: Cape Breton University Press, 2012); Jerry Bannister, "Atlantic Canada in an Atlantic World? Northeastern North America in the Long 18th Century," *Acadiensis* 43, no. 2 (Summer/Autumn 2014): 3–30; Alan Blackstock and Frank O'Gorman, *Loyalism and the Formation of the British World, 1775–1914* (Woodbridge, England: Boydell and Brewer, 2014); Mary McCarthy, "Mixed Race Identity: Black and Maliseet: My Personal Narrative," *Acadiensis* 43, no. 1 (2014); Catherine M. A. Couttreau-Robins, "Searching for the Enslaved in Nova Scotia's Loyalist Landscape," *Acadiensis* 43, no. 1 (Winter/Spring 2014); Mary-Ellen Kelm, "Living as a Treaty People: Lessons from the Mi'kmai'ki and Beyond," *Acadiensis* 43, no. 1 (Winter/Spring 2014); Jason Hall, "Maliseet Cultivation and Climatic Resilience on the Wəlastəkw/St. John River During the Little Ice Age," *Acadiensis* 44, no. 2 (Summer/Autumn 2015); Harvey A. Whitfield, *North to Bondage: Loyalist Slavery in the Maritimes* (Vancouver: University of British Columbia Press, 2016).

West Africa

For the African world the Trelawney Town Maroons encountered, see Claude George, *The Rise of British West Africa, Comprising the Early History of the Colony of Sierra Leone, the Gambia, Lagos, Gold Coast, etc. etc., with a Brief Account of Climate, the Growth of Education, Commerce, and Religion and a Comprehensive History of the Bananas and Bunce Islands* (London: Houlston and Sons, 1904); Eveline C. Martin, *The British West*

African Settlements, 1750–1821 (New York: Longmans, Green, 1927); Robin Hallett, *The Penetration of Africa: European Exploration in North and West Africa to 1815* (New York: Frederick A. Praeger, 1965); Robin Hallett, ed., *Records of the African Association, 1788–1831* (London: Thomas Nelson, 1964); B. W. Hodder, "Periodic and Daily Markets in West Africa," in *The Development of Indigenous Trade and Markets in West Africa,* ed. Claude Meillassoux (Oxford: International African Institute, 1971); A. G. Hopkins, *An Economic History of West Africa* (New York: Columbia University Press, 1973); S. C. Ukpabi, "The Military in Traditional African Societies," *African Spectrum* 9, no. 2 (1974): 200–217; Igor Kopytoff and Suzanne Miers, "African Slavery as an Institution of Marginality," in *Slavery in Africa: Historical and Anthropological Perspectives,* ed. Suzanne Miers and Igor Kopytoff (Madison: University of Wisconsin Press, 1977); Martin Klein and Paul E. Lovejoy, "Slavery in West Africa," in *The Uncommon Market: Essays in the Economic History of the Atlantic Slave Trade,* ed. Henry A. Gemery and Jan S. Hogendorn (New York: Academic Press, 1979); Paul Lovejoy, Igor Kopytoff, and Frederick Cooper, "Indigenous African Slavery (with Commentary)," *Historical Reflections: Roots and Branches: Current Directions in Slave Studies* 6, no. 1 (Summer 1979): 19–83; Ellen Gibson Wilson, *John Clarkson and the African Adventure* (London: Macmillan, 1980); Philip D. Curtin, "The End of the 'White Man's Grave'? Nineteenth-Century Mortality in West Africa," *Journal of Interdisciplinary History* 21, no. 1 (Summer 1990): 63–88; Christopher Fyfe, "Introduction," in *Our Children Are Free and Happy: Letters from Black Settlers in Africa in the 1790s,* ed. Christopher Fyfe (Edinburgh: Edinburgh University Press, 1991); Gareth Austin, "Indigenous Credit Institutions in West Africa, ca. 1750–1760," in *Local Suppliers of Credit in the Third World, 1750–1960,* ed. Gareth Austin and Kaoru Sugihara (New York: St. Martin's Press, 1993); Toyin Falola and Paul E. Lovejoy, "Pawnship in Historical Perspective," in *Pawnship in Africa: Debt Bondage in Historical Perspective,* ed. Toyin Falola and Paul E. Lovejoy (Boulder: Westview Press, 1994); A. G. Hopkins, "The 'New International Economic Order' in the Nineteenth Century: Britain's

First Development Plan for Africa," in *From Slave Trade to 'Legitimate Commerce': The Commercial Transition in Nineteenth-Century West Africa* (New York: Cambridge University Press, 1995); Robin Law and Paul Lovejoy, "The Changing Dimensions of African History: Reappropriating the Diaspora," in *Rethinking African History,* ed. Charles Jedrej, Simon McGrath, Kenneth King, and Jack Thompson (Edinburgh: Centre of African Studies, 1997); Suzanne Miers and Martin A. Klein, "Introduction," in *Slavery and Colonial Rule in Africa,* ed. Suzanne Miers and Martin A. Klein (London: Frank Cass, 1999); Ismail Rashid, "'Do Dady nor Lef Me Make Dem Carry Me': Slave Resistance and Emancipation in Sierra Leone, 1894–1928," in *Slavery and Colonial Rule in Africa,* ed. Suzanne Miers and Martin A. Klein (London: Frank Cass, 1999); Paul E. Lovejoy and Richard Richardson, "The Slave Ports of the Bight of Biafra in the Eighteenth Century," in *Repercussions of the Atlantic Slave Trade: The Interior of the Bight of Biafra and the African Diaspora,* ed. Carolyn A. Brown and Paul E. Lovejoy (Trenton, N.J.: Africa World Press, 2011).

Sierra Leone

A. B. C. Sibthorpe, *The History of Sierra Leone* (1868; repr. New York: Humanities Press, 1970); J. J. Crooks, *A History of the Colony of Sierra Leone, Western Africa* (London: Frank Cass, 1903); Thomas Nelson Goddard, *The Handbook of Sierra Leone* (London: G. Richards, 1925); Eveline C. Martin, *The British West African Settlements, 1750–1821* (New York: Longmans, Green, 1927); Francis A. J. Utting, *The Story of Sierra Leone* (Freeport: Books for Libraries Press, 1931); E. J. Wright, "Remarks on the Early Monetary Position in Sierra Leone with a Description of the Coinage Adopted," *Sierra Leone Studies* 1 (1953); A. P. Kup, *A History of Sierra Leone, 1400–1787* (Cambridge: Cambridge University Press, 1961); N. A. Cox-George, *Finance and Development in West Africa: The Sierra Leone Experience* (London: Dennis Dobson, 1961); Christopher Fyfe, *A History of Sierra Leone* (Oxford: Oxford University Press, 1962); Christopher Fyfe, *A Short History of Sierra Leone* (London: Longman, 1962); Christopher Fyfe, "The Countess of Huntington's Connexion in

19th Century Sierra Leone," *Sierra Leone Bulletin of Religion* 4, no. 1 (1962); M. C. F. Easmon, "Sierra Leone's Connection with Royalty," *Sierra Leone Studies* 16 (1962); Rev. E. G. Ingham, *Sierra Leone after a Hundred Years* (1894; repr. London: Frank Cass, 1968); Christopher Fyfe, *Sierra Leone Inheritance* (London: Oxford University Press, 1964); P. E. H. Hair, "Sierra Leone and Bulama, 1792–94," *Sierra Leone Bulletin of Religion* 6, no. 1 (June 1964); John Peterson, "The Enlightenment and the Founding of Freetown," in *Freetown: A Symposium*, ed. Christopher Fyfe and Eldred Jones (Freetown: Sierra Leone University Press, 1968); R. J. Olu-Wright, "The Physical Growth of Freetown," in *Freetown: A Symposium*, ed. Christopher Fyfe and Eldred Jones (Freetown: Sierra Leone University Press, 1968); Christopher Fyfe, "The Foundation of Freetown," in *Freetown: A Symposium*, ed. Christopher Fyfe and Eldred Jones (Freetown: Sierra Leone University Press, 1968); J. McKay, "Commercial Life in Freetown," in *Freetown: An Interpretation of Sierra Leone History, 1787–1816*, ed. Christopher Fyfe and Eldred Jones (Freetown: Sierra Leone University Press, 1968); John Peterson, *Province of Freedom: A History of Sierra Leone, 1787–1870* (Evanston: Northwestern University Press, 1969); Richard West, *Back to Africa: A History of Sierra Leone and Liberia* (New York: Holt, Rinehart and Winston, 1970). Cyril P. Foray, *Historical Dictionary of Sierra Leone*, African Historical Dictionaries 12 (Metuchen, N.J.: Scarecrow Press, 1977), provides useful summations. On more recent works, see David Skinner, "Sierra Leone Relations with the Northern Rivers and the Influence of Islam in the Colony," *International Journal of Sierra Leone Studies* 1 (1988); Winston McGowan, "The Establishment of Long-Distance Trade Between Sierra Leone and Its Hinterland, 1787–1821," *Journal of African History* 31 (1990): 25–41; Akintola J. G. Wyse, "The Place of Sierra Leone in African Diaspora Studies," in *Peoples and Empires in African History: Essays in Memory of Michael Crowder* (London: Longman, 1992); Philip D. Curtin, *Why People Move: Migration in African History*, Sixteenth Charles Edmondson Historical Lectures (Waco: Markham Press Fund, 1994); Akintola J. G. Wyse, "The Krio of Sierra Leone: Perspectives and West African

Historiography," in *Rethinking African History,* ed. Charles Jedrej, Simon McGrath, Kenneth King, and Jack Thompson (Edinburgh: Centre of African Studies, 1997); Suzanne Schwarz, "Zachary Macaulay and the Development of the Sierra Leone Company, 1793–94" (Part 1: Journal, June–October 1793), in *University of Leipzig Papers on Africa, History and Cultural Series,* no. 4 (2000), and (Part 2: Journal, October–December 1793) in no. 9 (2002); Starr Douglas and Felix Driver, "Imagining the Tropical Colony: Henry Smeathman and the Termites of Sierra Leone," in *Tropical Visions in an Age of Empire,* ed. Felix Driver and Luciana Martins (Chicago: University of Chicago Press, 2005); Isaac Land and Andrew M. Schocket, "New Approaches to the Founding of Sierra Leone Colony, 1786–1808," *Journal of Colonialism and Colonial History* 9, no. 3 (Winter 2008); Kehinde Olabimtan, "Church Missionary Society Projects of Agricultural Improvement in Nineteenth-Century Sierra Leone and Yorubaland," in *Commercial Agriculture: The Slave Trade and Slavery in Atlantic Africa,* ed. Suzanne Schwarz, Robin Law, and Silke Strickrodt (London: Boydell and Brewer, 2013).

Abolition

Eric Williams, *Capitalism and Slavery* (Chapel Hill: University of North Carolina Press, 1944); George G. Mellor, *British Imperial Trusteeship, 1783–1850* (London: Faber and Faber, 1951); Philip D. Curtin, *The Image of Africa: British Ideas and Action, 1780–1850* (Madison: University of Wisconsin Press, 1964); Martin Duberman, ed., *The Antislavery Vanguard: New Essays on the Abolitionists* (Princeton: Princeton University Press, 1965); R. A. Austen and W. D. Smith, "Images of Africa and British Slave-Trade Abolition: The Transition to Imperialist Ideology, 1787–1807," *African Historical Studies* 2 (1969): 69–83; Wylie Sypher, *Guinea's Captive Kings: British Anti-Slavery Literature of the 18th Century* (New York: Octagon Press, 1969); Ralph A. Austen, "The Abolition of the Overseas Slave Trade: A Distorted Theme in West African History," *Journal of the Historical Society of Nigeria* 2 (1970): 257–74; Stiv Jakobsson, *Am I Not a Man and a Brother?: British Missionaries and the*

Abolition of the Slave Trade and Slavery in West Africa and the West Indies, 1786–1838 (Lund: Gleerup, 1972); Philip D. Curtin, *Economic Change in Precolonial Africa: Senegambia in the Era of the Slave Trade* (Madison: University of Wisconsin Press, 1975); Howard Temperley, "Anti-Slavery as Cultural Imperialism," in *Anti-Slavery, Religion and Reform: Essays in Memory of Roger Anstey,* ed. Christine Bolt and Seymour Drescher (Kent, England: Dawson, 1980); Stanley L. Engerman, "Some Implications of the Abolition of the Slave Trade," in *The Abolition of the Atlantic Slave Trade: Origins and Effects in Europe, Africa, and the Americas,* ed. David Eltis and James Walvin (Madison: University of Wisconsin Press, 1981); David Eltis and James Walvin, eds., *The Abolition of the Atlantic Slave Trade: Origins and Effects in Europe, Africa, and the Americas* (Madison: University of Wisconsin Press, 1981); Ronald Robinson and John Gallagher, *Africa and the Victorians: The Official Mind of Imperialism* (London: Macmillan, 1981); Seymour Drescher, "Public Opinion and the Destruction of Slavery," in *Slavery and British Society, 1776–1846* (Baton Rouge: Louisiana State University Press, 1982); David Eltis, "Abolitionist Perceptions of Society after Slavery," in *Slavery and British Society, 1776–1846,* ed. James Walvin (Baton Rouge: Louisiana State University Press, 1982); David Richardson, ed., *Abolition and Its Aftermath: The Historical Context, 1790–1916* (London: Frank Cass, 1985); Fiona Spiers, "William Wilberforce: 150 Years On," in *Out of Slavery: Abolition and After,* ed. Jack Hayward (London: Frank Cass, 1985); Seymour Drescher, "The Historical Context of British Abolition," in *Abolition and Its Aftermath: The Historical Context, 1790–1916,* ed. David Richardson (London: Frank Cass, 1985); Seymour Drescher, *Capitalism and Antislavery: British Mobilization in Comparative Perspective* (New York: Oxford University Press, 1987); Ronald Kent Richardson, *Moral Imperium: Afro-Caribbeans and the Transformation of British Rule,* Contributions in Comparative Colonial Studies, vol. 22, no. 22 (New York: Greenwood Press, 1987); M. J. R. Ward, *British West Indian Slavery, 1750–1834* (Oxford: Clarendon Press, 1988); C. A. Bayly, *Imperial Meridian: The British Empire and the World, 1780–1830* (London: Longman,

1989); Michael J. Turner, "The Limits of Abolition: Government, Saints and the 'African Question,' c. 1780–1820," *English Historical Review* 112, no. 446 (1997): 319–57; Gad Heuman, "Slavery, the Slave Trade, and Abolition," in *The Oxford History of the British Empire: Historiography,* ed. Robin W. Winks (New York: Oxford University Press, 1999); David Lambert, *White Creole Culture: Politics and Identity During the Age of Abolition* (New York: Cambridge University Press, 2005); Christopher L. Brown, "The Politics of Slavery," in *The British Atlantic World, 1500–1800,* ed. David Armitage and Michael J. Braddick (New York: Palgrave Macmillan, 2002); Christopher Leslie Brown, "From Slaves to Subjects: Envisioning an Empire without Slavery," in *Black Experience and the Empire,* ed. Philip D. Morgan and Sean Hawkins (Oxford: Oxford University Press, 2004); Deirdre Coleman, *Romantic Colonization and British Anti-Slavery* (Cambridge: Cambridge University Press, 2005); Christopher Leslie Brown, *Moral Capital: Foundations of British Abolitionism* (Chapel Hill: University of North Carolina Press, 2006); John Oldfield, "Abolition and Emancipation," in *Representing Slavery: Art, Artefacts, and Archives in the Collections of the National Maritime Museum,* ed. Douglas Hamilton and Robert J. Blyth (Aldershot, England: Lund Humphries, 2007); Gad Heuman, "The Historiography of Slavery and Abolition in the Anglophone Caribbean," in *Beyond Fragmentation: Perspectives on Caribbean History,* ed. Audra Diptee, Juanita de Barros, and David V. Trotman (Princeton: Markus Wiener, 2006); David Brion Davis, *Inhuman Bondage: The Rise and Fall of Slavery in the New World* (New York: Oxford University Press, 2006); Eric Robert Taylor, *If We Must Die: Shipboard Insurrections in the Era of the Atlantic Slave Trade* (Baton Rouge: Louisiana State University Press, 2006); David Beck Ryden, *West Indian Slavery and British Abolition, 1783–1807* (New York: Cambridge University Press, 2009); Michael Barnett, *Empire of Humanity: A History of Humanitarianism* (Ithaca: Cornell University Press, 2011); Neil Ramsey, *The Military Memoir and Romantic Literary Culture, 1780–1835* (Burlington, Vt.: Ashgate, 2011); Bronwen Everill, *Abolition and Empire in Sierra Leone and Liberia* (London: Palgrave Macmillan,

2013); William Mulligan and Maurice Bric, eds., *A Global History of Anti-Slavery Politics in the Nineteenth Century* (London: Palgrave Macmillan, 2013); Emily Conroy-Krutz, "Dissenters from the Mainstream: The National and International Dimensions of Evangelical Reform," in *The World of the Revolutionary American Republic: Land, Labor, and Conflict for a Continent,* ed. Andrew Shankman (New York: Routledge, 2014).

After Abolition

On the era after the abolition of the slave trade and slavery, see Philip D. Curtin, *Two Jamaicas: The Role of Ideas in a Tropical Colony, 1830–1865* (Cambridge: Harvard University Press, 1955); Monica Schuler, *Alas, Alas, Kongo: A Social History of Indentured African Immigration into Jamaica, 1841–1865* (Baltimore: Johns Hopkins University Press, 1980); Sidney W. Mintz, "Labor Needs and Ethnic Ripening in the Caribbean Region," Woodrow Wilson Lectures, no. 137 (1982); Mary Turner, *Slaves and Missionaries: The Disintegration of Jamaican Slave Society, 1787–1834* (Urbana: University of Illinois Press, 1982); Sidney W. Mintz, "Epilogue: The Divided Aftermaths of Freedom," in *Between Slavery and Free Labor: The Spanish-Speaking Caribbean in the Nineteenth Century,* ed. Charles H. Vance (Baltimore: Johns Hopkins University Press, 1985); Monica Schuler, "The Recruitment of African Indentured Laborers for European Colonies in the Nineteenth Century," in *Colonialism and Migration: Indentured Labour Before and After Slavery,* ed. P. C. Emmer (Dordrecht: Martinus Nijhoff, 1986); Stanley L. Engerman, "Servants to Slaves to Servants: Contract Labour and European Expansion," in *Colonialism and Migration: Indentured Labour Before and After Slavery,* ed. P. C. Emmer (Dordrecht: Martinus Nijhoff, 1986); Suzanne Miers and Richard Roberts, eds., *The End of Slavery in Africa* (Madison: University of Wisconsin Press, 1988); Suzanne Miers and Martin A. Klein, eds., *Slavery and Colonial Rule in Africa* (London: Frank Cass, 1999); William A. Green, "Plantation Society and Indentured Labour: The Jamaican Case, 1834–1865," in *Colonialism and Migration: Indentured Labour Before and After Slavery,* ed. P. C. Emmer (Dordrecht: Martinus Nijhoff, 1986);

Nemata Amelia Blyden, *West Indians in West Africa, 1808–1880: The African Diaspora in Reverse* (Rochester: University of Rochester Press, 2000); Rosanne Marion Adderley, *New Negroes from Africa: Slave Trade Abolition and Free African Settlement in the Nineteenth-Century Caribbean* (Bloomington: Indiana University Press, 2006).

Acknowledgments

In studying the Trelawney Town Maroons, I have learned much about human tenacity and hope and also about multiple levels of cultural integration. The Maroons defy categorization.

Mavis C. Campbell's comprehensive work drew me to the Trelawney Town Maroons. I am indebted to the librarians in Mona, Kingston, and Spanish Town, Jamaica; in Halifax and Ottawa, Canada; in Freetown, Sierra Leone; and in Kew and London, UK. In the United States, I have benefited from the archives in Clements Library at the University of Michigan, the John Carter Brown Library at Brown University, the New-York Historical Society, the Gilder Lehrman Collection, the Schomburg Center for Research in Black Culture, and the Huntington Library. A fellowship from the American Philosophical Society provided timely funding for research in Britain. San Jose State University, the College of Social Science, and the History Department found resources and lent support, time and time again.

I remain grateful to Alan Taylor and Clarence Walker, both brilliant scholars and generous mentors, who chose to take a gamble on me. Robert Middlekauff read early drafts and nudged me to add "flesh" to the Maroons: the portrait that emerges would not have been possible without his intuition and his insights. Over a decade ago John Reid's and Elizabeth Mancke's sharply analytical works introduced me to the Maritimes and transformed my thinking about the Americas. Incisive feedback from anonymous reviewers encouraged me to forcefully establish the Maroons' place in world history. Sheila Skemp's friendship, intellectual curiosity, and adventurous spirit continually expand my horizons. Audra J. Wolfe's scholarly range and sensitivity to words and their nuances and Lawrence Kenney's care created a work that could be approached by nonspecialists. I thank Laura Davulis, who has since left Yale University Press, for her commitment to a stranger and to a strange new project.

Without Rahul, nothing would be possible. He knows this. Our parents texted recipes and jokes, parceled sweets and rotis, sent prayers as well as songs and photos of pink and purple flowers. My sons, to whom this book is dedicated, became teenagers during my years with the Trelawney Town Maroons. It seems only fitting that this work comes to a close as our younger son, Ahab, joins his brother, Zoey, on the East Coast, moving away from home to begin his own journey.

Index

Page numbers in *italics* indicate illustrations.